Faith in the Shadows

The Other Side of the Fence

KEITH HARRIS

KEITH HARRIS

"Faith in the Shadows: The Other Side of the Fence" offers a refreshing and timely perspective on faith and disability. Challenging our traditional understanding of "being" and presenting innovative faith statements, Faith in the Shadows sparks important—necessary conversations on disability and faith within our church communities.

The principles expounded and outcomes proposed in Faith in the Shadows pave the way for a more inclusive and expressive approach to faith and disability. As we embrace this new understanding of faith, we can create church communities that value the contributions of disabled individuals, fostering a rich and diverse spiritual journey for all."

FAITH IN THE SHADOWS

 A catalogue record for this book is available from the National Library of Australia

Library of Congress Control Number: 2023907166
Dewey Code: 248.4/8.06 FIS:HA
BISAC: 062000 / Spirituality / Faith / Worship / Inclusion

Cover Design: ©Jesus Cordero, Anointing Publications
Interior Design: © RiverView Publishing

RiverView Publishing
BEYOND BARRIERS

Published by © RiverView Publishing,
PO BOX 6029, LPO, Riverview, QLD, 4303, Aust.
ABN: 38375709802
E: *info@keithharristoday.com*
W: *https://www.keithharristoday.com/*

ISBN: 9780645366402 (h)
ISBN: 9780645366440 (e)
ISBN: 9780645366457 (p)

10 9 8 7 6 5 4 3 2 1

Printed in Australia, 2023.

COPYRIGHT

COPYRIGHT © 2023 Keith Robert Harris

No part of this publication may be reproduced, distributed, or transmitted in any form or by any other means, including prototyping, recording, or other electronic or mechanical methods, without the prior written permission of the author, except in the case of brief quotations embodied in reviews and certain other non-commercial uses permitted by copyright law.

This book is a work of non-fiction. The author and publisher make no guarantees about the accuracy of the information in this book. The names of people, events, and places have been altered to protect individual privacy. All due care has been taken to acknowledge sources and copyright material, and any oversight is unintentional. Please advise the publisher of any errors.

Unless noted, Scriptures taken from the Holy Bible, New International Version®, NIV®. Copyright © 1973, 1978, 1984, 2011 by Biblica, Inc.™ Used by permission of Zondervan. All rights reserved worldwide. www.zondervan.com The "NIV" and "New International Version" are trademarks registered in the United States Patent and Trademark Office by Biblica, Inc.™

Scripture quotations taken from the ESV® Bible, (The Holy Bible, English Standard Version® (ESV®) Copyright © 2001 by Crossway, a publishing ministry of Good News Publishers. All rights reserved. ESV Text Edition: 2016

Scripture quotations taken from the Holy Bible, New Living Translation, copyright ©1996, 2004, 2015 by Tyndale House Foundation. Used by permission of Tyndale House Publishers, Carol Stream, Illinois 60188, USA. All rights reserved.

Scripture quotations taken from the (NASB®) New American Standard Bible®, Copyright © 1960, 1971, 1977, 1995, 2020 by The Lockman Foundation. Used by permission. All rights reserved. lockman.org"

Scripture quotations taken from the Holy Bible: Easy-to-Read Version™, the HOLY BIBLE: EASY-TO-READ VERSION™ where noted are copyright © 2006 by Bible League International and used by permission.

NOTES

In the Bibliography, references to resources used are listed in the order of their appearance in each chapter in the text.

A Glossary and references to Internet articles, Software, and helpful Website addresses are at the end of this book for your information and help.

Due to the dynamic nature of the Internet, Websites, and resources — URL addresses cited in this book may have changed and no longer be available. However, you can search for the article by title. All due care has been exercised to ensure that the references listed are current at the time of publication.

Also, note that all Internet links have been "deactivated" in the eBook versions of this book. Please copy the link 'text' and paste it into your internet browser's "URL" bar or search box. A search for the file nametag, i.e., "*Human Condition*," in search engines, in most cases, will locate the document.

https://en.wikipedia.org/wiki/Human_condition

In a work of this size and complexity, all due care has been exercised to reference sources and published works. Any oversight is unintentional, and if a source is not referenced or notated correctly, please advise the publisher.

All citations from the Internet are in APA format and checked at the time of printing. Please note that the dating of citations from websites, where noted, follows the format: Cited, dd/mm/yyyy.

The views expressed in this book are solely those of the author and do not necessarily reflect the views of the publisher, and the publisher hereby disclaims any responsibility for them.

THIS BOOK IS DEDICATED TO MARY,
WHO IS THE REASON FOR ITS
EXISTENCE.

Contents

Copyright iii
Notes iv
Contents vi
Illustrations x
Acknowledgments xi
Foreword xii
Abbreviations xiii
Introduction 1
Chapter 1 The Shadow World 9
Chapter 2 The Fence 12
    What Fence? 12
    Fence Sitting 16
Chapter 3 A Brief History 19
Chapter 4 Defining Being 25
    What Is Life? 25
    Physical Life 27
    Ontological Life 28
    Spiritual Life 30
Chapter 5 Defining Disability 34
    Physical Disability 35
    Sensory Disability 40
    Intellectual Disability 44
    Mental and Emotional Disability 48
    Developmental Disability 52

Spiritual Disability	56
Just Coins	60
Chapter 6 Defining Faith	**64**
A Secular Definition	64
A Religious Definition	65
A Biblical Definition	68
A Salvic Definition	77
Just Notes	86
Chapter 7 Reality of Faith	**90**
Why Discuss This Here?	90
Historical Views of Faith	96
The DSM-5 Disconnect	105
A Fact of Faith	107
Just Pourers	113
Chapter 8 Actualising Faith	**116**
Actualising Faith in a Neurotypical World	117
Can We Actualise Faith in the Shadow World?	120
Limits to Actualising Faith in the Shadow World	126
Faith Remains Consistent	130
A New Language for Actualising Faith	132
Just Hands	141
Chapter 9 Living Faith	**146**
Faith Transcends Disability	146
A Theology of Faith in the Shadow World:	156
The Feet of Him Who Brings "Good News"	165
The Paradox—God's Part and Our Part in Evangelism	170
Chapter 10 Faith in the Shadows	**173**
Norman	174

Susan	177
Julie	179
Mary	180
Two Bottles	186
Chapter 11 Encouraging Faith	**190**
Fearfully and Wonderfully Made	190
Grace in the Shadow World	203
Hope in the Shadow World	205
All God's Children by Faith	211
Just Wings	212
Chapter 12 Accountable Faith	**218**
Three Bottles	225
Chapter 13 Conclusions	**228**
Chapter 14 Postscript: On Our Side	**237**
Who Built the Fence?	238
There Is No Fence to Faith	240
Removing the fence	243
Bibliography	**246**
Introduction	246
The Shadow World	246
The Fence	246
A Brief History	246
Defining Being	248
Defining Disability	248
Defining Faith	254
Reality of Faith	256
Actualising Faith	258
Living Faith	259

  Evangelism in the Shadows 261

  Encouraging Faith 262

  Accountable Faith 263

Conclusions 264

Postscript 264

Glossary 266

Internet Links 274

Software Resources 277

Appendix I 279

  Disability, Religion, and Spirituality Resources: 279

  Web Sites 280

  Articles 284

  Books 289

Appendix II 297

  Email: Jody Plecas 297

  Questions 298

Appendix III 299

Additional Books Accessed & Read 299

Endorsement 303

  Jason Forbes, Jericho Road 303

ILLUSTRATIONS

Fig. 1	The other side of the fence[1]	Page 5
Fig. 2	Man is a spiritual "being"	Page 32
Fig. 3, 4	Just coins[2]	Page 61,62
Fig. 5, 6	Just bank notes[3]	Page 87
Fig. 7	Circle diagram[4]	Page 102
Fig. 8	Spirit pourers[5]	Page 114
Fig. 9, 10, 11	Just hands[6]	Page 142-144
Fig. 12, 13	Two different bottles[7]	Page 188
Fig. 14	Aircraft wing aerodynamics[8]	Page 213
Fig. 15, 16, 17	Angle of Attack	Page 213-215
Fig. 18	Three different bottles[9]	Page 226
Fig. 19	Faith is Spirit[10]	Page 230
Fig. 20	All God's Children	Page 236
Fig. 21	God, Faith, and Mary	Page 242
Fig. 22	There is no Fence	Page 244

---

[1] Fig. 1, 2 © Gerard Maille, Art On Walls 2020, All rights reserved. Used with permission.

[2] Fig. 3, 4 © Royal Australian Mint, Deakin, ACT, All rights reserved. Used with permission.

[3] Fig. 5, 6 © Reserve Bank of Australia, All rights reserved. Used with permission.

[4] Fig 7 © Gerard Maille, Art On Walls 2020, All rights reserved. Used with permission.

[5] Fig. 8 © Cameron Fowles, Drift Zone Photography, All rights reserved. Used with permission.

[6] Fig. 9, 10, 11 © Gerard Maille, Art On Walls 2020, All rights reserved. Used with permission.

[7] Fig. 12, 13 © Cameron Fowles, Drift Zone Photography, All rights reserved. Used with permission.

[8] Fig. 14, 15, 16, 17, © Gerard Maille, Art On Walls 2020, All rights reserved. Used with permission.

[9] Fig. 18 © Cameron Fowles, Drift Zone Photography. All rights reserved. Used with permission.

[10] Fig. 19, 20, 21, 22, © Gerard Maille, Art On Walls 2020, All rights reserved. Used with permission.

Acknowledgments

To my awesome wife, Jocelyne, who read the early drafts of this book, reread and edited its many revisions, encouraged, supported, and advised me over the years, often reminding me of the importance of this work, I am deeply thankful. She is as essential to this book getting done as I am.

I would also like to acknowledge the many who have contributed to this work and helped me in the task of writing.

To Mr. Allan Templeton and Ms. Jody Plecas for their support, comments on this manuscript, and help in improving the theme of this book over the years of its development.

To Roy Rolley, my prayer partner of fifty years who, while dealing with personal disability, has walked with me over the years of this project from academic paper to book manuscript.

To Loughlin Patrick (Editorial Assistant)[11] for the courage to edit this manuscript and make positive changes that have improved the presentation of this book and its message of faith and grace to all who will read it.

To my graphic artists, Jesus Cordero (cover), Gerard Maille (illustrations), and photographer Cameron Fowles, my thanks for their help and creativity in displaying the theme of this book.

To Stefanie Evans for her support to our family, especially the opportunity to share this work as a paper—revision II—at the ASA Third National Conference in Brisbane, 2015.

And thanks to the countless friends at Grace Christian Church, Redbank Plains, and on Facebook, who have endured my moments of passion and rhetorical reflections on what is, to me, essentially, a matter of the heart.

Finally, and certainly, my thanks and praise to God, who is above all and in all things and who, by His Spirit, brings faith and life into the Shadow World of disability. Glory be to His name alone.

---

[11] Loughlin Patrick: *https://twitter.com/loughlinptrck*

FOREWORD

When I read the early drafts of Keith's paper (now this book), I thought it was a great idea to educate our people (Christians) about the importance of gaining an insight into the plight of the disadvantaged in achieving recognition within the church: first to accept that the severely disabled can indeed possess true faith, to endeavor to understand the depth of that faith, and ultimately to encourage the growth of the faith of that disabled person. These are more than sufficient reasons to read this book.

However, as I progressed to read and discuss with Keith more of what he had to say, I began to realise that this work had far greater potential. I became aware that Keith had been entrusted with a much broader and deeper mission than he had realised. I believe that the final result has seen him triumph in fulfilling that commission, which is to challenge and encourage every one of us to reassess the entire basis of our own personal faith.

Most of us go through our Christian walk almost totally oblivious to many of the realities of scripture. We base our faith and belief system on what we know, and then we take this (quite often distorted) understanding and teach it to others in much the same manner as it was taught to us by those whose cognitive dialogue matches our own.

In God's eyes, the only "fence" that exists between Him and us is the fence of weak or misguided faith. Read this work and be challenged to check that you haven't unwittingly created a fence between you and your Heavenly Father. When I originally wrote this piece many, many months ago, I said, "Brother, I really do pray that your work is published and distributed widely. Not just for the sake of people in the Shadow World but also for those who think they reside on the other side of the fence. There needs to be an awakening. My advice is to immerse yourself in this exposé of pure faith and be challenged about who you are as a Christian."

Allan W. Templeton, BA (psych).
Christian Counsellor; Sunshine Coast, Qld, Au

ABBREVIATIONS

NIV: New International Version
ESV: English Standard Version
NLT: New Living Translation
SPD: Sensory Processing Disorder
SID: Sensory Integration Dysfunction
IDD: Intellectual Disability Disorder
MED: Mental Emotional Disability
COD: Compulsive Obsessive Disorder
CFD: Cognitive Dysfunction Disorder
DID: Dissociated Identity Disorder
DD: Development Disorder

Introduction

Faith in the Shadows asks and answers the question: "Can a profoundly disabled person have the same personal, joyful, fruitful, spiritual faith relationship with God as the neurotypical person would have and experience in life?"

It's a big theological question with a complex and profound answer that I certainly didn't arrive at overnight. In fact, over the years of developing and editing this book—questioning the ideas and concepts within—my own understanding of faith and spirituality evolved beyond what I ever imagined possible.

There's no better demonstration of this than a conversation I had with my friend Jack, who is autistic, in late 2021. Occasionally, I like to meet with a group of disabled guys and their caregivers for coffee, discussion, and prayer at a coffee shop in my town.

On this day, Jack was there with his friend-caregiver. The group wanted to hear about my book and what it was all about. As I showed the guys the book's outline, Jack saw the illustration "God, Mary and Faith."[12]

Jack had been talking about his frustration with the mask rules adopted for the CovID pandemic and how masks interfered with his ability to "see" people's faces and interact with them. With his auditory-sensory disabilities, Jack partially needs to lip read to know what someone is saying.

Jack fixated on the diagram, excited and distressed at the same time, returning to it repeatedly in the conversation, saying how the illustration revealed truths about himself and his experience of church.

"This is me," Jack said, "this is how I feel in church, fenced in without fully expressing myself and understanding what others are saying to me."

"Now I understand myself, my relationship with God, and my friends at church. I can see why I get so frustrated trying to get

---

[12] See "God, Mary and Faith," page 242

through the fence (of my disabilities) to express how I am, and I understand why people get frustrated with me, but God, whom I love, has no such problem."

After such a heart-wrenching moment—declaration—Jack was almost in tears, asking: "Why hasn't someone told me this before? Now I understand me."

As Jack sat there, his caregiver-friend began to analyse, psychologically,[13] Jack's response to the diagram, carefully explaining to Jack why he felt and thought the way he did. The more Jack's friend analysed him, going into great detail, the more animated Jack became and revealed that he had finally found, at the same time, a way of understanding himself (with his unique view of the world) and his relationship with God.

It was a most enlightening moment for me and will stay with me forever. I did not realise the importance of this exchange for a few weeks until it came to mind while I was on my way to another meeting about this book. It revealed to me hidden anxieties that often go overlooked in our exchanges with the disabled.

It was then that I realised the cover art of this book has two interpretations—two sides to the fence. Jack crying out from his side of the fence for acceptance and understanding, and his friend-caregiver putting up the fence of psychoanalysis, tradition, and social isolation without any intended animosity,[14] as a barrier [15] between them.

I asked myself, as I recalled the exchange, who was the person in the shadows in this meeting at the coffee shop, Jack, or his caregiver-friend?

---

[13] Jack's friend and caregiver is a qualified psychologist. I need to state here that there was no malice in this exchange. Jack's friend was trying to help Jack understand why he felt and reacted the way he did to the diagram and what the diagram had revealed to him.

[14] I would say even lovingly with every intent to help Jack understand himself. And this is my point; Jack understands himself; he lives with himself: the problem is that we think that Jack should live as we do. We need to step over the fence and live in Jack's world for a moment to see Jack as Jack sees himself.

[15] I am still working out, in my mind, if this fence-building is something we neurotypicals do intentionally. At times, yes, as a self-protection or avoidance mechanism. Also, it is sometimes involuntary due to years of convention and what is regarded as acceptable social conduct.

Sometimes, we are the ones in the shadows; we are the disabled ones trying to communicate across a fence to our friend in his/her world with our neurotypical analysis—paradigm of the life of the disabled. We have to reassess which side of the fence we are on and who is living in the shadows, those we call the disabled or we ourselves, who are often unable to see the fullness of life, faith and God in the life of those who live in the "Shadow World."

This book will examine that question and more. We will look at how disability impacts upon and interracts with the spiritual nature of a person so that we may discover new theological and practical guidelines for faith communities, parents, and families in the wider community.

We will be approaching this question, and the subject of faith and disability, from a Christian perspective; however, this does not exclude its investigation from the realm of other faith systems. It can provide helpful means for a progressive discussion on this important topic of care and love for the disabled.

We will examine the question of faith, disability, and inclusion from both sides of the fence: our world and the world of the disabled person. We will take note of historical models as we examine life, disability, and faith from a new perspective— discovering that faith is spiritual. Identifying faith in this new paradigm, we come to realise that the spiritual inclusion of the disabled within our faith communities is not only necessary but essential for the social and spiritual growth of the church body. We also look at means of and limitations to spiritual inclusion within our fellowships—taking a step of faith toward removing the "fence" that divides both worlds while initiating healing in the body of Christ on earth.

With faith, defined as no longer the property of intellect but God's Spirit in the life of the disabled person, we step back into our world with real-life examples of inclusion that have added to and enhanced the spiritual faith experiences of the disabled person and the church fellowship to which they belong. The challenge we face in accepting that faith is a spiritual attribute is to positively act upon this realisation through full inclusion, in spirit, word, and deed within the sacramental and social fellowship of our churches and faith communities.

Faith in the Shadows is an exploratory study. It is written from the perspective of personal research and discussions with medical and care professionals. The wide use of materials currently available on the internet and journal sites, as well as in printed media, has been made to bring this discussion to the forefront.[16, 17]

Key elements in this discussion are identified and quantified: life, being, disability, faith, the veracity of faith, and objectivity in faith, as well as real-world fundamentals associated with the topic. Theological and practical definitions were formed to clarify boundaries and set criteria by which people could assess and interact with its outcomes—concerning faith and disability—discussed in this book. Intellectual disabilities can be disruptive in the management of thought processes and adaptive behaviors within an individual; however, many so affected can and do remain valued participants whose contribution represents a positive element within the life and fellowship of their faith communities.

The principles expounded and outcomes projected in this book recommend a new approach to our definition of "being"—of faith and disability—that requires some innovative thinking. The book proposes a new language and new forms of dialogue that are needed to facilitate engagement, interaction, and discussion within established doctrinal and liturgical models of religious life in order to *fully* recognise and accommodate the faith statement and experiences of the disabled within the life and fellowship of their faith community.

We will approach the subject of faith and disability from the inside outward and answer questions from the other side of the fence—from inside the spiritual life of the disabled person. This has benefits for families, caregivers, friends, and faith communities where questions of life, hope, and faith concerning

---

[16] This book is the outcome of several revisions of the initial paper on faith and disability, first delivered at the Australasian Conference for the Academy and Church, Emmanuel College (QTC) St. Lucia in 2011; the second edition was presented to the ASA Third National Conference in Brisbane in 2015.

[17] A list of resources used in writing and the revision of this paper is attached in the bibliography and the appendix.

their loved ones, or those they care for, exist. It is a long journey that we have ahead, but the rewards are great, not only for the disabled but for everyone, as we, together, look forward to that day of full inclusion in faith and fellowship, not only in this world but the next to come with God.

Before we begin, let us take a moment to look at the diagram below.

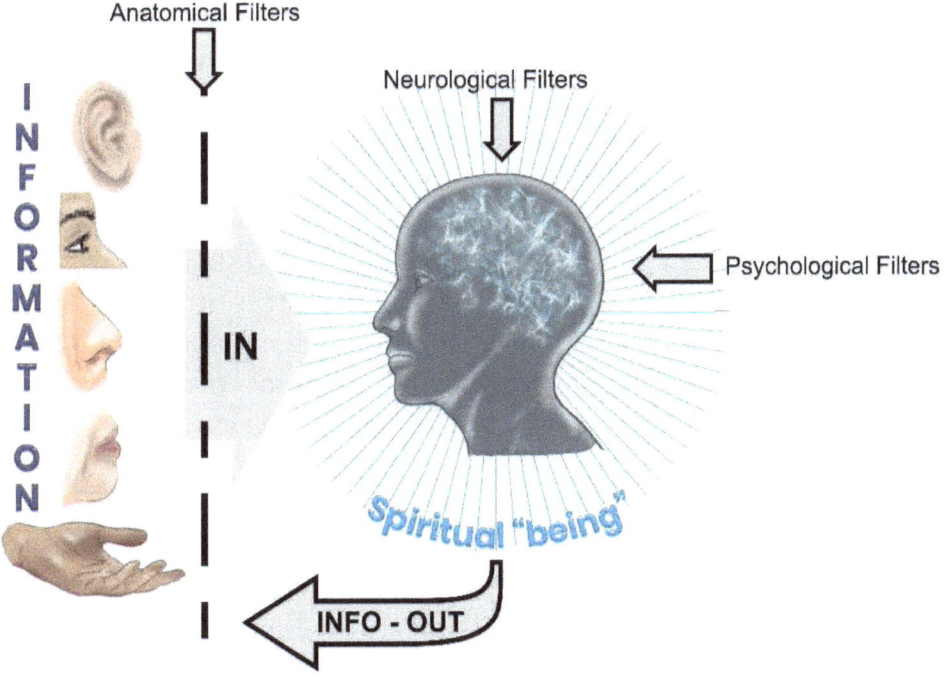

THE OTHER SIDE OF THE FENCE

It gives an overview of the issues that can have an impact on the life of a disabled person concerning their ability, or lack thereof, to understand, experience, and communicate thoughts, emotions, and feelings, and make decisions that we can both comprehend and accept in the world of the neurotypical person. With this understanding of their world, we can begin to examine faith and disability in a deeper sense in *Faith in the Shadows: The Other Side of the Fence*. The diagram, then, expresses, in picture form, our starting point.

On a personal note, having established a traditional care model of support programs and people networks for our disabled daughter in 2010, my wife and I began to think about life outside the conventional boundaries of finances, health, housing, and lifestyle that are usually associated with the care of the disabled.

Today—although new care models, services, and financial supports are becoming more readily available for the disabled, which is a great thing—we discovered that spirituality, faith, and one's sense of being was somewhat lacking in importance in these treatment models and the organisational systems usually associated with the care of the disabled.

A secondary issue—associated with our topic of faith—is that we live in a world where a person's value is frequently assessed through their perceived capabilities or external attributes. Disabilities, whether visual, intellectual, biological, or psychological, can create significant challenges or barriers to acceptance and recognition for disabled people in their community within a "face-value model" of social status.

Thus, in order to engage fully in our discussion on faith and disability, this book looks at faith and disability from the inside out—that is, starting with the circumstances of one's disability, we investigate and discuss the links between disability, spirituality, and faith. In the end, we propose a new paradigm of what it means "to be," "to believe," "to have faith" primarily as a spiritual living human being so that we may facilitate inclusion for and enhance the spiritual life of the disabled within their social and faith communities.

Experiencing the disassociation—both socially and culturally—that is, often felt by the disabled, and observed in the life of our disabled daughter, this book is then the outworking of questions raised, and challenges met and overcome in our journey with her toward inclusion and acceptance within her church and faith community. [18]

Understanding the life and experiences of the disabled within our faith communities then requires us to re-examine life, being, disability, faith and spirituality, and work through the difficulties

---

[18] While this book comes from a Christian perspective, this discussion on spirituality, being, and disability is relevant to all faiths.

our disabled people experience in their interaction with us within our churches and faith communities.

In the chapter titled "Encouraging Faith," we observe that the experiences of inclusion and fellowship for the disabled may not have been as fulfilling as they may desire or is at least required for them to have a personal sense of belonging in our churches and faith communities.

As this book reads in the Conclusion:

> The Shadow World of disability is, at times, a place where customary liturgical and creedal practices used in our faith communities are often inoperative or at worst ineffectual. In the Shadow World, we need to learn a *"new language"* if we are to understand, recognise, and process the faith responses of those we love and care for. Particularly when their disabilities may prevent them from communicating or expressing their faith in a neurotypical, cognitive, vocal, volitional, sentient[19] manner that we are accustomed to, or accept as a reality, in our world.[20]

Essentially, this book asks and answers the questions:

> "Is disability a barrier to faith in God?"

And the associated question:

> "Can a disabled person have the same joyful—fruitful spiritual faith relationship with God as a neurotypical person would have and experience?"

In providing answers to these questions, we will enter on a journey into the world of disability that is both challenging and encouraging as we discover that faith is real in the "Shadow World." This book will ask us to rethink our priorities on how we deal with disability, faith, God, and life.

I will also propose that new dialogue is necessary in our perceptions of value with respect to the disabled of our community recommending a new paradigm of inclusion and acceptance based

---

[19] See "Glossary" – sentience, page 272
[20] See "Conclusions," page 228

on the inherent internal spiritual reality of a person rather than their functional or external abilities. This opens a pathway to the realisation of a new and much healthier understanding of faith, disability, and the world in which people with disabilities live.

Our conclusion—and answer to the important question above—is that faith in God is real, experiential, and personal regardless of the "world" one lives in. This conclusion, of course, presents us with some challenges of engagement and active interaction with those who live in the world of disability. That is, on the other side of the fence, as depicted in the final diagram that concludes my discussion on this topic.[21]

Back on the neurotypical side of the fence, the acceptance of new paradigms in faith will open a pathway to the acceptance of a new and much healthier understanding of the real-world environment, both spiritually and materially, in which people with disabilities live.

So, let us have a look at the Shadow World.

---

[21] See "All God's Children," page 236

Chapter 1

The Shadow World

In this book, I frequently use the phrase "the Shadow World," but what does this phrase mean? I use the phrase "Shadow World" to describe the place where people with disabilities, especially those with neurological incapacities, often live in relation to their social and religious identity.

The word "shadow" has a sense of mystery about it; it conjures up the concept of something indistinct, vague even—something less defined in contrast to a clear objective reality. By definition, a shadow is a representation of something that is tangible but is not the substance of that reality. A shadow looks like an object it projects from—or represents (often in a distorted sense) but does not have the full substantive properties of that object.

Also, shadows can be places where seeing or perceiving things clearly is difficult. Outlines are there but not as distinct, and we can stumble walking about in the shadows. From the outside, where we have light, looking into a shadowed area is hard; and it is, at times, difficult, or at worst, impossible to "see" distinctly what is going on hidden there in the shadows.

It is in this aspect that I refer to the world in which the disabled often live as the Shadow World. This does not mean that I regard those who live there as intangible or not real—positively not! Yet, the Shadow World of disability is frequently a place where a communication barrier exists, where the common language of our neurotypical world is often inoperative, or at worst inappropriate.

My argument is that from our neurotypical world, looking across the fence into the Shadow World of the disabled, what we perceive as "reality" for those who live there might not be so for them. Conversely, what those living in the Shadow World perceive of our world is often similarly clouded in uncertainty.

Therefore, the following points are worth noting:

- First, in the Shadow World, we will need to learn a "new language,"[22] their unique individual language, if we are to understand and process the responses of those we love, who have a disability that prevents them from communicating with us in a normal cognitive, vocal, sentient manner.
- Second, the Shadow World is no less a place where God loves and cares for His children, regardless of their neurological abilities or disabilities. This is an important concept to recognise as this world of shadows is sometimes thought of as being out of God's reach, a place where the spiritual activity of God is muted, or at least limited by the disability of the person, or at worst is seen as a place where God is inactive or quiescent.
- Third, the Shadow World is sometimes a place of silent sounds, of black and white color, of illegible words, of distant touch, of bland fragrances, where people who live in the normal world are seen only as shadows—living in a distorted unique harmony.
- Fourth, although the Shadow World is a challenging place—just ask those who live there or care for those who do—it is also a place where we, as Christians, can show the love of God in real and tangible ways.
- Fifth, the Shadow World is a place where we can learn about the love of God as we see it in action in His grace and love daily in the lives of those whose life experience is so different from ours. It is also a place where we need to understand and engage with those who live there if we are to take the gospel unto the "ends of the earth," as we are commanded in Matt. 28:19, Acts 1:8.

---

[22] A term originated by Ms Susannah Mintz that defines the unique and individual language of a disabled person, identifying their individual and distinctive means of communication and comprehension.

In summary, there is much to be said for a reappraisal of "humanity," essentially the humanness of "being" and what defines "life" and "faith" for those who live in the Shadow World. In our narcissistic society where performance and appearances count for so much, those who live in the Shadow World of disabilities are often overlooked or regarded as lesser humans.[23]

As Diane Burgent states in *Spirituality and Intellectual Disability*: "Too often they are regarded as less than human, their movement is restricted, their existence is circumscribed, and they are denied access to much that society offers for a fulfilling life."[24]

This is not only an error of social conscience but one of basic anthropology.

Those who live in the Shadow World, along with those who share life with them there, can testify that this is a very emotive topic. I have, therefore, thought that to be nondenominational and non-creedal in my treatment of this subject would be of best assistance to those who live in that Shadow World, and for those who love, work with and care for them.

Finally, and most importantly, we need a reminder that the Shadow World is a place where real people live, where they experience joy and pain, gladness and sorrow, hope and disappointment, dreams and ambitions, faith and life just like you and me.

It can, at times, seem as if there is a fence between them and us, a barrier that clouds the view from our world into theirs, a fence that is hard to define and it is often embarrassing to admit that it exists. But we have to first define this fence and understand its reality before we can cross over it and, eventually, remove it forever.

So, let us look at this fence.

---

[23] Jeremy Rifkin, The Emphatic Civilization: The Race to Global Consciousness in a World in Crisis (Polity Press: Cambridge, 2010), 457

[24] William Gaventa and David Coulter, *Spirituality and Intellectual Disability* (Routledge: New York, 2011), 102 [Quoting Diane Burgent, *Come Let Us Go up to the Mountain of the Lord Isa. 2:3*, In Edward Foley, Ed., Developmental Disabilities and Sacramental Access: New Paradigms for Sacramental Encounters (Liturgical Press: Collegeville, 1994) 13–32]

Chapter 2

The Fence

WHAT FENCE?

It may seem odd at first to some that the concept of a fence between us and the disabled might exist, and it may be even offensive to some to suggest such, as we try to defend the traditional models of care and support that are currently given to the disabled.

But, as mentioned in the title, we are looking at faith as a spiritual concept and reality in the life of a disabled person, not just you and me living in a normal (neurotypical) world. This book examines spirituality and faith, essential elements in the life, care, and management of those who have a disability. Faith and spirituality within society, culture, and religion have historically, in general, not been seen as an important factor in the social care model or communal life of the disabled.

Is this important to note here? I think so. Fences are usually constructed by manual labor and consist of a material structure and form that is easily recognisable, but the fence bordering the Shadow World, in our case, can be invisible; it may be sometimes ideological or cultural or religious in its makeup.

When we speak of faith, we don't think of material structures like the fence that defines the boundary of our homes but usually of concepts of theological and ideological origin and forms of religious doctrine that were established over time that clarify, to us, the requirements of knowledge, understanding and comprehension that precede the inclusion and acceptance of one making a statement of faith within the communal life and fellowship of our churches and faith communities.

This process of setting criteria and examining a person's faith statements for inclusion within the communicant and spiritual fellowship of our communities is sometimes called "fencing" or guarding access to the deeper things of life, faith, and personal relationships with God that we consider essential to establishing the fact and veracity of that faith in God so declared.

In 2018, I was asked a question regarding 'age' in relation to faith, communion, and membership in our local church that has an important impact on this book and its discussion. As I thought about the question of the "age of accountability" I realised that this question is at the heart of this book's proposal on the inclusion of the disabled.

In our church traditions, for good reasons, we have associated participation in communion with church membership; one usually goes with the other. However, scripture does not teach this. Faith—belief in Jesus Christ—is a separate issue to membership of a fellowship and the management and decisional responsibility that that membership of a church entails.

The central criterion for participation in a service of communion is essentially the expression of confessing a personal faith in Jesus Christ,[25] and if we disassociate a person from communion on the grounds of their intellectual and cognitive ability that disables personal expression, then those who are so disabled and have faith in Christ either are or can be denied participation in a spiritual reality that their faith requires and enables—empowers—them to partake of within the spiritual fellowship of their church or faith community.

The challenge of the Apostle Paul in 1 Corinthians "to discern the body of Christ" (1 Cor. 12:27), requires much thought in our context. Does this discerning, this examining of oneself, mean only through the intellect, or reason, or knowledge? Yes, certainly we need to discern faith's existence within the life of a person, but what level of knowledge, reasoning, or intelligence determines their ability to participate in communion? Is this discerning of the body and blood of Christ tied only to the normative, neurotypical aspect of reason and knowledge of God, or can one disabled in normative intellect and knowledge rightly discern the body and blood of Christ?

---

[25] We often invite visitors of other denominations or churches who profess a faith in Jesus Christ to participate – share – in the communion service in our local church.

The word used for "unworthy manner"[26] in Paul's words to us is the Greek word ἀναξίως *anaxios* from which we derive the English word noxious, a bad smell, an unworthy thing. Is unworthy equal to intellect? Does one disabled in mind and intellect become unworthy by default even if faith, through the Spirit of God, exists within that regenerated and redeemed soul? Not so, I say.[27]

In tying together two things that are not associated in scripture, the normative intellect required for membership of a fellowship and the "discerning faith" for participation in communion within our church membership as the criteria for communion, we have put a barrier between the disabled and their ability—Christian right—to participate in the communion service with Christ that is central to the spiritual development of their faith and life with God.

While I advocate for normative reasoning to be essential for church membership, and decision making within that fellowship, I also advocate for communion participation for the disabled to be dependent upon the existence of "salvic"[28] faith, and its evidence through their language[29] as the sole criteria for the participation of the disabled in communion as a spiritual necessity for the spiritual life of both the enabled and disabled alike within our church communities.

There is a "good" (I use the term argumentatively not in a sense of moral good) reason for this fencing, and most faith communities observe and maintain key verses of their sacred documents, the Bible in our case, as stipulating what is and is not essential to in matters relating to faith leading to inclusion in our faith communities.

A key verse that is frequently used to establish criteria and covenants in defining and accepting what is identifiable and assured in areas of faith, that defines faith and provides clear

---

[26] 1 Corinthians 11:27 (ESV).
[27] This has an enormous impact, especially in the cases of believers suffering from Dementia and Alzheimer's.
[28] See "Defining Faith—Salvic Faith," page 85, para 5
[29] See "Reality of Faith," page 91, para 5

criteria for the acceptance of faith "statements" within the Christian denominational community, is Romans 10:9–10.

Romans 10:9–10 sets before us the basics of a pre-creedal confession of faith in Jesus Christ that we, living in a neurotypical world, can recognise and give assent to from our normative cognitive, volitional, sentient perspective of life.[30]

> That, if you confess with your mouth, "Jesus is Lord," and believe in your heart that God raised him from the dead, you will be saved. For it is with your heart that you believe and are justified, and it is with your mouth that you confess and are saved. (Rom. 10:9–10)[31]

These requirements—imperatives, shown here in Romans chapter 10, when interpreted in a neurotypical framework and used by many faith communities as a declaration of their faith, focus us on cognition (the ability to think in a logical, progressive manner) and comprehension (awareness of concepts and ideas), all of which are common elements of the neurological— "normal," everyday life experience for the enabled person.

In addition to these imperative requirements for faith, we are presented with a challenge in Hebrews 11:6 that adds an additional urgency to the subject matter of this book:

> Without faith, it is impossible to please God. (Heb. 11:6)

What, then, is the situation of the disabled person, the one who has a neurological communication fence to contend with in the expression and realisation of their faith? Especially the one who is not "normal" in the sense of the everyday neurological function in life and thought that we assume is necessary from our reading in Romans chapter 10 for both their personal faith (belief) and inclusion in a worship community.

This is one of the questions that parents of disabled children and adults are frequently faced with. How can they, the parents and friends, know that faith itself exists, that their disabled family member knows that faith, in a personal sense, where there exists

---

[30] See "Glossary" – page 266f
[31] All quotations, unless noted: Holy Bible, New International Version, (IBS: Colorado Springs, 1987) Used by permission.

this disruptive intrusive "communication" fence that impedes volitional expression and verification of faith within. And how, given that this communication fence exists, can the disabled person be fully understood and included, for their faith in God, within their church or faith community?

That is, how do we know that they know that what they know is real? (That, as they say, is the question and purpose of this book!)

FENCE SITTING

The mystery of "confess and believe"—"knowledge and knowing"—that we are presented with here in Romans 10:9, and in Hebrews 11:6, is a conundrum that sets before us some significant challenges regarding people with severe mental, neurological, and intellectual disabilities.

For this book, defining and actualising[32] personal faith, in this case, salvic[33] faith in Jesus Christ, for the disabled child or family member, using a neurotypical normative[34] model—narrative—of cognitive comprehension, recognition, and volitional response

---

[32] A key topic of this paper is the act of actualising the faith of the disabled person within their respective church or faith community. Actualising, in the sense used in this paper, is to make real, both in an inner and outward sense, the faith of the disabled person. Not only in a way that they know but that we accept and know what they know.

[33] My use of the word "salvic" is taken in the indicative mood; that is, it indicates a factual situation or statement. The word "salvific" refers to God's saving will or processes that lead to a saved situation—a reality for a person. The first, "salvic," states that God's saving work is complete, and the person lives in a redeemed position; the second word, "salvific", refers to the process and will of God to bring someone to the point of redemption. As this paper mainly deals with the fact of salvation for a disabled person, I use as preference the word "salvic" in most instances.

[34] Normative should be taken in this context to refer to the generally accepted practices of faith communities in acknowledging and accepting faith statements of their members, statements which are accepted as verifying the internal, heart and mind commitment that a person is making before the congregation or faith community fellowship. Normative also means the creedal and liturgical practices of a faith community that are accepted as indicative of their belief systems and dogma, which identify that community's spiritual and practical structures.

(with sentient acclaim), within their faith community is often at best uncertain or more likely to be impossible in many cases for those who live with neurological, biological, and psychological disabilities.

The question that is asked of us here is, is the salvific power of the Lord Jesus Christ sufficient to overcome the neurological, biological, and psychological disabilities a person may have, or is it more likely to be less possible in such cases?

That is, how can one disabled in either cognitive (neurological), or psychological (mental), and/or anatomical (sensory) areas of life conform to the requirements outlined in Romans 10:9–10, in order to meet the necessity of church dogma, practice, and be "pleasing to God" as we read in Hebrews 11:6. It is an important issue because how these verses are interpreted within our faith communities determines how we deal with the inclusion of the disabled within the communal and spiritual life of our faith communities.

It is hoped then that this book will be an encouragement to those who are disabled as well as those who love and care for them, and a challenge and enlightenment for all of us who see the need for a new approach to faith, disability, inclusion, and evangelism for those who live in the Shadow World of disabilities.[35]

This is an exhaustive subject matter with very emotive aspects that touch the heart of every family, person, and caregiver who interacts with and cares for disabled people, therefore:

- It is important to examine this topic from both sides of the fence,
- It is a long journey that lies ahead but there is a reward for those who travel to the end, and

---

[35] In the appendix, I provide extensive references to data on the internet, fully cited and noted. Online sources have been prioritised as, in my experience, parents, friends, and care givers of the disabled person will more often go to the internet than their local church or university library in their search for answers to this and other issues related to the disability and care of their loved ones. I encourage you to look at these sources in your own time to find further reading on the topics I address in this book.

- What we discover along the way will challenge and change how we look at faith and disability forever.

Our concluding chapter: "Postscript, Back on Our Side of the Fence" records these words:

> Faith in God has, is, and always will be a matter of "spirit"—spirituality and any other definition of faith is flawed, on both sides of the fence, for it dismisses God who is Spirit as the prime cause and facilitator of faith in those who believe, whatever "world" they live in, and marginalizes the disabled whom we may perceive to be incapable of facilitating that faith.[36]

Challenging words, so I hope, then, that you are prepared to continue along with me on this journey into the Shadow World, where we will discover new things, a bit like those brave souls whom Jules Verne characterised in *Journey to the Centre of the Earth*,[37] that discovered joy, wonder, and faced many challenges along their journey of discovery.

Now, for our next step, we must go back in time.

---

[36] See "Postscript," page 242
[37] Jules Verne, *A Journey to the Centre of the Earth*, (Griffith and Farran, 1871)—via Project Gutenberg.

Chapter 3

A Brief History

In this chapter, we will take a summary look at the history of how communities, both culturally and socially, have dealt with disability and consider their models of disability care over the course of time. In particular, we will look at the period from the time of the Reformation, circa early 1500 to 1600[38], to today, and how the disabled have been either included or excluded from participation in group activities and the fellowship life of their faith communities.

In *Present and Past Perceptions Towards Disability*, Chomba Wa Munyi[39] indicates that throughout the ages, social awareness and perceptions of disability have varied greatly, ranging from suspicion and judgment to exclusion and ritual cleansings.

In his study of disability over the past centuries Barnes, in *A Brief History of Discrimination and Disabled People*, indicates that to be precise in such a survey is almost impossible due to the variety of cultural precepts and lack of written materials on the treatment of disabled people within Western and Eastern cultures and societies.

---

[38] This period is generally viewed as the point in church history when denominationalism sprang up within the Christian faith community as an identifiable individual process. Faith communities did exist before the Reformation, and we will refer to them briefly. However, structural dogmatics and creedal statements essential to faith communities existing today primarily grew out of this period and express the core parameters and processes currently involved in acceptance, and the declaration of faith statements in today's multifaceted faith communities.

[39] All references to books, articles, and authors in this book are contained in the bibliography at the end and listed in the order in which they are quoted in the text. This helps uncomplicate the text for easier reading and allows further research if the reader desires. Some books will be in the footnotes as they are foremost in the discussion.

Commentary by Thomas, *in The Experience of Handicap*, 1982, and Hanks & Hanks, in *The Physically Handicapped,* 1980, introduces an economic element as a factor in determining society's practices toward the disabled, suggesting that their care and acceptance then becomes a function of what is fiscally viable versus what is necessary and required to address the needs and inclusion protocols within social structures.

On the perspective of religion, Schipper, in *Disability in the Hebrew Bible*, gives us an overview of the Old Testament (OT), suggesting that the OT writers viewed disability from the point of "purity"—of preserving the health of the sanctuary and the nation, in a holistic manner, through its liturgy, sanctions, and regulations surrounding its identity and culture.

On the other hand, Stiker, in *A History of Disability*,[40] takes an extremely negative view to the early New Testament (NT) era, suggesting that the relinquishing of the ceremonial and national laws of Israel left disability, and in the NT era of the church, floating on the waves of public opinion:

> The God relationship no longer entails religious prohibitions; the opposite is true. Our relationship to the abnormal, our relationship to disability depends entirely upon ourselves. [41]

That is, with no imperative *specific* dogmatic covenant conditions, Stiker comments further that there is nothing in the NT that stipulates a social order—care model for the disabled, the result of which is that the "Gospels then become a source of instability" for the disabled.

Barnes, in *Disabled People in Britain and Discrimination*, suggests that in the Middle Ages, the disabled were either classified as supernaturally endowed or the subject of

---

[40] Henri-Jacques Stiker, *A History of Disability* (University of Michigan Press: Michigan, 2007), xi, 36, 69, 76, 180.

[41] Ibid., 36–37. In a sense, Stiker assumes that following the removal of the ceremonial and Levitical OT stipulations, the condition—treatment of disabled people, or lack thereof, was at the liberty of the NT believer. This is not true, as many NT Bible verses stipulate the care and love of brothers and anyone else as essential to the creedal dogma of the NT church (Matt. 22:39, 1 Cor. 12:25, Gal. 6:2, etc.).

superstitions, persecution, or rejection from social and communal life. In general, disability was viewed (and treated) as something other than natural (i.e., children and adults with disabilities were ostracised from inclusion within their social, religious, and cultural communities). Perceptions then may have fallen somewhere between good or bad luck, punishment or cleansing of the soul, a battle between good and evil.

Entering into the Reformation period much has been said about Luther, Zwingli, Calvin and the reformers in a quite negative framework as in Stiker, in *A History of Disability*; yet in recent research and a review of this approach, Miles, in *Martin Luther and Childhood Disability,* has suggested that the reformers had an inclusive and compassionate approach to the recognition and acceptance of the disabled and their welfare within the religious and social community in which they lived.

However, little is said or written or known about in general Reformation literature on models of inclusion, spirituality, and faith as a composite of the approach of the Reformation to the issues of disability and faith.

Clapton and Fitzgerald in their essay, "A History of Disability; A History of Otherness," take a wider view of the history of disability, looking at models of management of disability in culture and society from three perspectives: a biblical model, a medical/genetics model, and a rights-based model, summarising how each model interacted over the ages concerning disability, care, and social awareness—inclusion.

Their opening statements indicate a progression from a cultural/tribal model preceding the church reformation at which time changes occurred within the social structures of Western society that opened new avenues of social inclusion and justice for the disabled.

Of note in their essay is a summary of the benefits and shortcomings of each "disability" management model, and comments on how we are still searching for a model of inclusion, acceptance, and justice that deals with the central issue of disability, identity, and equality in life and being.

Clapton and Fitzgerald challenge us to seek a model of disability that will remove the tag of "otherness"[42] and open up new avenues of existence and experience for those who live in the Shadow World of disability.

My summary of the models presented to us by Clapton and Fitzgerald in *The History of Disability: A History of Otherness*, with the main points, are as follows:

> **BIBLICAL**: Grounded in biblical references, the consequent responses and impacts of the Christian church following the Enlightenment still underpin the modern era. Themes of sin or sanctity formed in the dominant bases of Western thought following the Reformation. In the modern era of industrialisation and technology, these values and protocols were challenged by the uprising of reason and rationality. As George White states in *People with Disabilities in the Christian Community:*

As a note, George White writes, with some sadness, that there was an element in the early church that had a somewhat uncompassionate view on disability, its cause and effects on people, John 9:1f.

> Historically, many churches believed that disabilities were caused by sin in an individual's own life or their parent's lives. Today, many authors will strongly argue against that theory.[43]
>
> **MEDICAL/GENETICS**: A lack of adequate professional and material resources perpetuates a charity-based model that depicts certain "disabled" people in continual need of help, ostensibly as objects of pity being forever dependant upon others and resulting in them

---

[42] A term used by writers to identify the issues within society where disability is seen as a barrier to inclusion, thus, "otherness" or different—difference—to the normal scope of life and experience.

[43] George White, "People with Disabilities in Christian Community," *Journal of the Christian Institute on Disability* (JCID) 3, no.1, Spring/Summer 2014: 14.

often being viewed as children in the eyes of family and institutions. The inherent economic cost of a medical model further isolates the disabled, wedded to government fiscal policy, personal ability and capacity are often overlooked and assessed rather as incapacity and disability, determining care outcomes and a person's access to resources.

RIGHTS-BASED: More recently, disability has come to be conceptualised as a socio-political construct where, through the positive work of rights activists, the popular medical/genetics model above transitioned from a dependence model to that of an independence and outcomes-based model. The limits of this model were found in the concept that rights can be legislated, and are often necessary, yet the written legislation itself fails to break through the barrier of exclusion "otherness" in society leading us forward toward a model of inclusion and community acceptance.

SOCIAL: In their conclusions, Clapton and Fitzgerald suggest that the rise of genetics has the danger of isolating the whole of a person from society; the religious model has limitations in dealing with its purity mode, and the medical model has issues with fiscal policy while the rights-based model fails to empower inclusion. An enlightened society should be demanding a new model of disability that espouses that bodily differences should not be allowed to mask our essential humanity, especially for those who are disabled and find themselves isolated in a field of "otherness." Limitations of the construct of disability, whatever the model, inherently disable dialogue.

We can see from our brief skim over the surface of a historical view of the treatment of disability within human culture—from a religious, medical, and social perspective—that each model falls short of the care and inclusion ideal that each model seeks to provide.

This shortfall in the basic models of disability, as discussed above, and the historical search for an ideal, is in part the motivation for this book, which presents a new model of disability care and inclusion, a lifting of the veil,[44] engendering a new additional model of inclusion based on faith, a faith in God that is both inclusive and transitional, uniting all, enabled and disabled, in the pool of humanity who live on either side of the fence.

Our brief chapter on the history of disability treatment models has given us a broad overview of how the community as a whole has dealt with disability and issues of life and inclusion. But what defines life? Can defining what life is, what it means "to be"—"to exist"—help us better understand how faith and disability interact within life and thought, especially in the life of a disabled person?

Let us find out.

---

[44] Jody Plecas, Review comments email, 09/03/2018, used with permission.

Chapter 4

Defining Being

WHAT IS LIFE?

What does it mean "to be," "to exist," to live as a sentient being, a person distinct from another? What defines life? Are there any human characteristics that set us apart from the animal world, characteristics that define us as human beings, or are we just part of the organic collective of life on this planet?

It is a question that Hamlet ponders (Act 3, Scene 1) in a moment of reflection on life, "to be or not to be."[45] What is the purpose of life, and where does "life" itself reside? An important question to answer when dealing with disability, especially a disability that at times blurs the distinction between function and form, between our world and the Shadow World.

Wikipedia has this basic definition of "life."[46]

> The definition of life is controversial. The current definition is that organisms maintain homeostasis,[47] are composed of cells, undergo metabolism, can grow, adapt to their environment, respond to stimuli, and reproduce.

The article goes on to state that organic life exists, primarily, here on earth in various forms, but the sciences also propose that

---

[45] "To be or not to be" is the famous phrase that begins a soliloquy in Act 3 of Shakespeare's *Hamlet,* in which the titular character contemplates death and suicide, bemoaning the pain and unfairness of life but acknowledging that the alternative might be worse. The meaning of the speech is heavily debated but seems concerned with Hamlet's hesitation to directly and immediately avenge his father's murder (discovered in Act 1) on his uncle, stepfather, and new King Claudius.

[46] Wikipedia: Life: *https://en.wikipedia.org/wiki/Life*

[47] Wikipedia: Homeostasis: In biology, homeostasis is the state of steady internal, physical, and chemical conditions maintained by living systems. *https://en.wikipedia.org/wiki/Homeostasis* See glossary.

there is a form of life that is beyond the organic and has a separate listing for what we would term human life.

> The human condition is "the characteristics, key events, and situations which compose the essentials of human existence, such as birth, growth, emotionality, aspiration, conflict, and mortality. This is a very broad topic which has been and continues to be pondered and analyzed from many perspectives, including those of religion, philosophy, history, art, literature, anthropology, psychology, and biology."[48]

Human life or simply "life" may refer to in philosophy as the human condition or "conditio humana"[49] and discusses the meaning of life and personal life, as the course of an individual's life, especially when viewed as the sum of personal choices contributing to one's personal identity.

Other forms of life considered in articles to be sentient,[50] individual, and/or self-aware, are sometimes termed artificial intelligence, such as animals, computers, algorithms, robotics, and biochemistry that endeavor to simulate certain aspects of human "life," the "condition humana" but do not achieve the sapient[51] aspect of life, that spark of life that creates spontaneous awareness of self and independent moral thought that is essentially only existent in the human form of life.

Although some aspects of artificial life, or artificial intelligence, can be helpful in the world of disability they do not

---

[48] Wikipedia, Human Condition "conditio humana," https://en.wikipedia.org/wiki/Human_condition

[49] See "Glossary" – conditio humana, page 267

[50] Wikipedia, Sentience: Sentience is the capacity to feel, perceive, or experience subjectively.[1] Eighteenth-century philosophers used the concept to distinguish the ability to think (reason—see sapience) from the ability to feel (sentience). In modern Western philosophy, sentience is the ability to experience sensations (known in the philosophy of mind as "qualia"). In Eastern philosophy, sentience is a metaphysical quality of all things that require respect and care.

[51] Wikipedia, Sapience: "noun of sapient, is the ability to think and to reason. It may not seem like much of a difference, but the ability to reason is tied more closely to sapience than to sentience." Most animals are sentient (yes, you can correctly say your dog is sentient!), but only humans are sapient.

constitute "being"—sapient life itself, life as we know it, in the sense of our identity as human beings.[52]

When answering the question "what is life?" we must search beyond the organic, the visual, the physical life, the external outward appearance of a person to the inward evidence of life. And it is here, in the inward person, their inner spiritual being, that we have to enter into this discussion of what it means to be, to exist, in the Shadow World of disability.

PHYSICAL LIFE

However, before we start looking beyond the organic, let's first establish what we mean by "physical life," as a definition of life. This is usually understood as the DNA of life, the material physical structures that create the biological and anatomical (chemical-material) framework that establishes the details of the external, physical body, or outer person that we see and interact with, in and through that body each day.

It seems overly simple to state, but our sense of "being," how we are perceived by and how we accept others as human beings, depends a lot upon this external box. My reason for stating this is that sometimes people with disabilities are seen as less than human, yet they have the same foundational DNA-based organic structures—basis for their lives—as we do. They are, essentially, whatever their external appearance or function, made of the same "stuff" as we are.

Although, in many cases, their external body, due to anatomical and neurological disabilities, may not exhibit the same form—shape or function—as that of an average "normal" (neurotypical) person, their existence as a human being, their conditio humana, is evidenced in the observation that their "being," their true inner humanity, exists just the same as ours and that they have and experience life within a functioning, although disabled, living human body.

---

[52] As noted, this paper comes from a Christian standpoint on matters of life and the definition of being. The origin of life in God is both sentient and sapient; God the Father, Son, and Spirit, each being a distinct sentient personality, are sapient in their relationship, self-aware morally, transcendent yet individual in existence within the godhead.

The issue becomes more apparent to us in this discussion when we see that what is viewed on the outside, the external box, is often used to determine whether life is, or is thought to be, of sufficient quality (function and presence) on the inside as "conditio conscius,"[53]—that is, the normal consciousness condition of human life.

Can "conditio humana" then be said to exist when "conditio conscius"—neurotypical conciousness—does not seem to exist, at least from our external viewpoint? That is, can the human condition be reckoned to exist, in the fullness of its expression of humanity, in the life of one disabled in the basic functions of expression of life through their neurological and anatomical disabilities?

Particularly as the one depends upon the other. Life in this world needs the body, and the body needs inner life to exist in conditio humana. In this world in which we live, bodily, the inner self (the soul and spirit) of a person requires the physical external body to sustain a conditio humana existence.

It is to this interaction (and interdependence) between the necessity of physical (outer) and the inner spiritual concepts of life in this world that we address our discussion on life—"on being"—in this book. This inner life is defined in this book as ontological life, "the wholistic nature of being." But what is ontological life? [54]

ONTOLOGICAL LIFE

Ontological life[55] is the definition of life in relation to one's being, one's existence as an individual independent of the

---

[53] See "Glossary" – condito-conscius, page 267

[54] Biological and ontological life is an extensive discussion outside the scope of this book. My view is that life is a state of "being," and the essential element of this "being" is spiritual (ontological) in nature, and that this "being" is essentially independent of the body but nevertheless dependent upon the body for function and recognition in this physical material world.

[55] Ontological life: Ontology is the philosophical study of the nature of being, becoming, existence, or reality, as well as the basic categories of being and their relations. [1] Traditionally listed as a part of the major branch of philosophy known as metaphysics, [2] ontology often deals with questions concerning what entities exist or may be

empirical, experiential, and external attributes of life and defines the reality of our existence as a person separate from observable physical evidence.

Ontological life is also the foundation of one's being. It necessitates an understanding of life that is not wholly based on the visual, biological, external, or physical realities (evidences) of one's existence in this world.

It reaches beyond the physical outer body to the inner self that defines one's "true being" and thus one's reality in life as a person. Ontological life is, therefore, in some ways independent of the body within which it exists.

This is an important distinction, as we will learn later in this book because one's existence, essential being, while dependent upon a body in this mortal life, is not limited by the condition (conditio humana) of that body for "life" itself. Recent social and scientific studies are re-evaluating what defines "being," existence, and reality and are looking to the ontological aspects of life for a better understanding of who and what we are as conditio humana.

We will need to look further at this, but a 2012 article by the Center for Systems Philosophy on what defines life touches on the link between ontology and being, between being and spirituality and reads:

> Beyond this, there is also a growing recognition in the "hard" sciences that Physicalism [external evidences] may be inadequate for explaining the fundamental facts about life, consciousness and mind.[56]

It is, therefore, necessary that we enter into this discussion on ontology and spirituality as they are interlinked in defining what

---

said to exist and how such entities may be grouped, related within a hierarchy, and subdivided according to similarities and differences.
See: *http://www.yourdictionary.com/ontology* Ontology; the branch of metaphysics dealing with the nature of being, reality, or ultimate substance; gives a particular theory about being or reality.

[56] Centre for Systems Philosophy; About the Philosophy of Spirituality: http://www.philosophy-of-spirituality.org/about-philosophy-of-spirituality.htm?i=1

life is, and how life is to be perceived, both in the world of the neurotypical and the Shadow World of the disabled.

How then does one's ontological state of being relate to spirituality? Are they the same thing, or are they different or concurrent?

SPIRITUAL LIFE

While a clear and precise definition of ontology—one's being in the area of philosophy and the humanities—may be elusive, a definition of spirituality and life is not.

This book takes the viewpoint that one's ontological existence and spirituality, although distinct properties, are interrelated in their function of defining what it means "to be," to exist as a person in this world.

As the universe has a beginning so too does one's existence, "one's being." A key issue for life, and throughout this book, is when does one begin "to be," and if there is a beginning of "being," is there an end?

Ontologically, one's being has a beginning, and that "being" is articulated and identified as their unique individual spirituality, their personal soul/spirit[57], that "part" of them that although invisible to the human eye, is the core of their existence—that essential element of life that identifies them as a human being, conditio humana, and establishes their conditio conscius.[58]

That is, ontologically, I exist as an individual "being" because I am a spiritual human being, but how?

---

[57] "soul/spirit" – "spirit/soul" Throughout this book, I hold the view that a person has a spiritual nature that identifies them "specifically" as human, separate from animals and other forms of life that this planet may contain. My use of this phrase changes from time to time, sometimes "spirit/soul," other times "soul/spirit." If I am referring to cognitive or emotional issues, the order is "soul/spirit"; if I am referring specifically to the "spirituality" of a person, it is usually "spirit/soul."

[58] "I think, therefore I am." Rene Descartes: A beginning step, but where does the capacity to think come from? That is the essence that this book aims to reveal in the following chapters.
https://en.wikipedia.org/wiki/Ren%C3%A9_Descartes

This book takes the Judeo-Christian view of humanity, both body and soul (spirit),[59] as a two-part unity that encompasses our "being" in this world; the spiritual essence, soul, giving motivation to and sustaining life in the body, and the body as that necessary "vehicle" in and through which that spirituality expresses itself into this world.[60]

The key Bible verse for this position is Genesis 2:7. There are two accounts of the creation of man in the book of Genesis. The first, in Genesis chapter 1, tells us of man's creation—material existence—position as part of the overall creation of the physical universe, our solar system, and world. The second account is in chapter 2 where we see the creation of man from the spiritual perspective.

> Then the LORD God formed a man from the dust of the ground and breathed into his nostrils the breath of life, and the man became a living being. (Gen. 2:7)

We will talk more about the spirituality of man and its importance in our discussion on faith in the chapter "Defining Faith," but it is sufficient here to acknowledge that man, as created by God, is a spiritual creature as well as a material one.

Thus, the spiritual enlivens the material and lives and expresses itself within that material body through the anatomical and neurological organs of that body. I exist then bodily in this world because I am principally a spiritual human being.

One's spirituality, defined as the human soul/spirit, animates and gives life to the body. This spiritual life that exists within the body defines a person's ontological reality in this world and is the source from which their personality, character, mind, emotions, and consciousness are established.

It also needs to be noted here that the essence of one's spirituality intrinsically consists of the same "stuff" whether that person is enabled or disabled in the body, either anatomically or in the mind, neurologically.

---

[59] Discovery of the human "spirit" is the key that unlocks the door to our identity; we are more than just a body; the human "spirit" is that unique identifier of our humanity. It is our true reality and life.

[60] Anthony Hoekema, Created in God's Image (Grand Rapids: Eerdmans, 1986), page 203.

MAN IS A SPIRITUAL BEING

Like the fuel stored in a service station's underground tank, it is the same "stuff" whatever car it is pumped into through the petrol bowser. How it operates in each individual vehicle may be different and is a property of the engine and features of that car; the fuel, though, one's essential spirituality, is the same whatever vehicle it is in.

Therefore, the ontological existence, "being," of a disabled person is fundamentally the same as any other person; their state of "being" is tied essentially to their spirituality, which is basically, and more importantly, the same as you and I.

From this short discussion, we can draw a clear conclusion. One who lives in the Shadow World of disability has the same ontological "being," is made of the same spiritual "stuff," and has the same conditio humana status as one who is physically, neurologically, and mentally regarded as "normal," living a neurotypical existence.

You cannot have one without the other. One is either conditio humana or not.

It was this very question of equality of existence (conditio humana), "being," that challenged me the most. How can one disabled in mind [neurologically] and body [biologically], who is unable to communicate in a manner that is understandable or recognisable to the outside neurotypical world, be the same, have the same sense of being, the same ontological existence, and inner spirituality as an able-bodied and 'conditio humana' neurotypical person?

Let us state it clearly here that "condito humana," the state of being – one's existential existence as fully human — is the same for the enabled person as it is for the disabled person, whatever the condition, ability or disability, of that person may be.

From this question of defining "condito humana," we now direct our discussion on disability and faith, to defining disability and faith anticipating, eventually, the discovery of "life" and "being" in all its beauty for those who live in the Shadow World.

CHAPTER 5

DEFINING DISABILITY

A broad definition of disability from the World Health Organisation gives a basic introduction to the various areas in which a person can, or may, be disabled. The WHO article, although brief, does point out that disabilities can be a complex area, and people can have a variety of disabilities that make treatment and socialisation a difficult and complex task for them.

> Disabilities is an umbrella term, covering impairments, activity limitations, and participation restrictions. An impairment is a problem in body function or structure; an activity limitation is a difficulty encountered by an individual in executing a task or action; while a participation restriction is a problem experienced by an individual in involvement in life situations. Overcoming the difficulties faced by people with disabilities requires interventions to remove environmental and social barriers. [61]

The article goes on to list the fundamental areas in which disability can present itself in the life, character, and nature "being" of a person. It also notes that a person may experience one or more impairments from a general category of disabilities. Generally, these categories can include physical disability, intellectual disability, mental or emotional disability and developmental disability. We will look at them (briefly) in conjunction with a category that I have added, which is termed, "spiritual disability."

---

[61] World Health Organisation, Disabilities;
https://www.who.int/topics/disabilities/en/
See also: http://en.wikipedia.org/wiki/Disability Cited, 01/07/ 2011.

PHYSICAL DISABILITY

First, we must define physical disability. Physical disability is a disability or impairment that limits bodily motor functions and diminishes the physical response available to the person to situational stimulants and/or impedes mobility in daily tasks.

Although physical disabilities are often visual, Charles Gourgey writes, in the *Journal of Religion in Disability and Rehabilitation*, that their effect on a person can go far beyond what is seen or perceived externally.

> The hardship of living with a physical disability goes far beyond the limitations imposed by the disability itself. The consequences of having a disability can profoundly affect not only the body but also the mind and spirit. This is because so much of our sense of well-being is dependent on the way others perceive us and the way we perceive ourselves.[62]

The importance of the link between the physical and spiritual, evident in the Apostle Paul's words in Romans 10:9, should not go unnoted in our discussion here. This link between body and self, along with the sense of 'personal' well-being that has risen in recent years, is essential to establishing one's sense of being, reality, and humanity.

Christ himself makes this link between the external material body and the inner spiritual state of a person, the spirit-mind-soul continuum[63] of a person, when He observes the invalid man in Jerusalem at the pool of Bethesda.[64] (John 5.2f)

Here the man's physical disabilities had so emotionally and spiritually weakened him to the point where, in response to the

---

[62] Charles Gourgey, "Faith Despair, and Disability," *Journal of Religion in Disability and Rehabilitation* 1, no. 3 (Haworth Press, 1994): 51–63.

[63] See "Glossary" – continuum, page 268

[64] We should not fall into the trap of Aristotle's dualism here, the separation of the material body and the spiritual soul, but clearly states that a person is a composite being, the spirit/soul and the material body held in a union that God creates. The 'spirit' of a person in this world requires the material body, and the material body requires the spirit of life (Gen. 2:7) to give movement, expression, and being to that person.

words of Christ, he could only cry out for some external, beyond his physical being, intervention.

The man's capacity to communicate to Jesus his full feelings and emotions was compromised; in desperation he cries out in the universal language of distress .

He says to Jesus:

> "Sir," the invalid replied[65], "I have no one to help me into the pool when the water is stirred. While I am trying to get in, someone else goes down ahead of me." (John 5:7)

Physical disabilities, also, can have an impact on a person's ability to respond to and assimilate information received, as we read in the encounter between Jesus and the deaf and dumb man in Mark chapter 7.

> And they brought to him a man who was deaf and had a speech impediment, and they begged him to lay his hand on him. (Mark 7:32)

There would have been some neurological issues associated with the deaf and dumb man, but the physical disabilities associated with the condition of his bodily organs, anatomically, would have been part of that mix not only in this case but in most observable cases of physical disabilities.

In relation to bodily anatomical functions, the World Health Organisation, in *Towards a Common Language for Functioning, Disability and Health*,[66], indicates that the expression of one's inner feelings and experiences can be severely limited and thus fundamentally limiting to one's concept—view—of self and life.

It is accepted—understood—that in biblical times disabilities were not as evidently identified (quantified) as they now are in DSM-4/5 (see *A Brief History* above); however, people would still

---

[65] As Frank Gabelein explains in *Expositor's Biblical Commentary*: "The people brought the deaf-mute to Jesus and begged Jesus to lay his hands on him. Although they did not explicitly say so, they obviously wanted Jesus to heal the man. 'They begged' (parakalousin) shows their concern for him, and Jesus responds to it. The deaf-mute could make no intelligible request for himself."

[66] World Health Organization, Geneva, "Towards a Common Language for Functioning, Disability and Health ICF,"
http://www.who.int/classifications/icf/icfbeginnersguide.pdf

have suffered from some if not all of the physical, neurological, and emotional disabilities we see and experience today. However, the reality of faith and disability, the central topic of this book in relationship to faith's expression and understanding, is still evident in the biblical record.

Where disabilities were once, biblically, seen as external realities, many of the physical disabilities addressed in the Bible would now be associated with genetics, autism, Downs' syndrome, epilepsy, or other disabilities.

J. Schipper in *Disability in the Hebrew* Bible[67] speaks about the ambiguities of the Hebrew language in specifically identifying disabilities by type or severity:

> The Hebrew word מְאוּם, usually translated as "blemish," refers to many conditions that we may consider a disability, such as blindness or lameness (cf. Lev. 21:16–23).

The Levitical regulations on diseases are more focused on how that illness or disability may affect the overall sanctity of the nation and the temple. The priests are charged with keeping the temple "clean" and ensuring that any "illness" is isolated from the general population. This does not mean that Old Testament Hebrew, as a cultural language, has no concern regarding disability; it is just that the focus of the language used is centered upon the purity of the religious and spiritual life of the people of Israel.

We are, and can be, thankful that disabilities of a physical and mental nature are addressed biblically today, and organisations and entities currently establish care models and protocols, such as the California State University, Northridge, who, in their human resources management protocols, define and assist those with physical disabilities in a biblical approach:

> Physical impairment refers to a broad range of disabilities which include orthopedic, neuromuscular, cardiovascular and pulmonary disorders. People with these disabilities

---

[67] Jeremy Schipper, Disability in the Hebrew Bible, Society of Biblical Literature, *https://www.sbl-site.org/assets/pdfs/TBv2i8_SchipperDisability.pdf*

often must rely upon assertive devices such as wheelchairs, crutches, canes, and artificial limbs to obtain mobility.

The physical disability may either be congenital or a result of injury, muscular dystrophy, multiple sclerosis, cerebral palsy, amputation, heart disease, pulmonary disease, or more. Some persons may have hidden (nonvisible) disabilities which include pulmonary disease, respiratory disorders, epilepsy and other limiting conditions.[68]

Whatever the physical disability we are considering in relation to a person, it would be agreed that physical disabilities do have an impact on the spiritual responses of the soul/spirit of a person to situations that they experience and, as a result, have an impact—effect—upon the person's interactions with God and other people.

There is, of course, a reality check that we need to address early in this book. While every endeavor is made to assist people with physical, and anatomical disabilities through therapy and surgery, it is noted that some physical disabilities cannot be overcome by human means.

In 2014, Australia's public broadcaster ABC News took up this challenge in a highly criticised article, written by Shane Clifton, "Disability and the Dark Side of the Positivity Myth." The article is sensitive and cautious but also critical of the feel-good presentations that can, inadvertently, mask the reality that no amount of positive thinking can resolve the basic issues of impairment in body and mind that present in many complex disability cases.

Shane Clifton writes, (referring to a presentation on a TV lifestyle show), that the "hidden" issue of reality in disability in these shows often remains unaddressed:

---

[68] Jessica Haenn, Succeeding Together: People with Disabilities in the Workplace. *http://www.csun.edu/~sp20558/dis/physical.html* California State University, Northridge, See also HRM Document: *http://www.calstate.edu/HRAdm/pdf2011/TL-EEO2011-05.pdf*

It's that disability can't be thought away; mind doesn't trump matter but is itself an embodied reality.[69]

While Shane Clifton is positive in that these TV shows do show that there is often a better side of life with a disability, they often miss the point that a person can live and not recover from an injury or be born with complex disabilities yet still have a good, fulfilling life while dealing with those complex disabilities.

We need to note Shane's words here when we come to deal with matters of faith and spirituality in a person with complex disabilities that the disabilities do not define the view of life that the person has from the inside. To evaluate "quality of life" on our neurotypical scale alone is an error, and a person with substantial disabilities can still "live a good life" despite and often notwithstanding their complex diagnosis.

In speaking of faith in relation to physical disabilities, the union of one's body anatomically with the spiritual (nonmaterial) human spirit/soul of a person is a key facet in defining true reality for those with physical (and neurological) disabilities. And the outcome of such physical disabilities ultimately impacting on one's sense of self—"being" as well as placing unseen challenges before those who will love, care for, and work with the physically disabled within our community.

However, it should be noted here that this book will propose later that the intrinsic spirituality, essentially the quintessence of the soul/spirit "being" of the "disabled" person, is not impaired by any physical or anatomical disability in its function as a human spiritual soul, but accepts that, that the soul/spirit can be impaired in the expression of its true being—self "spirituality" by a physically and anatomically impaired body. We acknowledge then that physical disabilities can, at times, impair the ability of a disabled person in the expression of that "essence" of their inner spirituality.

---

[69] Shane Clifton, Religion & Ethics; Disability and the Dark Side of the Positivity Myth, (Australian Broadcasting Corporation), *http://www.abc.net.au/religion/articles/2014/09/18/4090190.htm* Cited, 26/12/2016.

SENSORY DISABILITY

In addition to physical disabilities, sensory disabilities can also have an impact on the comprehension and expression of a person's spirituality. Achieve Australia provides a concise definition of sensory impairment:

> Sensory impairment is when one of the senses; sight, hearing, smell, touch, taste and spatial awareness, is no longer normal. Communication is the greatest challenge. A sighted and hearing person will explore their surroundings, a person with sensory impairments will need encouragement to explore and interact.[70]

As termed above, sensory impairment affects the sensory responses (mode) of a person. All five senses, areas of information gathering, are included, sight, sound, smell, taste, and feel—touch including spatial awareness. In addition to the debilitating effects of sensory overload, that many cases react to, there is the long-term effects of SPD[71] to be considered. In her article "Sensory Processing Disorder," published by the STAR Institute, Mim Ochsenbein informs us that SPD can be a lifelong disability,[72] and although coping strategies can be developed for the individual, the basic disability is often a lifetime condition.

Also, according to the House With No Steps article, "Sensory Disability,"[73] it should be noted that "sensory impairment" may

---

[70] Achieve Australia, "What is Sensory Impairment; http://achieveaustralia.org.au/people-we-support/what-is-sensory-impairment/ Cited, 26/12/2016.

[71] SPD—Sensory Processing Disorder.

[72] Mim Ochsenbein, "Sensory Processing Disorder: It's Not… Something You Outgrow" article listed at Star Institute, Centennial, Colorado. https://www.spdstar.org/node/1134 "Sometimes called 'sensory integration,' SPD refers to how the nervous system receives messages from the senses. Often aligned with Autism Spectrum Disorder, SPD is a condition that exists when sensory signals don't get organized into appropriate responses. Acting like a neurological 'traffic jam,' SPD prevents certain parts of the brain from receiving the information needed to interpret sensory information correctly, resulting in motor clumsiness, behavioural problems, anxiety, depression, and learning difficulties. SPD can affect people in one or multiple senses."

[73] House With No Steps: Sensory Disability. This is a good page with additional information on sensory disability. "Sensory impairment

mean heightened or lessened sensory response, thus stimulation from the senses might be lower than normal or much higher. A person with a sensory disability might have to wear colored glasses or earmuffs or gloves or avoid certain areas of a home or outdoor environment.

In addition, a person with a sensory impairment may have one or more of these essential areas of everyday information and evidence gathering affected, influencing their ability to process such sensory input and formulate a normalised response to sensory stimulation.

The term "she/he is having a meltdown" is usually seen as anecdotal but could have tangible realities in the overstimulation of one or more of the senses of the disabled person. These sensory disabilities can limit the capacity of a disabled person to respond to words, a comforting touch, an offer of food, or to be comfortable in their environment—all of which may heighten their anxiety when interacting with others.[74]

Robert J. Dorman, in his paper *"Neurodevelopmental Perspectives on Autism and Asperger's Syndrome,"*[75] discusses the complex relationships between physiology (body) and neurological (mind) development in early childhood pointing out that the interrelationships between the physical and mental development of a child is a paramount issue in determining if a young child is developing a neurological, or sensory disorder.

Specifically, Dorman links neurology and physiology with sensory disorders, either in over-sensory stimulation or under-stimulation, which can have a large effect on the child's

---

    can get very complicated; a blind person might have low eyesight sensory function yet a heightened auditory or sense of smell."

http://www.hwns.com.au/Resource-centre/Types-of-disabilities/Sensory-disability

[74] Although there are many services and programs for visual and hearing impairment as "classed sensory impairments," little is written on the sensory impairment that many on the autistic spectrum experience, especially Asperger's sufferers. Much needs to be done here for those on the spectrum who have multiple sensory issues.

[75] Robert Doman, Jr. Neurodevelopmental Perspectives on Autism and Asperger's Syndrome: Printed in the Autism Health and Wellness Magazine Volume 1 Issue 3 – Autumn 2009.
http://nacd.org/journal/0909_autism_spectrum.php

development in their ability to "think in pictures and words," which can have a lasting effect on their ability to process information and respond in a neurotypical manner to the same stimulations that the general "neurotypical" population otherwise would be able to do.

Dorman advocates for a progressive approach to defining and treating autism, specifically Asperger's syndrome, and campaigns for an approach to autism that first takes into account a person's neurological, physiological, and sensory mix before any treatment plan or management regime is established.

A strong theme in Dorman's paper is that we treat anyone on the autism spectrum, either high or low functioning, as a unique individual, a point he mentions several times in his paper, and warns us against a one treatment fits all mix in how we relate to and engage with people on the autism spectrum.

> Complexity of thought, conceptual thought, language, and global neurological and developmental maturity are critically linked. For those within the spectrum, the developmental delay produced from the sensory dysfunction creates both neurodevelopmental delay and an imbalance affecting these critical functions. This imbalance, if not addressed, can and often does have a devastating effect on the ability to process, understand, and utilize language, as well as the ability to think conceptually, thus impacting global function.

At times, words, thoughts, and concepts that are acceptable in a neurotypical sense might be inappropriate when interacting with someone who has a sensory disability, and if the impairment is visual, then body language cues may be redundant, and so on. Therefore, according to Susannah Mintz, "*Ordinary Vessels*"[76] understanding the effects of sensory disability on a person can be crucial to successful communication with them and our comprehension of what they are communicating to us in their own "unique language."

---

[76] Susannah Mintz, *Disability Studies Quarterly* 26, no. 3 (2006), "Ordinary Vessels: Disability Narrative and Representations of Faith," para 30 http://www.dsq-sds.org/article/view/722/899

Sensory disabilities are often harder to define as some are invisible like smell, touch, sound, and spatial awareness, but each and all can affect the way a person processes information and responds to their environment.

Disability Services Australia discusses sensory disabilities and the effect they have upon the personal and existential[77] experiences of a disabled person:

> Sensory Integration Dysfunction (SID) (also called sensory processing disorder) is a neurological disorder that causes difficulties with processing information from the five senses (vision, hearing, touch, smell and taste), the sense of movement (vestibular system), and/or sense of position (proprioception). Unlike blindness or deafness, sensory information is sensed normally by a person with Sensory Integration Dysfunction, but the brain perceives and analyses the information in an unusual way that may cause distress or confusion.

As external information and stimulation are usually received through one's anatomical sensory organs, distortions either as lows or highs can have an impact on the way information is received, neurologically, and processed as thoughts and responses by the mind.

Sensory impairment, therefore, as either SPD or SID[78] or both, places significant challenges before faith communities in how they present, evaluate, and actualise the faith responses of those so affected within their fellowship or community.

The neurotypical model of human understanding, cognizance, and experience, when applied to the words of the Apostle Paul in Romans 10:14 below, presents a significant difficulty to those who may have sensory impairments. We usually assume that responses

---

[77] *http://www.thefreedictionary.com/existential* Existential: of, relating to, or dealing with existence. Based on experience, empirical ("What we know about life from personal experiences"), the experience of living in this world, the interaction with external realities, and internal thought. Cited, 13/02/2015. See "Glossary" – existential, page 269

[78] SID: Sensory Integration Dysfunction: The manner in which one receives, absorbs, and quantifies - integrates sensory input.

to these verses in Romans need to comply with traditional "norm—neurotypical—protocols"[79] and answers of those whose sensory fundamentals are not disabled.

> How, then, can they call on the one they have not believed in? And how can they believe in the one of whom they have not heard? And how can they hear without someone preaching to them? (Rom. 10:14)

The question then for us is obvious. For a person who has sensory disabilities (often multiple) how can they hear if deaf, how can they respond if mute, how can someone preach to them that they may believe if they do not know their 'language'?

In our definition of being, 'self', (in Defining Being) we established that being human was a unity of body and soul/spirit; a unity that was essentially meta-spiritual in nature, and crucial to one's awareness of life and sense of self. The question then becomes how one communicates with someone with sensory impairments in a manner that is both "audible" and reasonable to them.

Also, the implication for our discussion on sensory disability is that as "being" is essentially a spiritual issue, the reality of Romans 10:14 still applies to the sensory disabled as well as the enabled. Thus, although sensory disabilities can have an impact on the existential experiences of the soul/spirit of a person, sensory disabilities cannot disable the spirit/soul of that person.

We have been discussing at length anatomical (bodily) disabilities and how they may impact upon the biological, expressional, and spiritual experience of the disabled. Now let us next examine briefly intellectual disability.

INTELLECTUAL DISABILITY

Sometimes cognitive—intellectual—development disorders, usually termed as Intellectual Disability Disorder (IDD), are frequently exasperated by associated sensory impairments that

---

[79] In this context, "protocols" is used to mean "conventions"—what we see as normal and acceptable responses to faith conventions and liturgy.

can intensify the impact that an intellectual impairment inherently has on cognitive and spiritual development.

Charles Thomas, in *Cognitive Defects and Spiritual Development,* writes:

> The degree by which one develops cognitively affects traditional educational issues and spiritual development[80]

It is at times difficult to establish a clear distinction—or a barrier—between individual diagnosis, but although intellectual disability may have multiple origins it can have a profound effect on the soul/spirit-mind of the disabled person.

Charles Thomas again writes:

> What then occurs in the spiritual development of one with cognitive disabilities? Paloutzain suggests that spiritual development is roughly parallel to the general stages of cognitive development. This would imply that one with cognitive (IDD) deficit would also be less developed in their spiritual development.[81]

Therefore, Intellectual Development Disability (IDD) presents a different set of issues, whereas one might have physical and sensory disabilities, which can in and of themselves present formidable barriers to communication, intellectual disability hits at the heart of a person's ability to gather, assimilate, and evaluate information and make personal relational decisions based on cognitive reasoning.

Intellectual disability can affect cognitive function, impairing the ability of a person to learn, to absorb, and to retain new information, and coordinate and communicate that information through neurological processes into a logical sequence affecting their ability to make an evaluative volitional expressional decision.

---

[80] Charles Thomas, Cognitive Defects and Spiritual Development: The Relationships between Cognitive Defects and Spiritual Development (Lynchburg, VA: Liberty University, 2008), 2.

[81] I would like to note here that although this may be true for the expression of that spiritual development in a neurotypical sense—model—this paper proposes that there is no impairment in the experience of that spirituality, in their personal spirit/soul, between that disabled person and God.

That is, not being able to effectually cognate information for themselves in the usual neurotypical manner, IDD affects the way the disabled person processes the information that they have received, in whatever manner possible, and then actualise[82] that information in order to determine an adaptive[83] response.

The terms acquired brain injury, neurodegenerative disease, cognitive impairment, and even the highly derogatory "mental impediment,"[84] are all associated with intellectual disability, and IDD, being inherently founded at the core of the human psyche, can therefore have major disruptive effects upon that person's ability to make a sound and reasoned decision.

A second issue with an intellectual disability is that in many cases it is often progressive and not static, rarely moving in the positive direction toward improved cognition but more often in the negative, compounding the person's inability to remember previous conclusions. This further impairs—impacts upon—their capacity to make decisions based upon analytical skills or intuitive processing of the information they have received.

The Centre for Developmental Disability (DD), Department of Health, Victoria (Monash University) has a prompt for its staff training regarding intellectual disability that sums up the impact of this disability on the life and nature of a person with an intellectual disability.

> The definition of intellectual disability requires that an individual has an IQ below 70 along with significant

---

[82] Actualise: the processes by which a person's cognates received information and sensory data within their mind (spirit/soul), bringing to actuality a response dependent upon that received information.

[83] Wikipedia, Adaptive Behavior: That process, or conceptual processes, whereby a person receives information and facilitates a response.

[84] I, personally, feel disquieted using this term as it can be dismissive of the beauty of life that is still a reality for those so disabled. However, while many in the field ceased using terms such as this, and its derogatory alternatives, in medical terminology long ago, it is still used by some even today. Notably, this term was still used until September 2013 by the US government in documentation relating to social policy. Historically—even subconsciously—this lingering terminology sits in our minds and can draw us away from recognising the beauty of every human being, whether enabled or disabled (Psalm 139:13).

difficulties in adaptive behaviors and daily living skills such as self-care, communication and community participation. The more severe the disability, the more likely it is that the person will have associated sensory impairments which further undermines their ability to engage and learn. Vigilance with respect to detection and attention to sensory impairment is therefore imperative.[85]

This issue of engagement is important if the ability of the disabled person to express their experiences of faith outwardly, particularly into the neurotypical world, is consequently limited as a result of them having IDD.

Intellectual deficit disability, briefly touched on above, covers a wide range of issues from cognition to assimilation of information and adaptive behaviors, all of which tend to place those so affected outside the range of accepted responses that we would otherwise suppose are required for one to make or express a statement of faith.

Certainly, intellectual disabilities can be disruptive in the management of thought processes and adaptive behaviors within an individual, but many so affected are still valued participants in the life and fellowship of their faith communities.

Our brief overview of cognitive disability has raised some questions about homeostasis[86] interaction—that elusive interface between body and soul/spirit in a human 'being'. One of these important questions was raised by Jody Plecas, a friend and helper, during the development of this book:

> Does this preclude the notion that a fully cognitive "spirit" or "soul" which is not of the (material) body is merely trapped inside an impaired vessel?[87]

This is certainly a difficult and emotional question to answer. Essentially, at the point of the act of the giving of life, the "breath

---

[85] Monash University, "Working with people with Intellectual Disability in Health Care," Centre for Developmental Disability, Health Victoria, CDDH fact sheet.
[86] See "Glossary" – homeostasis, page 269
[87] Jody Plecas, Review comments email, 09/03/2018, used with permission.
See Appendix II: Jody Plecas, Email, page 297

of God" (Gen. 2:7), in the creation of life in an individual, that persona's spirituality is united—wedded—with their body. In this union of material and spiritual, the spiritual remains complete (whole) and, despite what the construct of the material body is, whether enabled or disabled, the spiritual does not lack any inherent ability to understand and/or receive spiritually communicated information (i.e., for instance, faith from God who created that spiritual "life" in the first place).

The issue for an intellectually disabled person, then, here taken as a compound sensory and neurological impairment, is that spirit/soul within them is able, in a meaningful manner, to receive, express, and cognate a faith-knowledge relationship with God within the union of that person's body and soul/spirit.

Words, at this point, I find difficult to describe the empirical reality of a fully functional spirit/soul that is not impaired in its experience of God himself and of faith in Him and yet, on a "'persona'" level, struggles to express that relational reality within in this world in which they live. Trapped, I guess I struggle with this concept too, as Jody asks in her question above, but as we will explore further in our chapter on the "'Reality of Faith'," the reality of joy, love, and peace, all a by-product of faith in God, are real in an experiential certainty, and can be seen, even though not expressed or understood in a neurotypical manner, in their life and "language."[88]

So, intellectual disabilities can impair cognitive function and thus impair spiritual expression, but not necessarily the wholeness of the spiritual reality of the person in itself.

MENTAL AND EMOTIONAL DISABILITY

Now, let us look at mental disability. This is generally seen as a psychological or behavioral disorder that affects the reactions and thought patterns of a person resulting in behavior that is outside the cultural norm or behaviors that specifically prevent them from processing and responding to vocal, physical,

---

[88] Every person has their "language." Some people are vocal orientated, while others, through writing, art, creativity, and body language, in order to communicate—express their inner thoughts and feelings.

emotional, and sensory stimulation in a culturally acceptable—or neurotypically normative—"world" approved model.

Mental Emotional Disorders (MED) cover a wide area, including anxiety disorders, maladaptive behavior, eating disorders, sleeping disorder, developmental disorders, personality disorders, self-harm, compulsive—obsessive disorders (COD) and many others that are usually included under the umbrella of mental disorders.

A more complete listing of such disorders by the American Psychiatric Association [APA] can be found in the *Diagnostic and Statistical Manual of Mental Disorders* [*DSM-5*][89], which states:

> A mental disorder is a syndrome characterized by clinically significant disturbance in an individual's cognition, emotion regulation, or behavior that reflects a dysfunction in the psychological, biological, or developmental processes underlying mental functioning. Mental disorders are usually associated with significant distress or disability in social, occupational, or other important activities.

A full consideration of mental disorders is a vast subject and is out of reach of the short discussion we have on this topic of disability in an introductory book such as this.

However, we note here that mental disorders can be complex and affect the cognitive, sentient, and emotional functions of a person so disabling them that processing information and making a declaratory decision in a knowing and knowable manner may be seriously impaired.

J. K Trivedi, in his work *Cognitive Defects in Psychiatrist Disorders,* makes the point on cognition and psychological disorders that underlying physiological and neurological

---

[89] American Psychiatric Association: Diagnostic and Statistical Manual of Mental Disorders, fifth edition. Arlington, VA, American Psychiatric Association, 2013, 20.
"A mental disorder is a syndrome characterized by clinically significant disturbance in an individual's cognition, emotion regulation, or behaviour that reflects a dysfunction in the psychological, biological, or developmental processes underlying mental functioning. Mental disorders are usually associated with significant distress or disability in social, occupational, or other important activities."

disabilities can compound the issue surrounding the treatment of and recovery from psychological disorders. Perceptions and reactions to words and external stimulations can be derailed by cognitive deficits, and these can produce pronounced internal stresses and result in alleviative[90] mechanisms that the disabled person develops in order to cope with the complex issue of function and problem-solving resulting in a galette[91] or "flat"— passive response to the outside world.

Mark Millan, in his paper "Cognitive Disfunction in Psychiatric Disorders," details research that indicates that although drugs can alleviate some of the issues related to mental disorders, inherent cognitive impairments frequently associated with mental disorders remain.

He writes:

> Although certain symptoms of psychiatric disorders— such as depression, delusions and anxiety—are alleviated by current drugs, cognitive deficits are not usually improved, and may even be worsened.

This is a serious concern to us here, especially when issues of spirituality and faith are discussed in relation to someone suffering from a mental and/or emotional illness.

The concern here, particularly with a personality afflicted with Dissociated Identity Disorders (DID) is who is in charge, and if you know, at any given point in time, how do you communicate with a person who is suffering from a schizotypal personality or bipolar disorder?

John Grohol, in *The Difference Between Bipolar Disorder, Schizophrenia and Multiple Personality Disorder,* further complicates this issue of identity by saying that the key diagnostic and treatment options are complicated by "a comorbidity of several diagnosis" that personality disorders are usually

---

[90] Alleviative: a process of making a painful or distressing situation less frightening or severe—drugs, escapisms.
[91] 'Galette' is a term used in French cuisine to designate various types of flat, round or free-form crusty cakes.

associated with more "conventional" disorders like IDD and MED.[92]

Additionally, if you can communicate with a person diagnosed with DID, which personality is responding to your discussion, and in which "person" does the personal faith statement that you are trying to validate reside?

It is in this general area of mental-emotional disorder (MED) disabilities that our neurotypical "singularity"[93] cognitive approach to perceptive functions, and comprehended determination is challenged by a situation where trust and engagement speak louder than words.

A secondary issue to the treatment of MED disabilities is the expression of self. If the cogitative and volitional aspects of one's personality (character) are affected by MED issues, then the ability of one so affected, to process information and make decisions on a personal spiritual level and express the same may be impaired. Thus, mental disabilities may impair recognition and cognition of existential[94] realities impairing spirituality and its expression.

We conclude our brief overview of several diagnostic medical[95] disabilities with a look at developmental disability, a term that will be found associated with all the above, at least on some level, but is usually associated with physical and or neurological function.

---

[92] John Grohol, "The Differences Between Bipolar Disorder, Schizophrenia and Multiple Personality Disorder."
https://psychcentral.com/schizophrenia/did-vs-schizophrenia :p1, para 4. This is an easy read, a good overview, and an introductory article.

[93] Singularity: Neurotypically aligned people have one personality, they may have many moods, but cognition, adaptive behaviors, and general character are singular in nature. This allows decision-making.

[94] See footnote 77, page 43

[95] I make a distinguishment here for the purposes of this book. Under the term "medical" disabilities, I include those disabilities that impair cognitive reasoning and adaptive function in order to distinguish the metaphysical from the spiritual aspects of our being—humanity.

DEVELOPMENTAL DISABILITY

Development Disorders (DD), like most disorders mentioned above, covers a wide range of impairments from cognitive—to neurological—to physiological disorders that can occur in many combinations.

Developmental disorders are most challenging, for here we frequently engage with parents of babies and of young to grown children who are most vulnerable. Here we interact with parents who are sensitive to the loss of hope and often see the future potential for that child or young adult slowly fading into the shadows.

Developmental disorders frequently present at an early stage of a child's development and display gradually, such that missing the clues in delayed motor skills, sensory reaction, and communication development often leave parents and caregivers quite distressed, and discussions regarding issues of faith with their slow-developing child can present as an additional barrier separate from the child's disability/s alone.

Of genuine concern for parents, family members, and caregivers of those with a developmental disability is the fact that developmental disabilities are usually an ongoing issue, are often lifelong in nature, and have a descending prognosis. For most developmental disorders, there is little in the way of medical, as in prescription medicines, which can reverse the condition or significantly mitigate its effect on the individual.[96]

The causes of developmental disabilities are as varied as is their diagnosis and can originate from exposure to invasive chemicals, chromosome, or genetic abnormalities, pre—or post-pregnancy viral infections, early childhood illnesses, abnormal gut regimen, or delayed development as the result of a car accident. Also, drug abuse (including alcohol during pregnancy),

---

[96] As is stated by the Sydney University Centre for Disability Studies:
 "Developmental disability is a term that refers to a permanent cognitive and/or physical impairment that usually occurs in the early years of life but can occur any time before the age of 18 years. It usually results in a significantly reduced capacity in three or more major life activities, such as communication, learning, mobility, living independently, decision making or self-care, and the need for support, whether or not of an ongoing nature."

metaphysical changes at different stages of life, and socio-developmental environments and/or any combination of the above can contribute to this spectrum of disorders.

The vulnerability of people, both in childhood and adult years, in this spectrum of disability is a key issue, as most so affected have difficulties in assessing information and making cognitive sentient decisions with unambiguous congruent understanding.

Therefore, those who live in this Shadow World of developmental disabilities frequently have what is called "challenging behavior," a term often used to describe the response of people with developmental disorders to situations in life that they find overwhelming, intimidating, confusing, or demanding.

Here we need to comment on a review question raised by Ms. Jody Plecas:

> I note by its absence, any reference to an "evil spirit" which could be, although uncommon, disguised as a mental disorder rather than a spiritual disposition.

I believe this is a valid question to be answered. Although I have not addressed the good vs. bad spirituality in this paper, we need to consider that evil "spirits" do exist and can, at times, affect the mental and behavioral attitudes of a person who is under the duress of an evil spirit. Most faith systems do acknowledge the existence of "evil" as a spiritual reality in this dimension in which we live and have writings and dogma that addresses this issue.

I have, in this paper, tried to be neutral in my address of disability, and as different faith systems have radically different approaches to this topic, "of evil spirits," I will speak from the personal point of view that I have as a Christian. Biblically, from the Christian Bible in both Old and New Testaments, the existence of "evil spirits" is well attested. In the name of brevity, I would direct those interested to the scholarly articles at the sites below, as to address this topic in full would require a work of this length on its own.[97]

---

[97] Ref-01: *https://www.gotquestions.org/unclean-spirits.html* Cited, 16/04/2018.

Ref-02: *https://www.gotquestions.org/psychological-demon.html* Cited, 16/04/2018.

My approach here is that it may be possible but is an extremely rare occurrence only and is not a usual part of the daily life experience or disability of a developmental disordered or mentally disabled or intellectually development disabled person.

Developmental disabilities can therefore result in challenging behaviors and can question our neurotypical expectations of behavioral responses to verbal, physical, and sensory stimulations. In other words, their responses to stimulation or external sensory inputs, which may make no sense to us in our particular way of thinking, is not what governs or directs their spirituality. Their core spirituality remains independent of the neurological, mental, and biological constraints that their developmental disorders may place upon them from within.

Our understanding of the effects of developmental disabilities on the spirituality of those so disabled is marginal and is an area of psychology that is not much understood, and current research into the interaction between the biological and spiritual functions of a DD person is in an inaugural phase. Several papers below are recommended reading.[98]

Also, the effect of developmental disorders on how we perceive the spirituality of those who live in the Shadow World with DD should not be underestimated or dismissed as "too hard." This is more a situation of awareness and understanding as those with developmental disorders are not often intra-connected within the social sphere and by default are often not accommodated within the liturgy or worship practices of many faith communities.[99] So, developmental disabilities may present

---

Ref-03: *https://www.ncbi.nlm.nih.gov/pmc/articles/PMC3705683/* Cited, 16/04/2018.

Ref-04: *https://www.mentalhealth.org.uk/sites/default/files/impact-spirituality.pdf* Cited, 16/04/2018.

[98] Adair Menezes Jr., Alexander Moreira-Almeida, "Differential diagnosis between spiritual experiences and mental disorders of religious content," Research Center in Spirituality and Health (NUPES) at Federal University of Juiz de Fora (UFJF), Brazil.
See also: HTML Resource File;
http://vkc.mc.vanderbilt.edu/assets/files/resources/denominations.pdf

[99] Mary Kay Rizzolo, Council on Quality Leadership, "Personal Outcome Measures," 11, 45, 58, 64, 78,
http://www.aaiddreligion.org/files/CQL%20Quality%20in%20Practice-Spirituality.pdf

issues of communication and cognition that in and of themselves can impair the reception of spiritual evidence through normative processes.

In our neurotypical normalcy, we term their behavior as "challenging," which, of course, it is, but our challenge is to see their behavior as "normalcy" to them given the neurological and biological sensory input they are receiving and having to deal with.

Quoting John Swinton and Jessica Kingsley, Dr. Cornah, in *"The Impact of Spirituality on Mental Health,"* speaks of the interaction that takes place between biological and neurological disabilities and the spiritual nature of a person.[100]

This is a new topic that previous years have not engaged with and is welcomed by the faith community as a way forward to raising awareness of the complete person in dealing with developmental disabilities.[101] It is like a final link being placed in a chain. A chain that has not been anchored to its central point, the core of a human "being," their spirituality, and is a solid foundation for discussion when we are dealing with developmental disability because it offers hope beyond what is seen, expected, and previously thought possible.

Therefore, we need to look at new ways to address the shortfall between what we would like—need—to say to them and what can be understood by them; that is, what makes "most sense" to them not to us.

---

[100] As a further clarification, Swinton adds an essential element of the importance of community in the expression and experience of one's spirituality. Cornah goes on to say in her article: "Swinton argues that spirituality is an intra-, inter- and trans-personal experience shaped and directed by the experiences of individuals and of the communities in which they live their lives."

[101] Deborah Cornah, *The Impact of Spirituality on Mental Health*; [Quoting from; Spirituality and Mental Health Care: Rediscovering a Forgotten Dimension; John Swinton, Jessica Kingsley, 2001. ISBN 1-85302-804–5.]
https://www.mentalhealth.org.uk/publications/impact-spirituality-mental-health

SPIRITUAL DISABILITY

Now, before we can say we have defined disability in general terms, one more point needs to be addressed, and that is the issue I previously raised of "spiritual disability." What do I mean by spiritual disability; that is, a person being spiritually disabled?

Is it a clinically diagnosed disability like the neurological, mental, and or psychological conditions discussed above, or is it some arbitrary term that is found in a systematic theology, a faith community's dogma, or talked about in Bible discussions late at night?

What I mean by the term "spiritual disability" then is an impairment of the metaphysical interaction—the interface between the body, mind, and soul/spirit of a person. In our earlier discussion on defining being, we established that 'man' is a two-part "being," a unity of body and spirit, a spiritual (nonmaterial) soul in congruence with the body (material), which defines their (body and self) existence and experience of life in this world.

Creating the term "spiritual disability" has some hidden difficulties and may be easily misinterpreted. I think that a more preferred term would be "spiritual impairment" as we will see later in this book.

Not that people so disabled exist *in* some sort of lesser conditio humana status and are not a complete ontological (body and soul) "being" like any other neurotypical human being, as we have defined earlier,[102] their spirituality remains whole — untouched by their disability yet can be limited in its expression by their disability within their personal existence.

Where the normative operation—and interaction of the body-soul-mind continuum of a person—is disordered or impaired by the impingement of neurological and cognitive disabilities upon the expression of their inherent spirituality into the world around them, either vocally or materially, we could consider that the expressional spirituality of that person, in this manner, may be diminished.

---

[102] See chapter 4, "Defining Being," page 31, as presented at the Asperger's Services Australia Conference titled "Human: Being on the Spectrum." City Hall, Brisbane, Qld, Australia, 2015.

Disabilities that interrupt and dislocate the cognitive comprehension processes inherently necessary in volitional decision making within the ontological "being" of a person can frustrate the processing of information necessary for real-world decision making, resulting in an overall constricting effect upon the expression of spirituality that might not, at first, be visually or subjectively obvious to us or objectively comprehended or personally understood by them.

Professor Charles Gourgey, in his article in the *Journal of Religion in Disability and Rehabilitation*, writes about this:

> The hardship of living with a physical disability[103] goes far beyond the limitations imposed by the disability itself. One's sense of life's meaning can be gravely threatened by the presence of a physical disability.

I would add here, of course, that the disabilities discussed above in any combination of one or more would have an effect upon the expression of spirituality within the soul/spirit–mind ontological unity of the disabled person. The degree of that effect, seen here as spiritual impairment, is the subject of several recent papers that seek to evaluate the impact of disability on the spiritual sense and awareness of those who are disabled.[104]

As we have discussed above, the expression of that inherent spirituality is also significantly connected to the body in many ways that go beyond the metaphysical relationship that normally exists between the body and soul/spirit of a person.

Spiritual disability, in this context, is, of course, the hardest of all disabilities to access, understand, and resolve within a faith community because for those who live in the Shadow World of disability, it is unearthing, and recognition/understanding is

---

[103] Here, 'physical' in Prof. Gourgey's article is a general term that includes the neurological (biological) physical restraints placed upon a person's inner self.

[104] Deborah Cornah, D, "The Impact of Spirituality on Mental Health," quoting from *Spirituality and Mental Health Care: Rediscovering a Forgotten Dimension*; Swinton, J., Kingsley, J., 2001. ISBN 1-85302-804–5. https://www.mentalhealth.org.uk/publications/impact-spirituality-mental-health

often realised only by those who live there and not by those who communicate with them.

Also, visually there is little or no evidence of the impact of such "spiritual" disability in the life of a disabled person that we can recognise from this side of the fence, and this issue is often worsened by the complexity of communication between a disabled person and a neurotypical one.

With limited methods and means at our disposal to identify and/or overcome the effects of such a disability on the spirituality of a disabled person, we are often left feeling inadequate or deflated in our encounters with spiritual disability (as defined above), in those severely affected in their ontological self.

> Charles Gourgey again writes:
>
> Having a disability can thus be socially isolating, creating a sense of rejection and fears of abandonment, even abandonment by God.[105, 106]

This spiritual disability—impairment—frequently unseen by us, is the primary casualty of any physical or mental disability mentioned above.

However, although there might be some impairment of that spirituality in its ontological expression into the world in which a disabled person lives, I would propose that the spirit/soul of that disabled person itself has no such limitations.

That is, spiritual impairment in the expression of one's ontological self into this world can result from one or more of the disabilities mentioned above; however, the essential spirituality (the essence of that person's soul/spirit) within the disabled person remains untouched—intrinsically whole.

David Coulter writes:

---

[105] Charles Gourgey, "Faith, Despair, and Disability," *Journal of Religion in Disability and Rehabilitation* 1, no. 3 (1994), 51–63: [My Edit – This to One's] Charles Gougrey includes psychiatric disabilities in the discussion in his paper and is inclusive of this as affecting the physical abilities of those so disabled.
http://www.judeochristianity.com/disabled/faith.htm Cited, 02/06/2011.
[106] See "Introduction" Jack's story, page 1, para 8

> Similarly, spirituality is not lessened because conscious expression (in a neurotypical manner) is lessened, as for example following a severe brain injury. Consciousness may be a property of the brain, but spirituality is a property of the whole person (the subjective essence of being).

It is this issue that led me as a Christian church worker, pastor, and father of a disabled young woman[107] to grapple with this disjunction between disability and spirituality relative to faith. The metaphysical and ontological relationship between body and soul/spirit, between what can be understood and assimilated regarding faith and spirituality and what can be applied—realised—within the life (soul/spirit) of one living in the Shadow World, is where our discussion now heads.

Additionally, as Jody Plecas commented in her email asking is there an inter-relationship between spiritual disability and "evil"? That is, can the presence of an evil spirit be possibly disabling—impairing—of a person's spirit, or impair the "breath of God" within a person such that that person exists with a limited "spirituality"—that is, is a lesser human being so affected?

While we acknowledge that evil spirits (fallen angels) exist and are a reality in the human dimension, their interaction with people, in this material reality, is extremely rare. Not that we should discount their existence and influence upon people but that overstating their presence in the world of disability distorts the limited effect they are allowed to have in human relationships and the lives of people living in this world.

The human spirit/soul is an intrinsic whole, as it comes from God, is sustained by God, and is the prime element in life that defines us as human beings (Gen. 2:7, Eccl 12:7). The "spirit" of a person is eternal and remains wholly guarded by God (Ps. 25, 20; 86:2).

Spiritual disability, then, as defined in this book, relates more to the limitations that biological and neurological disabilities can place upon the interaction and interface between the physical

---

[107] Our adult daughter has multiple neurological and cognitive disorders diagnoses as Asperger's 'high functioning' on the Autistic scale.

body—sensory organs—and the neurological "mind" as the seat of the spirit/soul of a disabled person rather than an imperfection in the spirit/soul of that person. This "limitation":—or impairment, from a neurotypical perspective—can be seen as an impairment of the spirit of that person in their inability to communicate their existential experiences of faith into our neurotypical world.

Therefore, spiritual (disability) impairment in a metaphysical sense is what can result from a combination of physical, neurological, and psychological-mental disabilities that impact upon spiritual expression, and not the intrinsic spirit/soul of the person, as a whole reality, as such.

With this brief overview of disability and impairment, we can see that oftentimes there is limited capacity to apply normative precepts and faith principles in knowledge and understanding of religious concepts in a cognitive, sentient, adaptive, volitional manner (as we would understand) to the core of the being, the essential ontological anthropological "world" of a cognitive, neurological, and spiritually disabled person.

This, however, does not preclude, disable, or limit the existence of faith in the Shadow World of a disabled person, just its normative expression out into our world.

JUST COINS

Before we conclude this chapter, I ask you to consider one more idea: just coins. Coins are interesting objects. They come in a variety of sizes and values as we can see by the ones in the images below. Each coin is made of different material, has a different shape, different visual appearance and touch, and we can easily recognise them and their individual value.

Just imagine, for a moment that they represent mankind across the full strata of human experience encompassing various levels of cognitive, sentient, and volitional function, each one somewhere on the scale—spectrum of life.

Using the different shapes and images impressed on the "tail" side of each coin, we can line them up either by size, color, or perceived value. So, let us sort them out by what distinguishes them from one another.

Our picture shows several coins 'tails side' up. [108]

COINS-TAILS SIDE UP

Looking at this side of the coins, we can see that they have distinctively different value images impressed upon them. So now we have them sorted out by value, what next?

Which one would you choose? The 1-cent coin or the $2 coin?

Which one is of more value, to you and the community? Which coin can you do the most with? How would you evaluate them?

---

[108] These images are of Australian coins, with permission, and are deliberately used for the purpose of this illustration.

Now, turn them over! What do you see?

COINS-HEADS SIDE UP

Despite their different materials, shapes, colors, and values, they all have the same image impressed upon them—a picture of Queen Elizabeth II, Australia's constitutional figurehead, the queen of Australia. But what does this mean—or have relevance to our discussion on faith in the Shadow World?

Just this, no matter what each coin represents in perceived value, ability, or function they all have the same "image" impressed upon them that makes them valid, true currency of Australia without which they would just be metal disks of different shapes, material, and sizes. Worthless in currency and exchange for goods and services.

My point is, no matter what the ability or disability of a person may be, it is that essential, spiritual, identity—"image" of God— impressed upon them in their "spirit/soul" that makes them a valid human being. A person of value. That is, it is the "image of God"—this essential spiritual and eternal reality—that each person receives from God that defines who and what they are rather than any inherent ability or disability they may or may not have.

Likewise, spiritual expression from within the "being" of a disabled people may be impaired by various disabilities that affect the thinking and volitional processes of that disabled person, but such impairment does not negate the intrinsic completeness and full purity of the spirituality that they individually possess as human beings.

As we complete our short discussion on disabilities, we can reflect upon the following point: as disability can impair communication, disrupt knowledge, inhibit expression, and impede cognition, and disability can thus affect the expression of spirituality.

Nevertheless, there still lies at the heart of every disabled person a need for faith, saving faith in Jesus Christ, and this is now the ongoing focus of this book.

So, let us now examine that spirituality by defining "Faith".

CHAPTER 6

DEFINING FAITH

A SECULAR DEFINITION

Looking at "faith" is much like looking at a cut diamond. Faith has many facets and each time you look at it you see a different aspect of faith projected back to you. Whatever the angle or facet you view, faith from the core material of the diamond of faith remains the same—belief, trust, and hope. These three, belief, hope, and trust, are the core material that secular faith is built on, made up of, whether it be faith in a thing, a person, an ideal, an organisation, a religion or a divinity.

From a secular point of view, faith can be defined simply as trust, the trust one has in a person, an ideal, a principle of life. This definition we find in our secular lives—in worldly pursuits, in business and corporate areas of life, as a trust that one has in the work of others in producing goods or services, trust that one has in others or organisations to perform to their stated ideals or policies.

Faith, so perceived as trust, is also seen within relationships, person to person or relationships within families, in social friendships and work—professional situations.

We also express and experience—cognize plain faith unconsciously in material things like the chair we sit upon. We don't think about it very often, but we place our personal safety—trust—and exercise simple faith in the ability of the chair's designer-manufacturer-installer to produce an end product that will remain stable—safe as we sit upon it.

This simple generic concept of faith has many facets in the material and social world in which we live. One of the facets of this 'simple' type of faith that we know and experience—see frequently in the world of disability is the faith, trust, and hope that those living with a disability have in the one who cares for them.

Our hospitals and emergency responders are instances where this aspect of faith is often seen in real life. What is not often recognised in our society are the many examples of faith that are exhibited in homes where the disabled are cared for by family and friends.

There is, in a similar manner, "faith" as an inferred trust—an implicit faith that exists in the relationship that many who live in the Shadow World have innately, whatever their disability, placed in those who care for and support them. It is a daily reality that many people who live in the Shadow World are themselves exemplary examples of such faith.

When we engage in the Shadow World of disability, we discover that the people who live in the Shadow World of disability are at times the most trusting of all people on earth. Often is the case that with the increased complexity of the disability of a person, the greater this implied faith is that that person has and displays, in this secular sense, toward those who care for them every day.

For the disabled person, the secular everyday definition of faith expands beyond the material issues of life and embraces knowledge—knowledge understood as reliability, consistency, patience, certainty, care, and many other facets of this faith that make up their daily life.

So, faith in this secular sense [but not morally] exhibited by those who live in the Shadow World is synonymous with confidence, loyalty, allegiance, trust, and/or reliance upon a person or persons who provide support and confidence for them in daily living. In this way, the disabled exercise faith in a general and personal[109] sense daily.

A RELIGIOUS DEFINITION

When we come to a religious—spiritual—definition of faith, the waters can become a little muddied. Here, we could include a definition of religious and personal faith as described in Potter and Perry's *Fundamentals of Nursing*—an unlikely source, yes, but a noticeably clear definition of the distinction between knowledge-based faith and spiritual experiential faith.

---

[109] Here, "personal" means everyday tasks they require assistance within their daily living (i.e., personal care).

The concept of faith has two definitions in literature. In the first, faith is defined as a cultural or institutional religion, such as Judaism, Buddhism, Islam, or Christianity. The second deals with a relationship with a divinity, higher power, authority, or spirit that incorporates a reasoning faith (belief) and a trusting faith (action).

To this, we could add a submission to an ideal or faith in a person whom the "believer" sees as one who provides protection, hope, "salvation" and/or entry into a higher level of existence not experienced in this material-mortal world.

This belief, expressed as faith, can be experiential in nature or may be based upon knowledge or comprehension of the ideals or dogma of a faith system where each aspect of that faith is presented (or represented) as fundamental concepts of the systematics[110] of that particular faith—or religious system.

Some examples of religious systems and their faith creedal systems.

> **JUDAISM**: Central authority in Judaism is not vested in any person or group but rather in Judaism's sacred writings, laws, and traditions. In nearly all its variations, Judaism affirms the existence and uniqueness of God. Judaism stresses the performance of deeds or commandments rather than adherence to a belief system.[111]
>
> **HINDUISM**: Hinduism does not have a "unified system of belief encoded in declaration of faith or a creed but accepts various approaches to faith. Sarvepalli Radhakrishnan states that Hinduism is not "just a faith" but in itself is related to the union of reason and intuition. [112]

---

[110] "Systematics" here refers to the involvement of an internal system of doctrine within a given faith.
[111] *https://www.princeton.edu/~achaney/tmve/wiki100k/docs/Jewish_principles_of_faith.html*
[112] *http://en.wikipedia.org/wiki/Hinduism*

ISLAM: Islam is a complete, unquestioning submission to (Allah), which includes belief, profession, and the body's performance of deeds consistent with the commission as vicegerent[113] on Earth according to Allah's will.[114]

TAOISM: Taoism is better understood as a way of life rather than as a religion, and its adherents do not approach or view Taoism the way non-Taoist historians have done. Taoism is defined more as a way of life rather than an ideal in which followers place their faith.[115]

BUDDHISM: Faith in Buddhism centers on belief in the Buddha as a supremely Awakened being, on his superior role as a teacher of both humans and gods, in the truth of his Dharma (spiritual doctrine), and in his Sangha (community of spiritually developed followers).[116]

CHRISTIANITY: Faith in general in Christianity is seen as belief in God as the supreme being over all things, and in the revelation of that "being" in Jesus Christ. There are many denominations and belief systems in Christianity, but the central theology is centered on a resurrected Jesus Christ in an objective belief.[117]

Taking into account the many different faiths in the world, faith, in the religious sense, can mean vastly different things, from a dogma to a system of doctrine, to religious duty to an ascetic lifestyle. As John Bishop writes in the *Stanford Encyclopedia of Philosophy* article "Faith":

The notion of religious faith as the possession of a whole people is familiar, and arguably theologically primary in the theist traditions. Philosophical accounts of theistic faith typically focus,

---

[113] Vicegerent: a person exercising delegated power on behalf of a sovereign or ruler. A person is regarded as an earthly representative of God or a god, for example, the Pope.
https://en.wikipedia.org/wiki/Vicegerent
[114] *http://en.wikipedia.org/wiki/Islam*
[115] *http://en.wikipedia.org/wiki/Taoism*
[116] *http://en.wikipedia.org/wiki/Budhism*
[117] *https://en.wikipedia.org/wiki/Christianity*

however, on what it is for an individual person to have faith or be a person of faith. An initial broad distinction is between thinking of faith just as a person's state (of mind) and thinking of it as also involving a person's act, action or activity.[118]

A complex multifaceted topic at best, but one that we need to be aware of so that when we talk of faith in the Shadow World, we must be precise in what we define—or hold such aspects of faith to be. So, for the purpose of our discussion in the rest of this book, we will consider religious faith to be the belief in a system of dogma, doctrine, or lifestyle.

A BIBLICAL DEFINITION

However, in terms of the Judaeo-Christian perspective of this book, we can be a little more specific. Written from a Christian standpoint, but not emphatically, it is necessary for us in our discovery of faith in the Shadow World to take a look at a biblical definition of faith in addition to the secular and religious definitions.

What does biblical faith mean, then, and how is the word used in the Bible—Old and New Testaments? In discussing the etymology of the English word *faith*, in a biblical sense, the *International Standard Bible Encyclopaedia, Online*, makes this interesting point:

> The history of the English word is rather interesting than important; use and contexts, alike for it and its Hebrew and Greek parallels, are the surest guides to meaning. But we may note that it occurs in the form "feyth," in Havelok the Dane (thirteenth century), that it is akin to fides and this again to the Sanskrit root bhidh[119] "to unite," "to bind." It is worthwhile to recall this primeval suggestion

---

[118] John Bishop, "Faith," The Stanford Encyclopedia of Philosophy (Winter 2016 edition), Edward Zalta (ed.), *https://plato.stanford.edu/archives/win2016/entries/faith/* Point:4 See also; *https://plato.stanford.edu/entries/faith/*

[119] Note that "bhid" means "split" whereas "bhidh" means unite—the opposite of bhid(a).

of the spiritual work of faith, as that which, on man's side, unites him to God for salvation."[120]

Although not a complete definition of faith, the above statement points out that biblical faith, at its core, has the concept of binding of one mind to another—one spirit to another, a point of union between two spiritual entities (Gal. 3:3a, 4:6, and 5:4).

Here, for a moment, we need to recall our definition of "being," of what it means to be human, and how spirituality is the defining moment of "being," for without spirituality rationality and life in this world cease.

> Therefore, the ontological existence, "being" of a disabled person is fundamentally the same as any other person; their state of "being" is tied to their spirituality which is basically, and more importantly, the same as in you and me.[121]

This "binding" of the Spirit of God that the Apostle Paul speaks about in Galatians 4:6 carries with it a motif of spiritual identity, of God identifying with man and man with God. This binding is essential for those with neurological and intellectual disabilities where the cognizance of their "persona" is impaired, limiting the neurological interaction that is normally facilitated between the spirit/soul-mind of a neurotypical person and God.

This line of distinction requires careful words unless we falsely gain an opinion that a person with IDD or DD[122] is a "less—than" person (persona) whose spiritual reality is somehow defective in that cognizance and sentient functions are impaired. While cognizance and sentient function in a personal rational neurotypical sense may be impaired, the spirit-persona of that

---

[120] I would, from my perspective, add "nature" to the phrase "spiritual work of faith," as the nature of faith in a biblical sense, in its aspect of the operation in the believer, is to unite them spiritually with God. *https://www.internationalstandardbible.com/F/faith.html*

[121] See "Glossary" – ontological life, page 271

[122] IDD: Intellectual Development Disability; DD: Delayed Development Disability

person has full capability of spiritual interaction and relational experience with God.[123]

Galatians Chapter 4 verse 6 speaks to this situation.

> And because you are sons, God has sent the Spirit of his Son into our hearts, crying, "Abba! Father." (Gal. 4:6)

It is important to note then what the Apostle Paul says in Galatians 4:6, in responding to the concept of "faith by works" or knowledge (which is a type of works)—or for that matter neurotypical cognizance, makes the point that any relationship one has with God is essentially one of the "Spirit"; that is, a spiritual reality! A point confirmed by Romans Chapter 8 verse 16.

> The Spirit himself testifies with our spirit that we are God's children. (Rom. 8:16)

This spiritual engagement that Paul speaks of in Romans 8:16 is an individual—God to man—[124] spiritual and interactive relationship.[125]

It is in the ontological[126] nature of our being that this spiritual relationship with God is first established and maintained. It is also an interactive relationship, not a dormant nor static one, but one in which the Spirit of God and the "spirit" of man are fully involved (Phil. 2:12–13).

As J. Bishop writes in his article in the *Stanford Encyclopedia of Philosophy*, "Believing by Faith," on faith:

> An initial broad distinction is between thinking of faith just as a person's state and thinking of it as also involving

---

[123] Jody Plecas, Email: "Spirit & Body," Email questions, *Faith in the Shadows*—03/08/2018. Used with permission. See page 296

[124] Here, man is representative of all mankind, male or female, enabled or disabled.

[125] We experience life in this world in the material realm, which can mask our existence's spiritual reality. Likewise, when we say God is 'spirit,' we can, from our material experience of life, mask, as it were, the full reality of his existence as Spirit and overlook that God acts as Spirit, communicates as Spirit, and exists thus as Spirit.

[126] Ontological: Our daily sense of being. The study of "who I am and why I am, " both in spirit and body, constitutes our experience of and interaction with life in this world.
See "Glossary" – ontology, page 271

a person's act, action or activity. Faith may be a state one is in, or comes to be in; it may also essentially involve something one does.

We see the inter-activeness of faith in Noah in building the ark, in Abraham and Isaac trusting God at Moriah, and in David in his conflict with Goliath in the Valley of Elah, where faith is demonstrated both as an objective reality and in real action, through interaction and word in their allegiance to one another, man to God and God to man.

J. Bishop also writes that faith without action, confirmed in life and practice, is dead, nor can action alone produce faith by itself (James 2:18). For our discussion then an adequate account of faith, perhaps, needs to encompass both.

There are several Hebrew words for "faith" in the Bible, the main Hebrew word being *emuna*, אֱמוּנָה,[127] which covers a wide field ranging from fidelity in relationships (Jonathan and David, 1Samuel 18:1ff), to personal faith in God (i.e., David in Ps. 51:1ff, to a national-corporate concept of Israel's faith in God, Psalm 62:8). The Greek word generally associated with "faith" in the New Testament is *"pistis,"* 'πίστις',[128] and has the added connotation of conviction and personal trust in reaching out in a relationship with God.

J. I. Packer writes in the *Evangelical Dictionary of Theology* (Paternoster Press), in his article "Faith":

> The idea of faith in the Old Testament develops as God's revelation of grace and truth, on which faith rests, and

---

[127] *Brown-Driver-Briggs Hebrew and English Lexicon*, Unabridged, Electronic Database, Copyright © 2002, 2003, 2006 by Biblesoft, Inc. NASB; אֱמוּנָה faith (1), faithful (3), faithfully (8), faithfulness (25), honestly (1), responsibility (1), stability (1), steady (1), trust (2), truth (5).

[128] "Faith," Strongs dictionary; OliveTree, Ver. 6.0.17; "πιστις; from 3982; persuasion (i.e., credence; moral conviction (of religious truth, or the truthfulness of God or a religious teacher), especially reliance upon Christ for salvation; abstractly, constancy in such profession; by extension, the system of religious (gospel) truth itself—assurance, belief, believe, faith, fidelity."

develops throughout the patriarchal and National eras of Israel.

This, of course, does not preclude those living in Old Testament times from having a personal saving faith in God (Ps. 51:11), a point that the New Testament letter of Hebrews in chapter 11 certainly clarifies, but that the nominal portrayal of faith in God in the Old Testament era was usually in a national religious context.

It is with the advent of Jesus Christ that biblical faith in God matures and is seen in its fullness. In the Old Testament, faith was universally expressed in duty and cultural ritual in an external acknowledgment of a relationship with God based largely on national identity.

J. I Packer, in his article "Faith," also writes:

> The Old Testament variously defines faith as resting, trusting, and hoping in the Lord, cleaving to him, waiting for him, making him one's tower and shield, taking refuge in him, etc.

However, we need to caution separatists[129] who would dismiss "faith" in the Old Testament as a "cultural" phenomenon only, because there is no disjunction between the Old and New Testaments on the subject of faith on a personal basis.

The writer of the Letter to the Hebrews calls on examples from the Old Testament of personal faith in God; that is, "by faith Abraham," etc.

> By faith, Abraham obeyed when he was called to go out to the place which he would receive as an inheritance. (Heb. 11:8)

Faith, in the New Testament, goes through a transformation of identity and application, as J. I. Packer further writes:

> Whereas faith (in the OT) is portrayed as trust in God and the old covenant, faith, receiving God's new utterance in

---

[129] Those who see a disjunction between the religion and faith of the Old Testament and the New Testament

the words and deeds of Christ (Heb. 1:1–2) has become a knowledge of present salvation.

Biblically the same faith is present in both testaments, but it is testified to in different ways and contexts, and the application of "faith" in the two testaments has a different objective in the progression of God's revelation of himself in Jesus Christ in the New Testament.

This convergence from a national approach in the Old Testament to a personal one in the New Testament is purposed to direct our minds to the personal component of faith as Bishop, in his article on faith, brings to our notice and is a component of biblical faith that requires further mention.

As John Bishop writes in the *Stanford Encyclopedia of Philosophy* in his paper "Faith":

> In the Christian context faith is understood both as a gift of God and also as requiring a human response of assent and trust, so that their faith is something with respect to which people are both receptive and active.

This "active" component of biblical faith is what often confronts us when we approach the topic of disability and faith, particularly when we are interacting with seriously compromised individuals who have difficulties receiving, understanding, and affirming verbally (in a neurotypical sense) personal cognitive acceptance and recognition of faith.

Going back to our Bible verse in Romans, Romans 10:8–10, we affirm the biblical requirement of acknowledgment, knowledge, and confession in relation to statements regarding faith:

> But what does it say? The word is near you, in your mouth and in your heart (that is, the word of faith that we proclaim); because, if you confess with your mouth that Jesus is Lord and believe in your heart that God raised him from the dead, you will be saved. For with the heart one believes and is justified, and with the mouth one confesses and is saved. (Rom. 10:8–10)

Belief, knowledge, assent, and acceptance of these concepts are essential elements of biblical faith, for that faith to be real and tangible in the life of a person.

Bishop, in his paper on faith, raises some issues with the concept of affective cognitive action; in practical aspects with respect to biblical faith when dealing with faith and recognition, especially in cases where neurological and mental disabilities are present in the person.

There is, however, some tension in understanding faith both as a gift to be received and faith as essentially including a venture to be willed and enacted. A philosophical account of faith may be expected to illuminate this apparent paradox. One principle for classifying models of faith is according to the extent to which they recognise an active component in faith itself, and the way they identify that active component and its relation to faith's other components. It is helpful to consider the components of faith (variously recognised and emphasised in different models of faith) as falling into three broad categories:

- the affective,
- the cognitive, and
- the practical.

There are also evaluative components in faith—these may appear as indicated in the affective and/or the cognitive components mentioned above, according to one's preferred meta-theory[130] of value. [131]

Any biblical definition of faith has to invariably recognise, accept, and give assent to, the object of that faith, in our case God, and, as many papers and scriptural references acknowledge that God is "Spirit" then, faith, as a gift from God through the Holy Spirit, in its core reality and attribute is principally "spiritual."

---

[130] "meta-theory": the discussion of composing and examining a 'theory'- usually in philosophy. *https://www.merriam-webster.com/dictionary/metatheory* Cited, 17/12/2020
See "Glossary" metaphysics—meta-theory, page 270

[131] "value theory" designates the area of moral philosophy concerned with theoretical questions about value and goodness of all varieties—the theory of value. *https://plato.stanford.edu/entries/value-theory/* Cited, 17/12/2020.
See "Glossary" metaphysics—value theory, page 270, 273

The quintessential definition of biblical faith in God in the practical realities of this world, as a spiritual truth and reality, is, of course, found in Hebrews 11:1–3:

> Now faith is being sure of what we hope for and certain of what we do not see. This is what the ancients were commended for. By faith, we understand that the universe was formed at God's command, so that what is seen was not made out of what was visible. (Heb. 11:1-3)

We also need to note, from Hebrews 11 and other biblical references, that faith is invisible; it does not come with a maker's logo stamp, ID card, or license. However, it can be "seen" in action in the life of those who believe, as per the examples the writer presents in Hebrews chapter 11, but the concept of the nondimensional reality of faith leaves us without cause to ground biblical faith in dogma, doctrine, culture, or ritual.

A final clarification on biblical (theistic) faith in God from John Bishop's paper:

Theistic faith is essentially faith in God. In general, faith of the kind exemplified by theistic faith must have some intentional object.

The intentional object of biblical (theistic) faith is God. It is a faith that has a cognitive and experiential content—one where knowledge of God and God's knowledge of the believer are paramount.

As John Bishop writes, there is also a practical element in biblical (theistic) faith as we have already mentioned above:

> It is helpful to consider the components of faith (variously recognized and emphasised in different models of faith) as falling into three broad categories: the affective, the cognitive and the practical.[132]

The practical element in biblical (theistic) faith is one of action whereby the one who has faith, who believes in God, acts out the principles of that faith in daily life. The acting out of that faith in life gives assent and acknowledgment of the inner workings of faith within the spirit/soul of that person.

---

[132] Ibid, 5, para 2.

As John Bishop again writes:

> On a model that takes religious faith to consist fundamentally in an act of trust, the analogy with the venture of interpersonal trust is suggestive. When one person trusts another there seems typically to be both a doxastic and a fiducial[133] aspect—there is the person's belief as to the other's trustworthiness and also an active commitment or "entrusting" to the other.
>
> This is because, on the doxastic venture model, faith involves a deeper surrender of self-reliant control, not only in trusting God, but in accepting at the level of practical commitment that there is a God—indeed, this God—who is to be trusted.

Therefore, acceptance of the existence of God is essential to biblical faith, and as God is the object of biblical faith, as the premise upon which it stands, biblical faith reaches beyond what is visible to the human senses as we see in Hebrews 11:1–2. Biblical faith is principally doxastic[134] and directed toward God.

Much more could, and probably should be, said about biblical Christian faith, but it is sufficient to realise that it is remarkably different from our secular definition of faith, and it is a faith that is also distinct from our definition of religious faith, with its system of dogma and traditions as noted above.

While this book accepts the reality of faith in secular and religious terms in everyday life and embraces a biblical definition of faith, it seeks to go further than an external—social, religious, and biblical definition of faith in order to find out what faith in God means in a salvic[135] context, especially for the disabled, where

---

[133] Merriam-Webster: "fiducial," founded on faith or trust, having the nature of trust, a standard reference point. *https://www.merriam-webster.com/dictionary/fiducial*

[134] See "Glossary" – doxastic, page 268

[135] Pertaining to salvation. The essential—initial spiritual deposit of 'faith' from God that attains salvation for that person (Eph. 1:13–14). Salvation is defined within many Christian creeds and Systematics as the salvic process of God effectively bringing the gift of life (faith) to the believer through the agency of the Holy Spirit, Eph. 2:8.

the interaction of faith, as a personal reality, is often outside the boundaries of the neurotypically observable characteristics of faith in God.

A SALVIC DEFINITION

So, let us examine salvic faith. Why are we talking about this as if it were something distinct to or separate from biblical faith? Surely believing in God and the Bible is faith. If you have faith in the Bible, faith that God exists, surely that is enough?

In the Book of the Acts of the Apostles, we find ourselves confronted with creatures that "believe" that God exists but have no salvic relationship with God. In Acts 16:16–17 and 19:17–18, Luke tells us about spiritual creatures, demons, who recognised and believe in the existence of God, Jesus Christ, and the Apostle Paul, yet they were certainly not themselves saved salvic creatures.

Apostle James, in his letter in James 2:19, in a warning to those who say they have faith but do not live that faith as a reality in life, confronts us with the fact that belief in God and salvic faith in God are not always synonymous.

> You believe that God is one; you do well. Even the demons believe—and shudder! (James 2:19)

This is where that strange word I used above—*"doxastic venture"*—[136] comes into view. Saving faith (salvic faith), as apart from belief in the existence of God and Jesus Christ,[137] could be defined as the belief within a person that God, in Jesus Christ, has established a spiritual, redemptive, holy, and eternal relationship within that person, as an individual, based solely on that "faith."

The concept of biblical salvic faith—faith that leads to salvation, revealed in the New Testament in Christ Jesus, was

---

[136] *http://www.dictionary.com/browse/doxastic* Doxastic definition: (1) of or relating to belief, (2) denoting the branch of modal logic that studies the concept of belief. Word Origin; C18: from Greek, δοξαστικόν— doxastikos, having an opinion, ultimately from doxazosin to conjecture, consider, believe. Cited, 31/12/2016.
See "Glossary" – doxastic venture, page 268

[137] Succinctly, God the Father, God the Son, and God the Holy Spirit constitute the reality and personhood of the triune God as demonstrated in both the Old and New Testaments.

foreshadowed in the Old Testament and is directed toward Jesus Christ (Luke 24:25–27, Acts 4:12). In the person of Jesus Christ, God became personal to us, and faith in God, as a result, becomes more a personal matter, reality, than one of national, religious or cultural identity.

In Matthew's Gospel, Matthew records for us this shift in the focus point of Israel's national "faith" in God from a societal–national identity to a personal one, namely in the person of Jesus Christ, the Son of God, the Son of man.

> He [Peter] was still speaking when, behold, a bright cloud overshadowed them, and a voice from the cloud said, "This is my beloved Son, with whom I am well pleased; listen to him." (Matt. 17:5–8)

Salvic faith was still a personal reality in the Old Testament, like Enoch and David and others in Hebrews 11:1ff are clear examples; however, a new dimension is added in the New Testament in that the national subjective faith of Israel (as a nation) has a new objective reality in the person of Jesus Christ.

It is now in the objective reality of Jesus Christ, his personal death, at the cross, and resurrection, upon which saving *salvic* faith is now centered; that is, the resurrected person of Jesus Christ, in whom God dwells fully (see Col. 1:19, 2:9)

Christian saving faith, therefore, involves accepting, in a doxastic venture, Jesus Christ "not merely as a God-sent teacher" but as God incarnate who in his own person "provides the sole means of salvation" through his death and resurrection (Acts 4:12, Phil. 3:10).[138]

Saving (salvic) faith is also, and primarily, a spiritual attribute involving the "activity"[139] of the Holy Spirit enlightening the soul of a person to their need of salvation, empowering that soul to receive God's gift of life (Gal. 3:14, Eph. 1:13, 2:8–10), and enabling them to participate in a spiritual faith relationship (Rom.

---

[138] Walter Elwell, ed., *Evangelical Dictionary of Biblical Theology* (Paternoster Press: Grand Rapids, 1996); Faith and Spirituality, adapted, p401, para 3

[139] See "Glossary" – salvic, page 272

8:16) with God now and in eternity to come. As the Apostle Paul writes:

> The Spirit himself testifies with our spirit that we are God's children. (Rom. 8:16)

> For by grace you have been saved through faith. And this is not your own doing; it is the gift of God, not a result of works, so that no one may boast. (Eph. 2:8–9)

In Ezekiel, and elsewhere in the Bible, we are confronted by the direct spiritual activity of God upon the human soul. In Ezekiel, we read of the transforming work of God through the Holy Spirit.

> And I will give you a new heart, and a new spirit I will put within you. And I will remove the heart of stone from your flesh and give you a heart of flesh. (Ezek. 36:26)

Saving (salvic) faith in Jesus Christ is the means by which a person is justified (Rom. 3:28, Gal. 2:16, 3:8, 24), is the agency through which a person receives the righteousness of Christ (Rom. 3:22, Phil. 3:9), and the forgiveness of sins (Mark 2:5, Rom. 3:25), bringing eternal hope and salvation (Acts 16:31, Eph. 2:8) to that person.

With the advent of Christ, saving (salvic) faith in God became an objective reality in the substantive personal representation of the godhead in Jesus Christ.

> For in Christ all the fullness of the Deity lives in bodily form, and you have been given fullness in Christ, who is the head over every power and authority. (Col. 2:9–10)

Faith, salvic saving faith, was no longer to be found in subjective ideology—dogma or a national religious lifestyle but in the ontological whole of the person's heart and mind, ostensibly existent in their spirit/soul, engaging their full being in a redeemed personal relationship with Jesus Christ, the spiritual reality of which is evident to them in the veracity of the objective reality of God in Christ Jesus.

Gerald Birney Smith in *The Christ of Faith and the Jesus of History* writes:

> Jesus is the complete embodiment of this redemptive principle, and therefore is the objective ground of redemptive faith, but the real source of redemption is located in the spiritual identity of the Absolute with the spiritual activities of the finite throughout all cosmic history.[140]

Salvic faith is then the foundation upon which personal trust in the redemptive work of Jesus Christ at Calvary (Eph. 1:7–10) is founded and is realised in that personal relationship with Him applied to the ontological heart—"being" (soul/spirit) of a person bringing to them new life in God by faith.

> But now the righteousness of God has been manifested apart from the law, although the Law and the Prophets bear witness to it—the righteousness of God through faith in Jesus Christ for all who believe. For there is no distinction: for all have sinned and fall short of the glory of God, and are justified by his grace as a gift, through the redemption that is in Christ Jesus, whom God put forward as a propitiation by his blood, to be received by faith. (Rom. 3:21–26)

In addition to the redemptive, completed, work of faith another aspect of 'salvic' faith in Jesus Christ is that it is first and foremost a spiritual reality that transcends the material body and is embedded within the core of a person's "being"—spirit/soul as a spiritual truth.

In The Regeneration of Man; Christ in You Ministries James Fowler writes:

> Christianity is not just an epistemological belief-system of doctrinal data, despite the fact that fundamentalistic religious perversions often project it to be such. One does not "believe in the Lord Jesus Christ" (Acts 16:31), in the same manner as one might believe that George

---

[140] Gerald Birney Smith, *The Christ of Faith, and the Jesus of History*: The American Journal of Theology, Vol. 18, No. 4 (Oct. 1914), pp. 521-54. http://www.jstor.org/stable/3154962

> Washington was the first president of the United States of America.

Believing, 'salvic' faith in its essence, is an objective reality whereby a new relationship is formed between God and the believer, and this new relationship is essentially spiritual in reality and nature (Ezek. 36:26–28; Eph. 1:13–14, 3:16; Heb. 8:10).

> Blessed be the God and Father of our Lord Jesus Christ, who has blessed us in Christ with every spiritual blessing in the heavenly places—in him you also, when you heard the word of truth, the gospel of your salvation, and believed in him, were sealed with the promised Holy Spirit. (Eph. 1:13-14)

It is a spiritual relationship that the saved person has with God in the essence of their being, a union between the spirit of man (Job 32:8, Eccl 3:21) that is essentially the breath of God (Gen. 2:7, Job 33:3–4), and the intrinsic eternal ontological Spirit of God (John 4:24, 2 Cor. 5:17, Gal. 6:15) that is founded in a personal relationship between the believer and God incarnate, Jesus Christ (1 Cor. 2:12–16).

Samuel Vinay, in his article "God, Humanity and Disability, Transformation," stresses that "we should not reduce the incarnation to (just) a remedy for sinfulness and fallenness (p.15), and goes on to say, "rather it should be viewed as the recovery of true personhood in the midst of a world that is fallen."

Our discussion on faith, salvic faith, might seem to be off track here, but my purpose in this part of the discussion is to widen our view of faith and salvation, moving it from just a theological statement—discussion—to include a whole of life scope. We need to encompass a wider view that faith, as a specific spiritual attribute given to man from God, (Eph. 2:8) is unbounded by the biological and transcends disability and life itself.

To ensure that we do not go into a dualistic view of "being" here; that is, dissociate the body from the soul/spirit, we note what John Hull, in his article, "A Spirituality of Disability," writes to remind us of the link between the biological and spiritual, yet allowing the spirit within a person to be its own identity:

> When we speak of spirituality as transfiguring the biological, we refer to the fact that the biological is never left behind by transcendence. The body is not the antithesis of the spiritual but its organ. We should not contrast the spiritual with the material, nor should we regard the spiritual and the biological as being on altogether different levels. Rather, we should speak of transfiguration: the material infused with the spiritual, the body becoming the form of inter-subjectivity.

Picking up on Hull's comments above, we note from John 4:24 that as God is Spirit, and as God transcends all creation, so too does faith, faith that originates in Him as the giver of faith (Eph. 2:8) so that faith, in essence, transcends the material world including the biological and anatomical abilities or disabilities of a person.

> God is spirit, and those who worship him must worship in spirit and truth. (John 4:24)

We can state then, emphatically, from our study on faith these points.

- GOD is Spirit, and Faith is a gift from God (Eph. 2:8). Therefore, Faith is Spiritual—from the Spirit of God. (2Cor. 4:13) [141]

That is, at its essential core reality Faith is not a thought, it is not knowledge, it is not a 'feeling', it is not a doctrine, it is not intelligence, it is not liturgy, it is Spirit; it is that initial deposit of the Holy Spirit in the spirit/soul—regenerated heart—of the sinner that initiates an eternal faith based relationship with God built on the reality of the presence of the Holy Spirit.

---

[141] At this point, I genuinely feel inadequate to express what I mean by "faith" is Spirit. (The capital 'S' is deliberate.) I wish I could grab a handful of faith and hold it up for you all to see, but I cannot. Eph. 2:8-9,13-14 confirms that 'faith is Spirit', the gift of the Third person of God that God gifts to those He loves. There is nothing subjective about this gift of faith from God; it is a "Spirit" reality (a deposit of the Holy Spirit) that is implanted within the spirit/soul of a human being by the grace of God that constitutes itself within the spirit/soul of that person in perfect unity, sealing and regenerating that person to faith in God. (Ezk. 36:27, John 4:10, Eph. 2:6-8)

This 'spirit' property of faith, its ability to transcend the neurological and biological properties (features) of a person, brings a new facet to mind not previously thought relevant in a study on faith and disability.

Dr. Clare Cagnoni writes in her master's thesis, "Personhood, Human Brokenness":

> As a person who works in the area of mental health and disability, I find it encouraging that the rhetoric of training and development in this field, exemplified in the quote above, is focusing more and more on the importance and value of personhood which transcends the disability itself. Thus, the significance of personhood as an Eastern Orthodox theological principal is being emphasised throughout (my) thesis.

In speaking of personhood, Cagnoni raises the issue of what constitutes "self", one's being, the body or the spirit/soul or both, and returns us to the point—question, where does disability and spirituality interface—interact in the life of a disabled person?

Cagnoni seeks the same recognition I do here. That a person is not defined by what we "see" of them on the outside but by their God-given spirituality that is within them and defines them as a person. It is essential that we hold this view in expanding our understanding of faith, particularly salvic faith, in order to embrace disability and overcome the barrier it often presents to us in our understanding and acceptance of the reality of salvic faith in the life of an intellectually and or biologically disabled person.

Cagnoni also seeks to address that elusive interface between body and spirit/soul where the unity of body and soul/spirit is maintained but the spirit/soul of a person is self—sustainable, independent of the body and any disability that that body may contain. My point in stating this here is that although the material—the biological body may inhibit the "speaking out" of the spiritual reality within the spirit/soul of a person into our normative world that that "spirit/soul" within the person has no limitations in its conversation with God.

Thus, salvic faith for the disabled has the same applicable redemptive effect in the life, "spirit/soul," of that disabled person as it does have in the life of an enabled person. This means that salvic faith is fully "salvic," regardless of the vessel—body within which it is contained.

We have, therefore, established that biblical Christian salvic faith has an objective reality in the life of a disabled person in the personality of Jesus Christ, that not only transcends time and our metaphysical universe but disability itself.

We have also established that biblical Christian salvic faith is spiritual in its core identity, reality, and presence in the life of a believing person, whether that person is enabled or disabled.

A central theme of this book that comes out of this definition of salvic faith is that God, in Christ, can operate freely within the Shadow World transcending disability, whatever its composure, bringing faith, salvic faith, life, and peace (Eph. 3:19, Phil. 4:7, Col. 1:16–17), to the disabled.

Christian salvic (saving) faith can be identified then as that spiritual gift of faith that we receive from God (Eph. 2:8) in and through Jesus Christ His Son by the Spirit of God (Eph. 1:13–14) and is a faith that defines a new relationship with and position before God for all His children (John 1:12, Rom. 8:23, Gal. 3:26, 1 John 3:1). Saving faith is a faith that establishes a personal (salvic) spiritual relationship with God.

So, to summarise our discussion on faith: while faith is an everyday term in life in the sense that it is an essential part of any relationship, particularly with the more vulnerable, for the disabled, living in this Shadow World, such faith alone struggles to provide the necessary hope and comfort that their spiritual soul/spirit searches for and needs.

Although religious faith, systems of dogma, creed, and ritual can bring some comfort to the disabled, Margaret Hutchinson, in *Unity and Diversity in Spiritual Care*, writes that since the late '80s a new awareness of the spiritual needs of the disabled in the nature of their being, and awareness of the need for that spirituality to be fulfilled, have begun to surface in the care of the aged and disabled.

With regard to what we term as "salvic faith" in this book, that is, faith in Jesus Christ, there is no distinction or disjunction in its efficacy, character, and nature between that of an enabled person, here taken as the general neurotypical mass of humanity, and the disabled person living in the Shadow World.

That is, as it is the Spirit of God who affects the work of salvic faith (Eph. 1:13–14) in the spirit/soul of a person; and as it is the Spirit of God who knows both the mind and thoughts of man and God (Rom. 8:27), and as the Spirit of God can transcend the spiritual—material and biological being of a person, then, there is no barrier to the Spirit of God bringing that gift of faith, salvic faith, effectively into the spirit/soul and life, "being," of one who is disabled living in the Shadow World (1 Cor. 2:10–11, Eph. 4:24, Titus 3:5).

Faith in God, as defined in this book, is spiritual, a "spirit" gift of the actual[142] Spirit of God—given spiritually to the inner "spirit/soul" of a person—(Eph. 2:8), and this takes us a step closer to addressing and resolving the spiritual needs of the whole person, whether enabled or disabled, in and through a personal salvic spiritual relationship with God.

The perspicuity[143] of the gospels and scripture demands this.

> Salvation is purposed by the Father, accomplished by the Son, and applied by the Holy Spirit—Our salvation is *in* Christ alone. Our salvation is *by* his Spirit alone. [144]

Through the agency of the Holy Spirit, God transcends whatever is the metaphysical nature—or state that that person lives in (Ps. 19:4, 7; Eph. 3:18–19).

---

[142] In the academic paper on this topic (See footnote 16, page 4), I describe this gift of the Spirit of God in more significant terms. The word "actual" is the best I can offer here. In talking with a young man (Jade), I could explain that as a believing Christian young man, the divine Spirit of God is actually present within his (Jade's) spirit/soul.

[143] The meaning here is the transparency of the gospel and scripture. Disability is no barrier to the spiritual reality of faith, God, or the gospel; they can operate clearly within the Shadow World.

[144] "Salvation is purposed by the Father, accomplished by the Son, and applied by the Holy Spirit."
https://www.thegospelcoalition.org/essay/the-holy-spirit-agent-of-salvation/ (Cited, 17/04/2020)

> For it is by grace you have been saved, through faith—and this is not from yourselves, it is the gift of God—not by works, so that no one can boast. For we are God's handiwork, created in Christ Jesus to do good works, which God prepared in advance for us to do. (Eph. 2:8–10)

The gift of salvic faith from God (Eph. 2:8) surpasses both worlds, enabled and disabled, and renews spiritual life in man, bringing with it all the blessedness of a personal Spirit-to-spirit relationship with God (Eph. 1:1–20), whatever side of the disability fence a person lives on. Saving (salvic) faith is ultimately a personal believing spiritual relationship with God through Jesus Christ by the Spirit of God.

Before we close this chapter and discussion on the meaning of faith, I ask you to consider one more point. Earlier in this book, we discussed how coins can be illustrative of how, while everyone is different, we all have the same image of God inside us. So, to visualise the transcendence of "salvic" faith let us consider "paper money" notes.

JUST NOTES

In many countries paper currency includes a translucent monogram on the note that validates it and helps identify fakes (along with other security technologies).

Looking at the bank notes the Australian $5 banknotes pictured below we notice that each side of the banknote looks different. Yet, if we look closely at the bottom corner of each banknote, we will see that there is a translucent watermark, evident on each side of the note, and visible from both sides.

This "translucent" image on the banknotes is in the form of a 'hummingbird' What does this mean in our discussion? If we imagine for a moment that the "hummingbird" represents faith we first note that faith, symbolised on the banknote as a hummingbird, is visible on both sides of the banknote.

Secondly, it is also important for us to note that we can only see one side of the bank note at a time. Pick a side that represents the neuro-typical and a side that represents the disabled person.

The fact that you cannot see the "other side" of the banknote, does not preclude faith existing on the other side.

AUSTRALIAN $5 BANK NOTE

Our banknotes also illustrate that salvic faith in a disabled person, in their inner spirituality—spirit/soul, has a transparency in that that saving faith can be seen from both sides of the fence, or note, and we can "see" (spiritually) and identify with it objectively through the window of faith.

Thus, as we approach the conclusion of our chapter on "Defining Faith," we know that disability does not inhibit the exercise of, and or experience of, salvic faith in God and that salvic faith is a spiritual reality for both disabled and enabled alike.

The content of faith then, its ability to enhance life experience and bring to the believer a sense of purpose in life, cannot be denied; it is, in fact, this aspect of faith that is most relevant to those who are disabled and at times impaired in the secular expression of their faith. As P. G. Reed writes in *Potter and Perry's Fundamentals of Nursing*:

> The belief that comes with faith involves transcendence, or an awareness that one cannot see through or know through ordinary physical ways.

In our overview of faith, we have seen four dimensions of faith, dimensions that have revealed different aspects of faith.

- Common everyday faith is subjective and demonstrative.
- Religious faith is collective—dogmatic and intellectual.
- Biblical faith is objective—focused on God (in Christ).
- Salvic faith in Christ is spiritual—nondimensional and experiential.

There may be more aspects of salvic faith that we could further discuss, but these four elements cover most of the life experience that a believer has and gives us a sense that faith in Jesus Christ is an active pursuit in life, whatever dimension we are talking about; that is, faith in God is never passive in the life of a person.

It is clear that the first two dimensions of faith, common and religious faith, although a part of our daily lives are not in and of themselves sufficient for meeting our individual spiritual need for a personal association—relationship with God. This can only be achieved through a Spirit-to-spirit salvic relationship. True faith, salvic faith, in God in Christ is a spiritual attribute—reality.

If faith is spiritual in experience, and we cannot see it in a material, biological sense, how then can we know its reality, particularly in the Shadow World of disability? How can we say that faith is "sensibly present" where the normal means of communication and presentation of that faith are not available?

The answer is that faith, salvic faith in Jesus Christ, does not require an external affirmation of its existence to confirm its reality in the life of the believer. As faith is a spiritual matter, its presence in the "inner man," attested to by the Spirit of God (Eph. 1:13–14), affirms faith's existence and veracity.

Our discussion above leaves us with the knowledge that faith is tangible, objective, and has a reality that can be quantified in how it interacts with the believer spiritually through the object of that faith.

As P. G. Reed writes in her article "Spirituality and Faith" in *Potter and Perry's Fundamentals of Nursing*:

> It gives purpose and meaning to a person's life. A trusting faith deals with the inner resources that allow a person to act.

It is in this acting out of faith that the question of practicalities arises, and we need to deal with this question of acting out—the factuality—the veracity—of faith in and the life of a disabled person that leads us to our next discussion.

Our journey into the Shadow World of disability continues.

CHAPTER 7

REALITY OF FAITH

WHY DISCUSS THIS HERE?
For those old enough to remember, a '60s pop group called the Monkees had a song titled, "I'm A Believer."[145] While the lyrics have little to do with our topic of faith and disability, the title is a good introduction to the reality of faith. That is, the song title, "I'm a believer," is a statement of fact. In our discussion on disability and faith thus far, we have not discussed the fact of "faith" in relation to the perception of and the reality of faith in God in a personal and objective sense for those who live in the Shadow World.[146]

The uncertainty or inability of us at times to identify and verify the actuality of their faith in God in neurotypical terms, from within their Shadow World, often leads to a disconnect where the disabled are inhibited or further disabled, in a personal and volitional sense, from engaging in the act of identifying and verifying their faith within their faith community.

Not only do those with neurological and biological disabilities have to overcome communication difficulties in expressing their faith; they also have to deal with the effects that their disability may have on their inner self—being, their understanding (cognitively) of their own personal reality, spirituality, and belief.

It is important, then, in such cases of neurological and biological disability that we work hard at confirming their faith as Margaret Coombs, in *Spirituality and Mental Health Care* writes:

---

[145] © The Monkees, "I'm a believer," lyrics, Neil Diamond, Screen Gems-Columbia Music (BMI), 1966.
http://en.wikipedia.org/wiki/I%27m_a_Believer Cited, 22/11/2014.

[146] A large part of the struggle for recognition of spirituality and faith for the disabled person comes from this period, where we see significant changes in culture and worldview taking place. The pretentiousness of "connecting" with one's inner self disengages us from the need to connect with one outside ourselves—namely God.

> Rejecting people's needs to explore (and identify) their spiritual experiences may inhibit their ability to make sense of and come to terms with powerful inner (faith) experiences.

The divide, this fence of disconnection, that disability can so often present in such cases can be discouraging. Is it worth the effort of going into this world in order to extract personal, and sometimes painstaking avowals,[147] if at all possible, in order to confirm the reality of faith in a neurologically and biologically disabled person? Can faith be real in such situations of neurological and biological disorders?

It is difficult to translate my thoughts into words here, to clearly articulate what I am trying to communicate, and it may be beyond my ability to do so, but in essence, although the disabilities that a person may have might impair their cognitive understanding of faith, within their soul/mind, their core spirituality—their true "inner spiritual" being has no such limitation.

This does not mean that the disabled experience some type of Platonic dualism, a separation of body and spirit/soul, but that the vessel in which their spirituality—"being" lives may impair faith's realisation in cognitive, sentient, and volitional terms; but their disabilities, whatever their composition, do not impede the veracity or reality of that faith, which is, in all reality, spiritually theirs.

Therefore, it is with this understanding that we do need to discuss the veracity (factualness) of faith in the Shadow World where the neurotypical language we use—in dogmatic, liturgical, and creedal practices within our churches or faith communities—is often irrelevant or at best inappropriate in defining the veracity of that faith.

As we mentioned in the previous chapter, "Defining Faith," salvic faith is like a can of spray paint; it is of the same "spiritual" substance—stuff—whatever surface it is sprayed upon. In fact "faith," as that life-giving salvic agent every human soul/spirit needs consists of the same life-giving spiritual (spirit) essence

---

[147] See "Glossary" – avowal, page 267

whatever the neurological abilities—status of the biological "vessel" within which that faith exists.

The foundation of that faith, in the life of a disabled person, is also consistent with what we accept in our neurotypical world. Faith, as we have defined it in our previous chapter, is the proactive work of God through His Spirit (John 3:15; Eph. 1:13–14), which brings to the enabled and disabled person alike that— same gift of faith and life that all who believe experience (John 1:12), a factual faith that exists within the spiritual reality of their ontological "being" (Eph. 2:8).

> But when the kindness and love of God our Savior appeared, he saved us, not because of righteous things we had done, but because of His mercy. He saved us through the washing of rebirth and renewal by the Holy Spirit, whom he poured out on us generously through Jesus Christ our Savior, so that, having been justified by His grace, we might become heirs having the hope of eternal life. (Titus 3:4–7)

> Blessed be the God and Father of our Lord Jesus Christ! According to His great mercy, he has caused us to be born again to a living hope through the resurrection of Jesus Christ from the dead to an inheritance that is imperishable, undefiled, and unfading, kept in heaven for you, who by God's power are being guarded through faith[148] for a salvation ready to be revealed in the last time. (1 Pet. 1:3–5)

James Fowler, in "The Regeneration of Man: Man, as God Intended Series," writes:

> Thus, it is that Peter can declare that "God has caused us to be born again to a living hope through the resurrection of Jesus Christ from the dead" (1 Pet. 1:3), evidencing the

---

[148] My point in this paper is that if faith is synonymous with 'belief,' then no one is saved, or guarded by belief, for we all experience moments of doubt and lack of belief in God. Faith has to be a permanent and enduring reality established in our spirit/soul beyond the frailty and subjectiveness of our human nature, Eph. 1:13-14, 2:8.

> pre-requisite of the historical resurrection of Jesus, with which we identify spiritually in regeneration.

As James Fowler further writes in his article "The Regeneration of Man," the origin—the source of life in us as human beings—comes from God, who gives to each "person" the gift of "spiritual" life, the breath of God— נְשָׁמָה - nesama,[149] that defines humans and establishes humankind as a primarily "spiritual" *anima vita*—living being, thus creating our distinctive and fundamental humanity (Gen. 1:27, 2:7).

> Then the Lord God formed the man of dust from the ground and breathed into his nostrils the breath of life, and the man became a living creature. (Gen. 2:7)

Life as we know it originates in God, who is Spirit (John 4:24, 5:26), and as He, God, remains that essential source of personal life in one's being, then all humanity exists, as separate from all other forms of life on earth, sustained by God himself.

> Yet he is actually not far from each one of us. For in him we live and move and have our being[150]; as even some of your own poets have said, "For we are indeed his offspring."[151] (Acts 17:27b–28)

---

[149] Thus, if taken literally, Neseama, sometimes synonymous with Ruah - רוּחַ, is God's anima vita, the anima of life, that is inspired into each human being He creates and, while present, enables each person to live in this world (Gen. 2:7). When released from the mortal body on death this "breath of life" does not dissipate but ultimately returns to God who created it (Eccl. 12:7). When with God, awaiting the resurrection and a new body, the "spirit" of each person retains its identity and spiritual characteristics free of any disabilities associated with its life in the mortal world. Ruah – רוּחַ more generally refers to the life form in animals, land, sea, and air, that do not have certain human characteristics that are present in humans (1Cor. 15:39).

[150] The Greek verb εἰμί is a primary verb that, when used in reference to persons, denotes existence, I, of persons, exist; II, to be, to be fact or the case; II, of the real world, be, become; IV, be the fact or the case with certainty as understood.

[151] The Apostle Paul, possibly citing from Epimenides and Aratus of Crete.

Paul quotes two maxims from Greek poets to support this teaching about man.

It can be seen from this passage in the book of Acts that not only does our spiritual existence depend upon God but as well the physical material-ontological body in which the spirit/soul (spirituality) of a person lives, moves, and has its "being" in this world.

Thus, any discussion on faith and life must consider the words of the Apostle Paul above and requires us to address the makeup of humankind. What makes the difference between humankind and the animal world? Is it essential to our understanding of disability, spirituality, and faith?

Yes, it is.

In our chapter "Defining Being," we discovered that God is the source of life (spiritual life) that we all receive, in essence, our soul/spirit; but God is also the creator of our material self, our bodies in which we live and move and have our being (Job 12:10; Dan. 5:23; [Heb. 2:11]), in this world.[152]

> And he made from one man every nation of mankind to live on all the face of the earth, having determined allotted periods and the boundaries of their dwelling place, that they should seek God, and perhaps feel their way toward him and find him. Yet he is actually not far from each one

---

The first comes from a quatrain attributed to the Cretan poet Epimenides (c. 600 BC), which appeared first in his poem Cretica and is put on the lips of Minos, Zeus's son, in honour of his father:

They fashioned a tomb for thee, O holy and high one—
The Cretans, always liars, evil beasts, idle bellies!
But thou art not dead; thou livest and abidest forever,
For in thee we live and move and have our being" (M.D. Gibson, ed., Horae Semiticae X [Cambridge: Cambridge University, 1913], p. 40, in Syriac; italics mine).

The second, *"For we are indeed his offspring's."* comes from the Cilician poet Aratus (c. 315–240 BC): "It is with Zeus that every one of us in every way has to do, for we are also his offspring [italics mine]" (Phaenonlena 5); which is also found in Cleanthes's (331–233 BC) earlier Hymn to Zeus, line 4.

[152] Edward Gaebelein, Ed., OliveTree, Bible+, Ver. 7.1.1, Expositors Bible Commentary, Acts 17:24-32: (M.D. Gibson, ed., Horae Semiticae X, [Cambridge: Cambridge University, 1913], p. 40, in Syriac. Cited, 20/04/2017.

of us, 'for in Him we live and move and have our being'. (ESV-Acts 17:26-28)

Our phrase, "In Him we live and move and have our "being," in verse 28, takes on a significance that goes unnoticed if we just allegorise these words:[153]

- "live and move," creates the foundation for the composite "being" of humankind.
- our "being"—anima vita—consummates our existence as a rational person.

This body-spirit union is not some platonic "dualism" or Aristotle's nexus of "forms" as known—written about in Greek anthropology.

As the Apostle Paul clearly states, "being"—living in this world requires all elements, to "live" (spirit) and to "move" (body) to be in a constant union to define one's sense of being, of their humanity, of self—of being a fully human person in this world.

Greek "dualism," on the other hand, requires a separation of the two elements, body (material) and soul/spirit (spiritual) viewing the body and soul/spirit as separate entities and the spirit/soul of man, which resides in the body doing so in a somewhat detached manner, like water in a bottle, a rider on a horse, each existing separate to the other.

In the biblical model followed in this book, our personal existence in this world, our being, is defined as a congruence of body and spirit/soul, each dependent upon the other for "life"—existence—being in this world.

The spiritual (non-dimensional) nature of man, essentially sustained by God as the human spirit, requires expression and interfaces with the material (biological) body of man for the expression of thought and word, the body being necessary as the

---

[153] The verb structure in this sentence is, present active (live), present passive (move), and present active (being); thus, they combine so that we "move" at the grace of God. OliveTree, Bible+ 6.1.1; Robinson's Word Pictures: "For in him (en autoi gar). Proof of God's nearness, not stoic pantheism, but real immanence in God as God dwells in us. The three verbs (zomen, kinoumetha, esmen) form an ascending scale and reach a climax in God (life, movement, existence)."

vehicle of action through which concepts and ideas are communicated from the spirit/soul of the person into the outside dimensional, visual, audible world.[154]

Faith in God, in Christ Jesus, as we have previously mentioned, exists as a spiritual valid construct within the spirit/soul of a person in this world, engaging the believer as a whole person, body—spirit/soul, whether one is enabled or disabled.

It is this spiritual definition of the fact of faith that we will take forward from here into our discussion on its reality and veracity in the world of disability. The reality of faith in God in the Shadow World as we will discover is, ultimately, not dependent upon the vessel but on God.

A historical-generalised overview of how faith communities have dealt with verifying the fact of faith in the life of the disabled will help set some guideposts that we can aim for in our support of the need to verify the reality of faith in the life of the disabled in our faith communities.

HISTORICAL VIEWS OF FAITH

Dr. Matthew Schuelka has an excellent paper, "A faith in Humanities," on this point and summarises various world religions and their approaches to inclusion or exclusion, as the case may be, in various faith systems and religious groups with respect to spirituality and faith within the life of their community and the individual disabled person.

Speaking of world religions, Schuelka divides them into general categories: those that think somewhat positively about people with disabilities, those that are somewhat dismissive of people with disabilities, and those that are ambivalent regarding the inclusion of people with disabilities.

---

[154] The "spiritual" nature of man although dependent upon a body for its existence in this "material" world can exist without that body and does so upon death awaiting the resurrection at the return of Jesus Christ when that "spirit" will attain an eternal body. (1Cor. 15:35-58, Phil. 3:20)

Looking at religious "sacred" writings, or texts[155], Schuelka, in *"A Faith in humanness: disability, religion and development"*[156], determines that where a particular religion fits into the below categories is often a matter of interpretation that changes over time.

> **ANTIQUITY**: disabilities were often seen as a judgment or the whim of the gods, and faith, as such, was relegated to appeasement or requests for allevement. The agrarian nature of most societies in antiquity demanded participation in pastoral pursuits rather than support and many with disabilities, either from birth or from war or accident or illness were largely unheeded in a society where the pressures of "the collective" survival of the community were paramount.[157]
>
> **JUDEO-CHRISTIAN**: Schuelka sees Levitical laws as draconian, but in fact, Judaism had a wide acceptance of people with disabilities. Schuelka sees the Bible's presentation of disability as a "result of sin" or the displeasure of God. With the advent of Christ, Schuelka states, there occurs a shift in acceptance, but

---

[155] Various terms describe the prime documents different religious systems and groups used. Each group holds its "core" documents in high regard and refers to them in matters of life and practice. There are, however, some distinctions made between the term "sacred and religious texts," the latter could be dogma and doctrine related, whereas the former is usually given to documents deemed to be "inspired" or authored under a divine mandate.

[156] Matthew Schuelka, (2013) "A faith in humanness: disability, religion and development," *Disability & Society* 28, no. 4, 500–513, DOI: 10.1080/09687599.2012.717880.

[157] It is worth noting that during the Industrial Age, the birthplace of technology, initially, disability was seen as a detriment where a person with a bodily or cognitive disability might not be able to contribute to the overall benefit of an "industrial" society. Thus, the birth of the "sanatorium" was the place where many with complex disabilities were assigned. Today's significant achievement is that we have support systems addressing past failures and concerns, resulting in improved attitudes toward disability support, care, and social inclusion.

he still holds to a view that disabilities were seen overall as a burden. [158]

ISLAM AND MIDDLE EASTERN: Schuelka sees Islam as initially having a kinder face toward disabilities and that disability is seen as a "necessary suffering" at times in order to experience the grace of Allah. However, Schuelka says, later interpretations of the Koran "lead to negative cultural realities" that placed disability as an obstacle to grace as the result of displeasing Allah.

EAST ASIAN RELIGIONS: Asian concepts of humanness and spirituality are fluid, and disabilities are variously seen as an impediment to "spiritual" enlightenment, or often confounded by the concept of "karma." Schuelka takes a view that Eastern religions, without a monotheistic model of God, were open in their definition of the human state. This viewpoint did create a conflict with the "need to meditate" as a manner of spiritual identity and "realisation" of the ultimate state for those disabled in biological and cognitive facilities.

RATIONALISM AND RELIGIOUS DEVELOPMENT: Schuelka traces the interaction of rationalism and religion in the Middle Ages on into the Industrial Age determining that a conflict arises where eugenics, the pursuit of the "normal," and rationalism displaced religious compassion and care as the "social model." Disability then came to be seen as a "rights-based" issue that, paradoxically, had a "negative impact" on the life, development, and re-habitation, the de-initialisation, of the disabled within society as society struggled to define an acceptable model for normalising—or

---

[158] I would be at variance with some of the basic suppositions of Dr Schuelka. In his excellent paper, he proposes the concept that "religion" per se is ambivalent and, at times, rather hostile in its approach to and engagement with the spirituality and faith needs of disabled people. In particular, his hostile attitude toward Biblical Christianity as encompassing an inadequate model of comprehension, compassion, and inclusion for the disabled person is concerning.

defining what was to be the new "normal" within the existing structures resulting from models of the previous ages.[159]

What Schuelka's paper does indicate is that one's religious concepts largely affected one's approach to and response toward disability and, as a result, the acceptance of faith and thus the recognition of the faith statements of the disabled person living in the Shadow World of disabilities.

At one point in his discussion, Schuelka concedes to Luther's viewpoint that the disabled are and have "full human value" and concludes that "the religious views of a faith community have a significant impact on how faith is actualised within that community."

This is an essential point to note as we look at the veracity (truthfulness) and fact (as an actuality) of faith in the life of a disabled person.

Before we can verify the reality of faith, saving faith, in the life of the disabled person, we have to accept then that faith, belief in Jesus Christ, in my viewpoint, is verifiable and constitutes a process that the disabled person understands—spiritually, in their soul/spirit "ontological" being, within the dimensions and limitations of their disability.

John Swinton, in "Restoring the Image," writes:

> Real affective apprehension of the divine must take place at a much deeper level than our personal comprehension. The exclusionary effect of assumptions that link wisdom with complexity and insight with abstraction can deny a person with profound cognitive disabilities full inclusion and participation in fellowship and as such must be treated with the utmost seriousness.

---

[159] Overall, Schuelka takes a favourable view of Eastern and Asian religions over a generalised model of Western and Middle East religions in regard to the acceptance and integration of disabled people using the Eastern "body-mind" holism model approach, which, void of a specific "ontological" model devalues their humanity and leaves then adrift of that essential ontological "spirit" reality that is essential for us to see them as "normal" human beings.

A key element in understanding Swinton's concept of the "deeper level" at which God communicates with "man" in the inner being (soul-spirit) of a person is found in Genesis 1:26.

> Then God said, "Let us make mankind in our <u>image,</u> in our likeness, so that they may rule over the fish in the sea and the birds in the sky, over the livestock and all the wild animals, and over all the creatures that move along the ground." (Gen. 1:26)

It is the phrase "in our image" that speaks to us of the deeper inner workings of a human being, on the spiritual level. The interaction between the Godhead, the Father, Son, and Holy Spirit, which existed before the foundation of time, establishes a timeless principle of life, of rational communication and existence on a spiritual level before man existed.

This "spiritual" three-way communication—relationship within God is called a "perichoretic" relationship because it encircles the three persons and nature of the godhead—Father, Son, and Holy Spirit—within the Trinity, maintaining the individual identity of the persons in the Trinity yet establishing the unity of God as one.

John Swinton, in "Restoring the Image," writes:

> Perhaps a key concept, which will enable us to examine critically such intellectualisation of faith ... is that of the "image of God in man."

In his discussion in Restoring the Image, Swinton writes that the image of God in man is not limited to the intellectual, that the divine transcends the cognitive and intellectual nature of man and therefore faith, as a spiritual reality, can exist where the intellect and cognitive aspects of human nature are limited or impaired.

I wish to suggest that adopting such a line of thinking is not only necessary but essential in order to identify one aspect of human nature for our consideration. It is also necessary, when dealing with neurological disabilities, to concentrate our attention upon just one facet of God's nature, His omnipresence. Undoubtedly omniscience and omnipotence constitute a significant dimension of the nature of God, but they are by no means the full essence of His divinity.

If we understand the image of God in man as being primarily based in acts of human reason, then our dealings with others will be basically of an educative and cognitive nature; the implications then for those unable to participate cognitively in such human exchanges, as a human "being," will lead us to a position of exclusion and devaluation.

However, I wish to argue here that if the image of God is understood in terms of personal "spirit-based" relationships, God is a relational—spiritual being and omnipresent as Spirit, then our theological understanding of God's relationships with "man" will revolve around the development of a truly "spirit"—based relational theology, a theology based on criteria independent of, or at least not determined by, neurological intellect, reason, or knowledge.

Here is our preparatory point.

Each and every mortal human "being" has a spiritual nature, a "spirit/soul," the gift of life (רוּחַ rûaḥ—נְשָׁמָה neshamah in the Hebrew, and πνεῦμα pneuma in the Greek) from God (Gen. 2:7, Job 33:4, Eccl. 12:7). In "man," living in this world, the physical and spiritual interact, and a diagram by Don Samdahi helps us see this inter—relationship.

The diagram (opposite) that Don Samdahi supplies on his web page below[160] takes us through the discussion on our "being" in this world to the only conclusion possible.

The human spirit/soul is an eternal entity created by God at conception that enters into this world to live here within a "body," and, at the death of the mortal body, that spirit/soul moves on into eternity.

---

[160] Concept design, © Samdahi D., Doctrine.org: *https://doctrine.org/nature-of-man* Cited, 08/03/2021. Graphic adaption © Gerard Maille, Art On Walls 2021, All rights reserved. Used with permission. See also:
http://www.talentshare.org/~mm9n/articles/man2/4.htm

The human soul united with its body is the root or radical principle of all man's acts, habits, and powers. Because man is both corporeal and spiritual, certain of his powers are organic (i.e., belonging to body and soul), and others are inorganic (i.e., belonging to the spirit/soul alone).

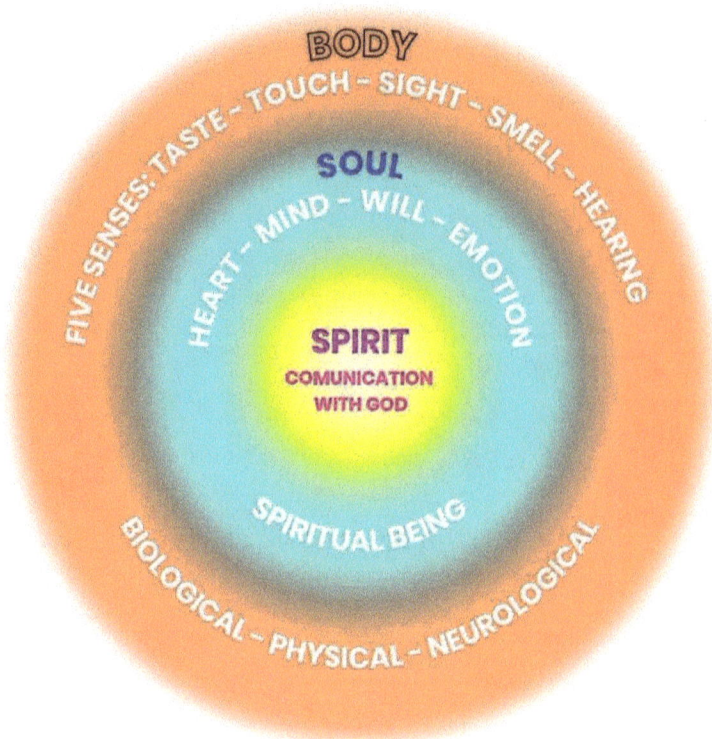

CIRCLE DIAGRAM[161]

Our biological abilities of sight, taste, sound, smell, speech etc., use organs in the body that can either fail or become

---

[161] Andrew Nimmo, Centre for Thomistic Studies, "*Souls and Spirits, Human Soul*": http://www.cts.org.au/2000/soulsandspirits.htm Cited, 20/04/2017. [Original article is no longer listed, see link below] http://www.talentshare.org/~mm9n/articles/man2/4.htm
"The human spirit is the 'breath of God' that gives and sustains life in man. The human soul is the principle of life—as spirit— and has the properties of intellect and will. The spirit/soul of man can exist without the body." Original diagram adapted by Gerard Maille, ©Art On Walls, All rights reserved.

impaired—disabled. Our human qualities of thought, intellect, will, emotions etc., however, are spiritual in nature, having no organic dependency on the human body and exist within the spirit/soul of a person, and continue to do so even when that person's human body is impaired—disabled or dies.

The "spirit," רוּחַ rûaḥ—נְשָׁמָה—neshamah "breath" from God, which gives us life and being, although interactive with the cognitive, intellectual, and biological nature of man, which I term as the "soul" of man, is independent of them in its existence.

As John Swinton goes on to write, in "Restoring the Image," "faith is a spiritual process" and as God is "spirit" (1 John 4:2–4) and every human being has this spiritual breath of God within, and is a spiritual being then faith, as a spiritual gift (Eph. 2:8) from God is constituted and exists as a spiritual reality in their life (resident within their spirit/soul).

Thus, there seems (should be) little doubt that God can communicate "spiritually" with the spirit/soul of a person and establish a faith-based relationship within the life of a disabled unhindered by the disability of that person, as we read in Romans 8:16

> The Spirit himself bears witness with our spirit that we are children of God. (Rom. 8:16)

So, can the "spiritual" nature of man transcend the biological function—or lack thereof—in the body and comprehend, in a spiritual sense, a perception of divine principles and experiences? One event in the Bible suggests so.

Though possibly not in the same context of our discussion on faith and disability, the response of the yet unborn John the Baptist to the presence of the unborn Jesus Christ (Luke 1:41, 44) is significant. Both were "disabled" in the biological sense in that they were not enabled, at that time, to express in a vocal cognitive manner their response to what they were experiencing on a spiritual level in their individual persons in this encounter.

It is also significant to note that the only mode of "communication and/or recognition" that the yet unborn John and the Christ had, as an awareness of the presence of each other, at this point in time had to be a purely spiritual one, and any communication, recognition, or exchange between them had to be on a purely spiritual level.

Also, this exchange between John the Baptist and Jesus Christ had to have elements of cognition, comprehension, and volitional act (John leapt for joy) even though at that time they were disabled, in a sense, from expressing such in an audible manner from within the womb of their respective mothers. Developmentally at six months (John) and one month (Jesus) of gestation, within the womb of their mothers, their cognitive powers would not have been fully developed at this stage. Yet, there is clear evidence that they "knew" or recognised the presence of each other (Luke 1:41).

We continually assume, in our neurotypical world, that the three elements of human rationale—cognition, sentient awareness, and volitional response—are essential to experience and knowledge in this world. Therefore, to be disabled in any one or three then would, under normal reasoning, render one unable to make what we assume to be rational decisions and or experience reality in a formative manner.

Speaking of a cognitively disabled person, John Swinton, in "Restoring the Image,"[162] writes:

> Secondly, I would dispute the suggestion that an inability to reason at a complex level is necessarily incompatible with meaningful spiritual experience and the development of authentic faith.

The exchange between John the Baptist and Jesus Christ leads us to only one conclusion—biological and sensory elements are not always necessary for spiritual interconnectedness. That is, the spirit of John the Baptist was able to "communicate" with the spirit of Jesus Christ sufficient for John to recognise and acknowledge who Jesus was even though both of them were still in their mother's womb.

The normal sensory and biological functions of their embryonic bodies were not enabled in the usual sense of one who

---

[162] John Swinton, "Restoring the Image: Spirituality, Faith, Cognitive Disability," *Journal of Religion and Health* 36, no. 1, Spring 1997, 23.

has been born, grown up, and developed reasoning capabilities like you and I would and could communicate in word, touch, attitude, or response to external stimuli. Isolated from the external world, pre-birth, John and Jesus were, in that sense, living in the Shadow World.

What we learn from Jesus and John, in Luke chapter 1 is that faith in, and recognition of, God is essentially a spiritual experience in the Shadow World, as it is in ours.

Before we move on to discuss actualising faith in the life of a disabled person, we need to take a moment to touch on what I term "the DSM-5 disconnect." What has DSM-5 to do with our discussion here?

THE DSM-5 DISCONNECT

The Diagnostic Statistics Manual of Mental Disorders, fifth edition, (DSM-5) is the manual, guideline, for identifying and treating a wide range of disabilities. Yet, in its attempt, by the authors, to be inclusive in its treatment of mental disorders, inadvertently DSM-5 brings with it a disconnect that is often unnoticed.

Previous to DSM-5, in earlier versions, some disabilities within the autism spectrum (as well as others) were identified *distinctly* from one another within the spectrum of autism facilitating individualised care models for those identifiable—with distinct characteristics of autistic disabilities.

While DSM-5's inclusive model of bringing disability-disabilities into mainstream humanity has some positive points, by default it is exclusive of, and in the case of some, dismissive of, the need to identify and communicate ideas and concepts in a special individual language that is frequently needed when communicating complex ideas and expressions of knowledge and experience of religious concepts, especially in the sometimes-vague amorphic world of autism.

This disconnect has an unfortunate flow on into the faith community not envisioned by the writers of DSM-5, but it is an issue that we need to address.

As John Swinton writes:

> The exclusionary effect of assumptions that link wisdom and complexity and insight with abstraction can deny a person with profound cognitive disabilities full inclusion and participation in (a faith) fellowship and as such must be treated with utmost seriousness.

Prior to the release of DSM-5, DSM-4 flagged different aspects of a disability category, thus generating a need to address individual care models—languages for disabilities with similar characteristics. In particular, placing autism and its derivatives somewhere on the "spectrum" of humanity reduces the urgency to address faith needs within autism, and by default, other disabilities within faith communities.

This language disconnect inherent in DSM-5 will have long-term effects on faith communities. It will be more difficult, with this inclusive model of disability, to convince leaders in our churches and faith communities of the need to have specialised programs, liturgy, and creedal statements that concord with the "language" of the Shadow World where the disabled live.[163] So, DSM-5, in its new one diagnosis fits all approach to autism, does no favors to our faith communities, but rather may inhibit the understanding of faith and its expression within faith communities.

However, as we have discussed above, the veracity and reality of "faith" in the Shadow World is not tied to any particular disability diagnostic model or system but is the function of a direct personal spiritual relationship between God and man, located in the spirit/soul of a person, whether that person is enabled or disabled as the situation may be.

Faith, its truth and acceptance within a belief system (as a faith community), as well as the expression of that faith in the life of a disabled person, by definition, now have to be seen to exist

---

[163] Many problems of the past are being resolved for people with disabilities who want to participate in religious communities. Physical barriers are being removed so that people with disabilities get past the parking lot, into the building, and the pews worshipping. Now, there are new challenges to overcome so that people with disabilities might not be present only but fully included.

existentially within that person as an independent reality. Our issue is to endeavor to see that the reality of that faith within their world complies with or is at least equal to, or harmonious with, the neurotypical, cognitive, sentient models of acceptance predominant within that faith community.

What evidence, then, of faith in the life of disabled people is necessary for us to verify and confirm such faith?

A FACT OF FAITH

John Swinton writes in his paper "Restoring the Image"[164] that it is the Spirit of God who defines faith, who transcends both worlds, God and "man's," and brings faith to be a reality in the life of a person on either side of the disability fence.

Beginning with the godhead, Swinton establishes that it is in the all-encircling "perichoretic"[165] nature of God, in the triune godhead, that spirituality is determined as the basis of His personality and verifies the reality that faith first existed as a relational concept on a spiritual level within the Godhead.[166]

> This perichoretic relationship between the transcendent (God) and the temporal (man)—(made) in the image of God—is restored as we participate in the dynamic circulation of the Spirit of God as it pervades the temporal (situation) and the transcendent enabling us to respond and relate on levels hidden from the intellect.

In plain English, this means that God, eternally existent and independent of our material-biological universe, operates interactively on a personal person-to-person (nonmaterial)

---

[164] John Swinton, "Restoring the Image: Spirituality, Faith, Cognitive Disability," *Journal of Religion and Health* 36, no. 1, Spring 1997, 23

[165] Perichoretic: from peri—to surround— and choreatic to embrace the all-surrounding, embracing relationship of the triune godhead, a term referring to the relationship of the three persons of the triune God (Father, Son, and Holy Spirit) to one another.

[166] The origin of "Faith" is in God, who is without beginning or ending, wherein the Father, Son and Holy Spirit interact with each other in a perfect example of implicit "faith," each person interactively and perfectly believing, trusting, and loving each other in all they do and say.

spiritual level of reality and existence, substantively and cognitively, within the triune Godhead.

It is also absolutely possible for God to step outside that perichoretic relationship, from within the triune godhead, establishing, communicating, and relating in a personal "ontological" relationship with a human being. This relationship is established in a spiritual dialogue, person to person, and connects that person with God, whether that person is enabled or disabled, establishing full understanding and communication, experientially—spiritually, within that person's spirit/soul "being" in their new (eternal), faith-based relationship with God.

Thus, faith, a gift from God, as proposed in this book, establishes a "spiritual" dialogue—communication between two individual people, God, and man (the human spirit/soul), that has both substance and reality in that personal interface between these two people. My point is that for the seriously compromised and disabled person, their relationship with God, through and by faith, is real and has an enlightening effect on that human spirit/soul, in their being—spirituality, such that they, the person, understands this within their personal "self-being," and is not something that just remains a conjecture or theory in religious discussions.

Disability, therefore, has no limitations on a God-sustained relationship.

The disconnect felt—implied in DSM-5 is no barrier to the soul/spirit of a disabled person in verifying the reality of their faith and their participation in the expression of that faith within their spiritual (faith) relationship with God, even if it is shadowed from those of us living in the neurotypical world. The criterion that defines faith in the Shadow World is precisely the same criterion that defines faith in the neurotypical world.

That is, it is the transcendence of God, inherent in this perichoretic spiritual relationship between the Father, Son, and Holy Spirit, that speaks through the universal divine spiritual language of faith that has uninhibited access to the soul/spirit "being" of that person living in the Shadow World and establishes that same faith relationship with the disabled as well as the enabled person alike.

As a result of this discussion, we realise that the language of God transcends the vessel in which the soul/spirit of a person lives. Even in cases of mental illness where the lines between material and psychological disabilities sometimes get blurred, there is no confusion in the reality and essence, spiritually, of that "faith" within a faith relationship between God and any human soul/spirit whom He, God, has created (Gen. 2:7, Job 32:8).

Therefore, faith, authentic[167] salvic faith, exists both existentially and ontologically, in the Shadow World of disabilities, as veritably as it does within the neurotypical world. Our humanity, our true essence—being is spiritual, and in the world of disability this is the key that opens the door to a new reality for faith in the life of a disabled person.

Samuel Kabue writes in his paper "Voices from Africa": *Disability, Society and Theology* that "true humanness transcends bodily (material) or cognitive faculties," and as such God's relationship with humankind transcends any disability.

> Material disability may present a whole range of social and cultural challenges and a sense of physical diminishment as stated elsewhere. But, it does not in any way diminish true self, that is, the image of God. Above all else, it is as spiritual beings that we are the very image of God, (and define our true humanity).[168]

As we go forward from here, our problem now, in this book, is not that we can question the existence of faith in the Shadow World of disabilities but that we often cannot recognise its language, the "voice" of the conveyer, or its reality and existence in the life of a disabled person.

Language is often seen as the vehicle of life, a vehicle through which we engage in life and living every day with people. Through language, like the written English language used to communicate and facilitate this discussion in this book, we can exchange ideas and discuss concepts, and inform—communicate—new realities

---

[167] That is verifiable as truthful, factual, authentic from veracity—to verify—to establish as truth.

[168] Samuel Kabue, *Disability, Society and Theology*: Voices from Africa (Zapf Chancery Publishers: Limuru, 2011) p42

that help the reader to understand, hopefully, the thoughts of the writer. But how do we communicate with the disabled person when language either, spoken, written, or visual, presents a fundamental challenge to discussion and interaction with that person?

John Swinton writes to refocus us from the cognitive to the spiritual nature of a person and leads us into the discovery of a language that transcends disability.

> Consequently, all human persons can be seen to have spiritual potential. The absence of a certain level of cognitive capability does not exclude a person from experiential spirituality. Authentic religious faith thus understood is a matter of an existential commitment to the reality of the divine as made manifest within relationships, which determines the basic character of a person's life and (defines) existence.

So, what defines faith in the Shadow World is a personal, spiritual, salvic relationship with God in Jesus Christ in and through the work of God's Holy Spirit.

We need to "see" and accept this fact. It is important that we also accept that people in the Shadow World of disability are fully human, in every sense, and work at ways of helping them actualise their faith in their *unique* "language," a language that they can share with God, and us spiritually, within our churches or faith communities (John 10:10).

As we close our discussion on the reality of faith in the Shadow World, we know that it is no longer a question of factuality but is more a question of understanding, interpretation, and acceptance of the language of the Shadow World.

Examples are often used to demonstrate a point, and I am hesitant to put this one forward, as it is not prescriptive of all churches or faith communities, but I believe that I must.

A young woman, a member of a faith community, was being discussed along with other names in view of prospective baptism and membership. This young woman was disabled with a combination of Down's syndrome with additional autistic characteristics. While discussing the young woman's abilities to comprehend faith and express such in a congruent balanced manner, the remark "she only has the mentality of a five-year-old" was made.

Once I too would have agreed with this statement as it is a common approach made to those disabled in a cognitive or intellectual manner in our society today. I was aggrieved at this, but with this new knowledge of "faith" in the Shadow World, its veracity and reality in a God-sustained spiritual relationship made me weep inside, not only for the statement made about the person referred to but as well the person making that statement from unawareness or convention.

It was not that the speaker devalued the disabled young woman as a person but had missed the whole point of the transcendence of faith as a spiritual reality and the perspicuity[169] of the gospel that permeates all creation (Ps. 19:1f, John 4:24, 1 Cor. 2:11–12; 2 Cor. 3:17), including the Shadow World of disability.

This book is written then in order to generate meaningful discussion when dealing with the spiritual suitability, or readiness, of any disabled person seeking to participate in the sacramental life of their faith community.

As I stated above, I have some reluctance in raising this issue here, but this situation brings to my mind our frequent failure and inability as "mere humans" to put aside personal biases, or partiality, or dismissiveness of the subject of faith and disability.

Allan Templeton (psychologist) summarises this situation best in an email comment he made during the development of this book:

> "Being led by the Holy Spirit" is a wonderful catchphrase to fall back on in order to cover over often deep-seated bigotry or just plain ignorance.[170]

My point is that "faith," faith in the Shadow World, is not a matter of prescriptive practices or one of levels of intelligence or cognitive realities, but one of a dimensionally transcendent

---

[169] See "Glossary" – perspicuity, page 271
[170] Allan Templeton, Email: Re: *Faith in The Shadows* III – Final (27/1/2018).

interpersonal spiritual relationship with God. It is this gift of faith, spiritually, which comes from God and responds to God (Gal. 4:6), that exists within the life-soul/spirit, "being" and mind of everyone who believes, (Eph. 2:8, 2 Cor. 1:22), whether they are disabled or "enabled" as we would oftentimes prefer.

Another question that we raise here in this chapter is.

> "How do we determine that faith is wedded to the person with the disability, 'in their ontologically being', particularly in cases where the disability/s of that person precludes the expected general declaration of confessional faith in God that we have come to assume and rely upon in our churches and faith communities."

The customs and rituals that we have developed over the years, and have become accustomed to, regarding faith declarations within our churches and faith communities are acceptable and trustworthy, and we continue to use them for good reasons. However, in the Shadow World of disability these protocols and languages, that work in a neurotypical situation (sense), usually fall silent and leave us bereft of answers. This is because the "language" and communication barriers that disabilities can present to our neurotypical preferences for "vocal" intellectual objectivity, in the confirmation of faith, can allude us in the life of a disabled person who may have limited neurotypical abilities.

But there is no such "language" barrier existing between the disabled person and God who brings faith and life to that person. Note, in this instance, the perceptual reality is that it is us, on this side of the fence, who are in the shadows here, not the disabled person who has an eternal, person-to-person, intimate spiritual relationship with God by faith.

Like a can of spray paint, whatever surface you spray it on, whether it be wood, metal, plastic, or concrete, the paint is still the same; it consists of the same material substance. Whatever vessel faith resides in this world, the vessel does not define or validate the objective reality of that faith in the soul/spirit of the person. It is in their inner "being," ontologically, that God validates faith's reality and constructs within their own personal spiritual identity.

Faith is "spiritual" and is "co-existent" (coalescent)[171] within the spirit/soul of a person whatever surface (body) it (faith) is placed in—that is, in the spirit/soul "being" of that disabled believer. What defines faith in the Shadow World is essentially the same as that in our neurotypical world, a personal, objective, spiritual relationship with God. Thus, the reality of faith in the Shadow World is also the same as in ours; it is of the same spiritual essence, substance, and content. To answer our question on how to "determine" that faith is wedded to a person with disabilities, we need to learn and accept their "language" as valid and representative of their faith in their inner "being."

Our journey through disability and faith has led us to the conclusion that faith and disability can coexist in the life of those who live in the Shadow World of disability. It is the expression of that faith that presents genuine issues for the disabled, their families, and faith communities.

As we conclude this chapter, I leave you with another illustration to ponder. Like the coins and notes, this one will help us bridge the gap between concept and reality as we engage in this debate as to how we can recognise and actualise faith, faith that the disabled have and experience while living in the Shadow World.

So, have you ever been to a bar or hotel, or restaurant where the bartender uses a device called a "pourer" to dispense—mix—spirit drinks? The picture below might help you visualise what they look like.

JUST POURERS

Imagine for a moment that we have several bottles each containing a liquid that represents the "spiritual" nature, "spirit/soul," of a human being.

---

[171] The sense of the word in this paper taken here is to unite "two things" into one unified mass, body; faith becoming part of the constitution of the whole, inaugurating a new reality, in the being of a person, whether enabled or disabled. See "Glossary" – coalesce, page 267

The bottle and liquid "spirit" it contains combines to form the actuality and "being" of a person living in this world. In each bottle, "faith" exists within the liquid, "spiritual" nature, of that person.

The bottle pourers in our illustration (usually used on the tops of the bottles in a bar) below are all different and give different flow rates, some measuring, some limiting the volume—quantity of spirit that can be poured out at any one time. In some cases, the pourer is almost fully restrictive, allowing only the minutest drop of the "spirit" within the bottle to be poured over the counter into our world.

SPIRIT POURERS

Thus, what we can observe from our little illustration is that it is obvious that the existence of the liquid "faith," in the bottle, is not defined by the shape of the bottle itself, or the pourer attached to the bottle. Likewise, the veracity (genuineness) of the "faith" within the "spirit" in the bottle is not defined or limited in its spiritual relationship with God by the "pourer" attached to the bottle.

Nor is the disabled person's faith defined by the category of their "pourer." Nor does the "pourer" that they use to communicate their faith over the counter into our world, so to speak, affect the existence or their experience of that "faith" in God.[172]

Although the look of the "pourer and the "flow" of liquid may differ with each "pourer" attached to the bottle, the pourer pours out the same liquid, the same spiritual nature of that person, whatever the rate or restriction that the pourer places upon the bottle

On our side of the fence, in the neurotypical world, the bottles we normally experience usually have no pourer attached that can restrict the expression, communication, and validation of faith within our church or faith communities in accordance with the various practices and rituals commonly used to do so.

When a "pourer" is applied to the bottle, limiting, restricting, or blocking the flow of the "spiritual" expression of faith, a crucial issue arises for those who live in the Shadow World of disability.

How can their faith, a factual and spiritual reality for them personally within the bottle, be portrayed—expressed not only within themselves, essentially in their ontological being, but also within the faith community to which they belong?

To answer our question, how do we confirm their faith, our discussion now looks at how, and by what means, we can understand and accept the faith statements of those who are disabled in ways that are empowering to and inclusive of them within our faith communities.

---

[172] It is a very bold thing for me to say here, but I venture into this discussion that, in some cases, the disabled person may attain a higher spiritual awareness of 'faith' and God than those who live in the neurotypical world. Being a neurotypical person has its issues: perception, cognition, volition, and our human traits—characteristics can impede—get in the way—of our individual and spiritual experience of God. Not that it is a 'good thing' to be disabled, but we neurotypicals do not have the prerogative on personal relationships with God. Sometimes disabled people (like Mary) may have a relationship with God that is out of this world.

CHAPTER 8

ACTUALISING FAITH

By the term "actualise," I mean the act of recognition and acceptance of a faith statement in a manner that is both understood and acknowledged within the framework of a faith community by both that community and the disabled person alike as a regular part of that church's life and fellowship; specifically, in the case of this book, in relationship to denominational Christianity.

How then do we understand, view and accommodate those of our faith community who desire—seek to express the reality of their faith within the boundaries of their faith community's protocols and liturgy, yet are disabled having a restrictive "pourer" attached to their "being," albeit it in a body in which their God given spiritual identity and faith lives (in their soul/spirit)?[173]

On this point in our discussion on faith, this book will follow traditional Western Christian theological and liturgical practices and assumes that the statement of faith to be made by the disabled person is in the objective reality of their personal spiritual faith relationship with God in Jesus Christ.

The principles of affirmation, declaration, and cognizance of a faith statement developed in this book, and the concepts of a personal spiritual understanding of faith in the Shadow World, can be universally applied to whatever faith system—or faith community—that that person may belong to or be a part of.

---

[173] "soul/spirit": In this chapter, I am using the combination "soul/spirit." Here we are discussing the out-working activity of faith in the "spirit" of a person from within their spiritual-driven emotions, thoughts, and actions. That is, faith, in their 'spirit' is working outward through their mind and heart (soul) into the world around them.

ACTUALISING FAITH IN A NEUROTYPICAL WORLD

In the world of the neurotypical, the actualisation of faith within a church or faith community is usually achieved through traditional membership classes, rituals, baptisms, and/or membership services germane to that denomination or faith community.

Whatever the process involved in this actualisation, there is usually an outward assent—acknowledgment, either vocal and/or visual—as a statement of an inward belief, knowledge, or change in the spiritual life of that person, in most cases declaring faith in the objective reality of Jesus Christ within the ideology of that faith community, while giving assent to its liturgical and doctrinal protocols.

This actualisation process varies within churches and faith communities, but at the core of the liturgy, teaching, and doctrine of any denominational actualisation of faith, are three basic conventions, elements, or formula—practices that come together to make up the actualisation process: dogma, liturgy, and relational aspects that occur in any combination that make up denominational creedal norms in and through which this actualisation process occurs.

Dogma[174] here means faith as defined by the system of doctrine or teaching of a particular denomination or faith community. Liturgical[175] here means faith as defined by the custom and worship practices of a particular denomination or faith community. And relational[176] here means faith defined as trust in a person, in our case in Jesus Christ, within the doctrinal system of a particular denomination or faith community.

This process of actualisation is usually accompanied by a confession of sin, (dogma) an acknowledgment of surrender to Jesus Christ as Lord and Savior (relational), and a commitment to a new life within the church, both bodily and spiritually, in Christ (liturgical).

The rituals, sacraments, and or confirmation ceremonies in which this usually takes place confirms the confession of faith,

---

[174] See "Glossary" – dogma, page 268
[175] See "Glossary" – liturgical, page 270
[176] See "Glossary" – relational, page 272

affirms this new dimension in the spiritual life of that person so declaring their faith in God, and (congregationally) recognises that declaration of faith as such.

The ability to articulate in an outward, observable manner the inward change in the spiritual and moral life of a believer, who has come to believe in Jesus Christ, is a great blessing indeed but one which, due to the entwining, interactions of physical, biological, and mental disabilities, is often denied to those who live in the Shadow World.

While we acknowledge, in reality, that although God alone knows the heart and faith of a person, (Ps. 44:21, Acts 15:8, Rom. 8:26–28) the fruits of that faith are still there within the spirit and life of that disabled person, although often not visually or audibly apparent to us, even if its expression is in a "different language." Therefore, actualising such faith, from a spiritual point of view, not only affirms its existence but acknowledges the spiritual work of God in the life of the disabled person.

So here we are at the crux of the issue.

Is it necessary for the inward grace of salvation in the life of a sinner to be effective, in "saving that person," that such grace and faith be acknowledged in a declaratory auditory, intellectual, neurotypical manner as is usually the case in our denominational and faith communities, where such declaratory affirmation is modeled on, or carries elements of, the proposition of the text of Romans 10:9, in our introduction?

Romans 10:9 gives us two basic conditions (clauses) as defined by the Apostle Paul regarding the affirmation of faith:

> That if you confess with your mouth, "Jesus is Lord," and believe in your heart that God raised him from the dead, you will be saved. For it is with your heart that you believe and are justified, and it is with your mouth that you confess and are (will be) saved. (Rom. 10:9–10)

Our first conditional clause is "confess with your mouth," indicating affirmation in a verbal manner. Verbalising an internal belief, condition, or personal understanding is often outside the functional attributes of the biological—anatomical and neurological—environment that a disabled person might suffer from, as the impairment of their normative attributes that are required for verbalisation of their inward belief are often prohibitive of such verbalisation of that inward belief—faith in God.[177]

Our second conditional clause is "believe," indicating assent in a cognisant manner. In our normative world, cognition of thought, idea, or knowledge is regarded as necessary (required) in order to facilitate an understanding of conceptual realities, especially in relation to the subjective nature of faith declarations. In a neurotypical world, a declaration of faith usually involves cognitive assent and verbal communication.

We cannot see inside the soul/spirit of a person in order to determine if that faith statement is objective and valid. With complex disabilities, the presence of mental and psychological "filters" can interrupt or distort thought patterns and thus inhibit what we might call, in our neurotypical world, a knowing-believing declaration of faith in a formative manner.

Initially, then, it would seem that these two prerequisites or "conditions" of Romans 10:9–10, would exclude many disabled from participating in a personal affirmation and communication of their faith relationship with God within their faith community.

Or we ask, can a person disabled in body and soul/spirit[178], where that disability impinges upon their cognitive and volitional

---

[177] As I reviewed this book, I realised that Romans 10:9–10 is not set in a congregational framework, and no imperatives in the text require this declaration of faith in God to occur in a communal setting. More to the point, it is a personal, person-to-person (i.e., man-to-God discussion, the Greek word for 'confess - ὁμολογήσῃς you confess, is second person singular as is the remainder of the Greek sentence, as is "your heart—καρδίᾳ σου—your heart"). The translation of the Greek Romans 10:9 σωθήσῃ—"are saved"— is a bit loose; the verb is future indicative passive, which means "you will be saved." This sits well with the Apostle Paul's theology of a personal, one-to-one relationship with God, in person to person, and is the key in this paper that unlocks God's beautiful personal relationship with each individual who believes in "their heart," whether enabled or disabled.

[178] See the discussion of spiritual disability toward the end of chapter 5, "Defining Disability," page 59, para 6. Disabled in 'spirit' means, in my context, the impairment of expressing personal spirituality into

abilities—processes, know "in a salvic manner" the reality of faith in God, and comprehend and actualise that faith in accordance with the Apostle Paul's definition of declarative faith as it appears to be presented in Romans 10:9–10.

That is, in the Shadow World of disability, is such a declaration possible, even factual?

CAN WE ACTUALISE FAITH IN THE SHADOW WORLD?

We can see and understand, from our brief survey of the world of disability in "Defining Disability," in chapter 5, that disabilities can affect the way a person reacts, thinks, and responds both neurologically and spiritually to words and concepts they "see or hear" coming to them from the other side of the fence—that is, the neurotypical world.

As disability is no respecter of denominational boundaries or faith community dogma and liturgy, all Christian churches and faith communities encounter, experience, and will need to deal with the issue of faith and disability within the framework of their fellowship life, teachings, and practices.

All of this means that when we engage with someone who has a mental and or physical disability, our methods of communication will need to take into account that disability mix and its effect on that person, both in body and soul/spirit in our approach to and consideration of their confirmation, affirmation, and the presentation of their faith.

As mentioned earlier in our chapter "Defining Disability," each disabled person has their own unique "language" that they use as their personal means of communication whether it be verbal language, body language, or attitude or electronic assistance (or any other mechanism of communication) as their response to external and internal stimulation.

The issue of "language" and adaptable protocols for the acceptance and realisation of faith in the life of a complex disabled

---

our world in the normative manner that we readily recognise and accept. There is no disability, known or unknown, that can disable the 'spirit-נְשָׁמָה nᵉšāmâ' of life in a person such that it may impair God's personal relationship, by His Spirit, with that person's 'spirit.' See "Glossary" – spiritual disability, page 272

person is the key to opening the door to them for inclusion, and for us to recognise them as full members of our faith communities.

Susannah B. Mintz writes in her journal article in *Disability Studies Quarterly*, "Disability Narrative and Representations of Faith":

> It is possible, then, to narrate the conjunction of faith and disability in ways that avoid—or even directly challenge—attitudes toward physical impairment as symbolic evidence of divine wrath or favor, attitudes that perpetuate the cultural marginalization of disability. Eiesland writes that [e]mancipatory transformation must be enacted not only in history but also in imagination and language. Liberatory theology of disability is the work of the bodily figuration of knowledge.[179]

Charles Gourgey, in dealing with the practical aspects of faith affirmation in the life of a disabled person, in his *Journal of Religion and Disability* paper writes, regarding the spiritual care of the elderly, dementia, and Parkinson's syndrome patients at a nursing home he visits, loud and clear for all to hear:

> In the work of Mairs and Kuusisto, disability and faith are unmoored from their conventional symbolic association and brought together in unfamiliar, imaginatively radical juxtapositions that tell new stories of what it means to believe, to be disabled, to be a self.

For the disabled, on their part, although their particular disabilities may preclude them from actualising their faith in a manner recognisable and understood within the accepted normative neurotypical styled focused practices of the liturgy and creedal systems of their denomination or faith community, this does not preclude us from investigating "imaginatively radical juxtapositions"[180] that can help the disabled declare and actualise their personal faith within their faith community.

---

[179] Susannah Mintz, *Disability Studies Quarterly* 26, no. 3 (2006), "Ordinary Vessels: Disability Narrative and Representations of Faith," para 30.

[180] Ibid, para 42.

So how do we, understanding the limitations that can present in complex cases of neurological and mental disorders, achieve this goal of affirmation—actualisation?

First, we need to acknowledge along with Professor Charles Gourgey that "people with disabilities are no different from others in that we (they) need care for our (their) souls as well as for our (their) bodies."[181]

I take Charles Gourgey's term "care for our souls" here to encompass the full spiritual needs of a disabled person, where salvation is the primary need, inherent in their human soul/spirit, for them to find fulfillment in a loving spiritual relationship with God which is paramount within their life, family, and faith community.[182]

Yes, it may be fundamentally a different relationship in matters of cognitive and sentient awareness to that of the neurotypical person, but it is still a relationship in which the disabled person interacts with God in a manner that is spiritually meaningful, knowable, and "makes most sense" to them.

Second, we need to acknowledge that it is the Holy Spirit who is the agent of change in the life and soul/spirit of a person.

> Paul taught that the Holy Spirit, poured out in the new age,[183] is the creator of new life in the believer and that unifying force by which God in Christ is building together the Christians into the body of Christ.[184]

---

[181] Parentheses mine.

[182] There is a growing awareness amongst medical and care journals of the importance of "spirituality" in an increased understanding of and need to meet and support the spiritual needs of a patient seen as part of the overall holistic care of that person, abled or disabled alike.

[183] Note: "new age" here refers to the outpouring of the Holy Spirit at Pentecost, which inaugurated the "new age" of the church of Christ on earth and personalised God's interaction with man; not the "new age" of the '70s and '80 commonly referred to as the period of enlightenment in freedom of personal and religious conventions: https://www.britannica.com/topic/New-Age-movement Cited, 05/03/2021.

[184] Walter Elwell, *Evangelical Dictionary of Theology* (Paternoster Press: Grand Rapids, MI, 1995) 400, 1043.

In our chapter on "Defining Being," the diagram on page 32[185] shows us that man is spiritual, a spiritual being, whether enabled or disabled. Therefore God, who is Spirit (John 4:24), fully encompasses and comprehends all that is "spiritual" in the soul/spirit of the enabled or disabled person.

We have learned from our chapter "Defining Faith" that faith is Spirit, and faith, as a spiritual reality, when immersed within the soul/spirit of a person, in a union of the "Spirit of God" and the "spirit (breath of life) of man," constitutes a state of salvation.

Life in a spiritual sense (apart from our humanity on earth) is then the domain of God, and it is in and through His Holy Spirit that God brings new life as salvation through the gift of faith deposited into the spirit/soul-being of that person (Ezek. 36:26–27, 37:4; John 3:5–8, Eph. 1:13–14)

Third, we need a new understanding of faith, one that is not based solely on the normative neurotypical, cognitive, sentient models of faith common within denominationalism and our churches—faith communities. A model of inclusion that allows us to embrace those who are disabled in the above areas of their "being" and life, who have God's "salvic" gift of faith within their spirit/soul-being. A model that takes the additional step, having received salvation as the gift of "life" from God through that spiritual deposit of faith (Eph. 2:8), which allow us to actualise their "faith" in God within their church community.

> For it is by grace you have been saved, through faith—and this is not from yourselves, it is the gift of God—not by works, so that no one can boast. For we are God's workmanship, created in Christ Jesus to do good works, which God prepared in advance for us to do. (Eph. 2:8–10)

This new understanding of faith, as a spiritual issue over a purely declarative reality, is essential to accepting those who live in the Shadow World of disability and is the key to affirming their faith in God that, as such, also acknowledges and affirms the reality of their spirituality and being.

---

[185] See "Man is a Spiritual Being," page 32

We, therefore, need to acknowledge that the Holy Spirit can, and may need to, work in different ways within the life and "being," soul-spirit, of a disabled person to that which we may understand as acceptable from our normative neurotypical viewpoint of faith.

As Susannah Mintz discusses in her paper, "Disability Narrative and Representations of Faith," actualising faith in the Shadow World of the disabled will require some new thinking.

This does not mean that we need a new gospel or a new faith but a new way of understanding faith in Jesus Christ that transcends the "fence" that disabilities often create and allows us access to new ways of actualising that faith in the life of the disabled person who lives in the Shadow World.

As we will soon explore some examples of actualising faith in difficult and challenging circumstances, we need to be reminded that grace overcomes tragedy, and love summits the highest hills in life.

Susannah Mintz writes of Reynolds Price's *A Whole New Life* (1995) in the story of his journey into paralysis from a malignant spinal tumor, and his awakening to faith in Christ that led him to a new understanding of faith in the context of disability:

> The dysfunction that results from illness is hereby rendered inspirational—not an arbitrary corporeal event but a meaningful occurrence experienced as purposeful and planned.

Therefore, disability, which is often seen as an impediment to a relationship with God, can open doors not previously thought to exist for that person in life.

For example, this is a difficult point to place before us in this paper, but when we discuss "Mary," a totally noncommunicative young girl,[186] it is certain that she can perceive things around her like: light, color, smell, taste, touch, and sound. However, the cognition of these sensory inputs is undeterminable and perceptualizing concepts and thus ideas may be difficult for her to form, yet her relationship with God knows no undeterminable elements.

---

[186] See "Mary," page 180

I am convinced, along with the Apostle Paul, that she, Mary, has a unique and unfettered dialogue with God in her spirit/soul that is not inhibited by worldly temptations that so often intervene in our world to distract us from God, His love, grace and care.

At present, I admit that there are no easy answers to the question of actualising faith in the Shadow World of disability, but we need to begin the journey in order to discover ways and means that will be spiritually meaningful to the disabled person, true to the gospel of Christ in the Word of God and meaningful to the disabled person and their church community alike.

In one case that I am personally aware of, let us call him Bill,[187] when questions were asked of him when he took membership of his local church, he used very direct "unique" language to signify his understanding of the gospel and his response to it within his personal being.

In word pictures painted by him, Bill was able to express his faith in his personal language, a language that was accepted by his church and fellowship in actualising that faith as evidence and affirmation of his comprehension within himself of faith. Bill participated, up until his death, in communion and full fellowship within the life of his local church.

Actualising faith in the Shadow World, furthermore, requires of us a willingness to participate in a biblical-scriptural model of recognising salvic faith as a spiritual entity—a reality in the life of a disabled person that is both congruent with their world and honoring to Jesus Christ.

So, how can this be achieved?

Throughout this book, I have used terms like "new language," "new thinking," "new dialogue" and "new discussions" to

---

[187] Bill (real name withheld) was a man of sixty-four years of age who lived in Sydney. Bill suffered from IDD (amongst other things) and had been a pen friend of mine. Bill worked in a sheltered workshop in Sydnham, Sydney, NSW. It was a joy to hear from Mary (his mother) in 1982 that Bill had taken full communicant membership of his church. I had, at the time of writing this book, known Bill for approximately, thirty-nine years; Bill passed away in June 2021.

introduce the concept of faith and its actualisation in the Shadow World of the disabled.

But what do these terms mean? Do they suggest alternate methods or adaption of methods that already exist? Yes, in some cases both, some of which can be improved—adapted to meet the spiritual needs of the disabled person bringing assurance to that person within their faith community of the reality and acceptance of their faith so attested.

As Nancy Eiesland writes in *Encountering the Disabled God* concerning the need for a new "language" of faith.

> Eiesland writes that "[e]mancipatory transformation must be enacted not only in history, but also in imagination and language."

This means that actualising faith in the Shadow World is not impossible but will take new thinking. Whatever path is taken, the veracity and self-awareness of faith is to be tested. However, the "level" of faith expressed and known by one living in the Shadow World of disability is another issue that we need to discuss.

LIMITS TO ACTUALISING FAITH IN THE SHADOW WORLD

So, does disability impact upon some areas of personal faith "awareness" in the life of the disabled?

In a word, yes — and then no!

YES:

Professor Charles Gourgey in, Faith, Despair, and Disability, discusses this issue of self-awareness and neurological-cognitive disability. Charles tells us that the intra-dependant[188] relationships[189] between bodily (biological) and mental

---

[188] My use of *intra* comes from the presumption that as a human being, I (we) am (are)—form a single [intra] entity (i.e., an intrastate highway) on this earthly life. Inter means to transect between boundaries, and although we have boundaries between the spiritual and bodily self,—we are not "two parts" beings (i.e., interstate highways).

[189] A key issue in this debate is self-awareness and how it can be assessed within one in which neurological and psychological

(neurological) disabilities of a disabled person can and do affect the body-soul/spirit-mind interface (continuum)[190] presenting challenges to those so disabled that those of us who live our lives in the neurotypical world would not normally experience or consider as an issue.

Charles Gourgey writes:

> The consequences of having a disability can profoundly affect not only the body but the mind and spirit.

I have considerable difficulty in finding words that would describe here the mystery of our humanity—that is, the nature of our earthly existence (embodiment)—expressed in and through the intermeshing of our spiritual nature and the biological (material) body that constitutes our life "being" in this mortal world.

The best I can propose is likening this mystery of our current existence, in a primitive way, to the intertwining of the fingers of our two hands as they join together. As they touch, interact, and

---

disabilities may impair cognition and congruence. Just how much does the person know that they know, and is it paramount that they know that they know? This "geography" (See N. Worth: *The Significance of the Person Within*) of "being" is an area of theology that needs much work. It is also an area of mystery. Where does this interface take place? The Bible states that the "life" is in the blood. Does this mean that a person's soul-spirit "lives" in their veins? Personally, I don't think so but am more likely to accept 'Pauline' concepts of mind and heart, that the "spirit" of a person being nondimensional is self-aware and inhabits the anatomical dimensional body "neurologically" giving animation to thoughts and words that form within the spiritual nature of the person, which are then processed and delivered into the material world through the anatomical elements (organs) of the body within which that spirit of life lives.

[190] *https://en.oxforddictionaries.com/definition/continuum* Continuum; "a continuous sequence in which adjacent elements are not perceptibly different from each other, but the extremes are quite distinct." This definition gives the best sense of my use of the term continuum, as it retains the independence of the elements of our being while describing their inter-relationships. Cited, 24/01/2017.

"continuum": The mystery of 'conditio humana' details how the spiritual interfaces with the material on the cellular level. Continuum here means that interface between the spiritual and material that facilitates our existence in this world in which we "live, move and have our being" (Acts 17:28).

move together yet remain separate entities, the image comes somewhere near the mystery of life, our human life in this world, as created by God.

The only caveat I employ is that the material (biological) body requires the spiritual for "animation" and life in this world, whereas the spiritual (spirit/soul) of a person once created (by God) and infused in the material body (at conception) remains an eternal individual entity, a reality that can "live" spiritually as a rationally existent person even when the body dies and decays.[191]

Although referring to a different situation, Jesus Christ himself recognises the interrelationship between the state of the human body and the spiritual awareness—cognition of the soul/spirit in His disciples, in the garden of Gethsemane.

> Watch and pray so that you will not fall into temptation. The spirit is willing, but the body is weak. (Matt. 26:41)

There is, therefore, a link between the spiritual state of a person and their bodily condition—nature, and vice-versa, the more so as disabled people become physically and mentally frail with age, as in the case of Alzheimer's or dementia, when what was previously known,[192] i.e., their faith in God, is likely to have been either forgotten or is now obscure or construed in an entirely different manner.

Does this mean that faith once held is now lost because it can no longer be expressed in a manner that they understand, or we recognise or accept in our neurotypical world?

Does this mean that cognisance of faith is exclusive of a salvic condition for those in the Shadow World where their cognitive abilities and neurological comprehension may be impaired through their disabilities?

NO:

We have noted above that Charles Gourgey speaks of the "interactions" that can occur between the body-soul/spirit-mind

---

[191] See Eccl. 12:7 "and the dust returns to the earth as it was, and the spirit returns to God who gave it." (ESV)

[192] Here, I refer to their powers of cognitive recall from primary memory and their sentient awareness as the ability to rationalise and reason within themselves that their faith in God is real.

of a person in a restrictive manner where there is an element of impingement via the physical anatomical vessel (body) upon the spirituality it contains.

However, though this "impingement" may be true, I propose, conversely, that, on the other side of the fence in the Shadow World, there is no disjunction—discontinuity between the spiritual realities of faith in the life of a physically or cognitively disabled person, and their experience of that faith, in their spiritual salvic relationship with God.

James Ellor, in his article "Reaching Out to People with Dementia," asks the question with dementia (and Alzheimer's) patients, where does the persona of the person go to in cases of this disability? What remains, and what is known or not known. However, the consistent response to these questions is that the spirit/soul within that person that knows—knew God before their Alzheimer's or dementia or disability took hold still knows God. This is true even if the capacity of that person's "persona" to recall either in memory or emotions that earlier faith relationship, that faith relationship with God within their spirit/soul remains alive, active, valid and constant.

We have all been to a pub, restaurant, or bar where the bartender serves drinks containing spirits. The 'spirit' bottle usually has a "pourer" attached that restricts—measures the flow of the spirit into a measuring jar, or into the drinking glass. The restriction on the contents of the bottle is a reality, but it does not change the characteristics of the spirit—fluid inside the bottle.

Similarly, a disabled person may have a restriction, either biological and or neurological,[193] on their ability to interact with this world in a cognitive, sentient, volitional manner; but there is no such restriction on the spiritual (spirit/soul) nature of that person in their interaction with God. God does not have

---

[193] The liquid in the bottle represents that person's 'spirit/soul'. Once faith enters that 'spirit/soul", it remains and will always be once it exists in the bottle. However, if there is a restriction on that bottle limiting—preventing that 'spirit/soul' from pouring out that faith, either partially or entirely, as may be the case with Alzheimer's, dementia, or IDD, do we, then, assume that the faith in that bottle is weak, disabled, or non-existent because it cannot exit the bottle in a normative, neurotypically acceptable manner?

Alzheimer's or dementia, or IDD; He fully recognises and communicates, spiritually, with those who are His (Heb. 13:5).

This has important implications for those who interact with and care for the disabled, especially the elderly, within our churches or faith communities, in this sense that we, living on the other side of the fence, need to be aware of when we consider the spirituality and faith of those who live in the Shadow World.

Instead, we find that we can say a resounding no! There are no limits on, or within, the God—person (spirit/soul) spiritual relationship in and through faith. We can say this, emphatically, for once one receives Christ by faith, that faith remains as a spiritual, constant, reality whatever the initial or subsequent condition—ability or inability of the body-soul/spirit ontology (being) of the believer to recall from memory or express cognitively or volitionally their faith in God.

> And you also were included in Christ when you heard the word of truth, the gospel of your salvation. Having believed, you were marked in him with a seal, the promised Holy Spirit, who is a deposit guaranteeing our inheritance until the redemption of those who are God's possession to the praise of his glory. (Eph. 1:13–14)

There is little doubt that where the spirituality of faith is concerned, that faith (as a gift from God) exists fully within a person's being in their spirit/soul "being" apart—separate—from any disability, physical or psychological, they may, or may not, suffer from.

FAITH REMAINS CONSISTENT

So, faith remains; however, where a disabled person's cognitive, and more importantly their cognisance (awareness) capacities are impaired, then naturally yes, there will be some limits in actualising that faith from a normative neurotypical perspective.

Depending on the degree of impairment a person may have, there may be limits upon what is able to be understood and comprehended, on both sides of the fence, and on what decisions can be made by that person in a conscious manner that reflects or represents the veracity and existence of their faith in God.

Furthermore, in his paper "Reaching Out to the Spiritual Nature of People with Dementia," James Ellor writes:

> Reaching out to the spiritual is first and foremost an understanding that "to be is a blessing." For as long as the person is with us, they are a spiritual person and should be related to as such.[194]

What James goes on to tell us is that "being," our existence as a human person, is first a spiritual reality, and everyone enabled or disabled constitutes their reality in that sense of their "being" in the unity of body and spirit/soul; yet the body, being the "material" vessel as such, does not negate the spiritual but rather confirms its existence.

The challenge we face then is being willing to engage with a disabled person at their level of understanding, entering into their Shadow World—using "their language," accepting that there are some areas of faith that cannot be determined by what we might define in/through our normative, cognitive, neurotypical means.

Susan Mintz reminds us here, in her essay "Ordinary Vessels: Disability Narrative and Representations of Faith," that true humanity is more than an outward impression of the vessel we live in and challenges us to look to new ways of validating the faith of those who live in the Shadow World not merely as a "got to" but as an honest recognition of their true (full) humanity.

> Faith becomes not the end-point of a uniformly structured narrative but an intermittently recurring emphasis that serves to remind readers of the inextricable link between body and spirit.[195]

---

[194] Rev. James Ellor, "Reaching Out to the Spiritual Nature of Persons with Dementia, Ed., Journal of Religion, Spirituality and Aging, Professor: School of Social Work Director: Center for Gerontological Studies Baylor University, para 7, http://www.baylor.edu/content/services/document.php/60623.pdf

[195] Susannah Mintz, Disability Studies Quarterly 26, no. 3 (2006), "Ordinary Vessels: Disability Narrative and Representations of Faith." http://www.dsq-sds.org/article/view/722/899 :para 8.

Faith, in this sense, is fundamentally identified with one's spiritual "being," and everyone has a sense of faith, be it secular or religious. However, in the context of this book, faith is essentially identified with the object of that faith, Jesus Christ.

It requires us then, in our churches and faith communities, to find, discover, and implement new and exciting ways of actualising that faith, bringing it out into the open, accepting the individual, personal, spiritual "faith" responses of those who believe in God and live in the Shadow World.

To do this we may have to accept some limits to our expectations, but actualising faith in God for the disabled is essentially a recognition of their true humanity.

A NEW LANGUAGE FOR ACTUALISING FAITH

In "actualising" the faith of our disabled members, what is needed is an innovative approach to faith, a new way of understanding and actualising faith within our churches, as Charles Gourgey writes:

> The struggle is essentially a struggle for awareness: awareness of self, awareness of others, and awareness of God. And to address the question properly we need not to advance [new] theories about God, but to look into the possibilities of faith under extreme conditions.

When we looked at various systems of faith in our chapter "Defining Faith,"[196] we noted that faith in the Christian concept, saving (salvic) faith in Jesus Christ, was of a personal spiritual nature, one in which a person's mind-soul/spirit is involved.

The *Dictionary of Biblical Imagery* describes faith as follows:

> Faith is the means by which a person is justified (Rom. 3:28, Gal. 2:16, 3:8–24) and the action through which a person receives the righteousness of Christ (Rom. 3:22, Phil. 3:9). Faith is also the means by which they are sanctified (Acts 15:9, 26:18), and adopted into God's family (Gal. 3:26).

---

[196] See "Defining Faith," page 84, para 5

However, translating this definition of salvic faith in God into a "language" that is understandable, recognisable, and useful in the Shadow World of disability presents some difficulty because we often assume that disabled also means—equates to—an inability of the disabled to understand and/or comprehend their faith as an objective reality, particularly within the definitions we currently use in our religious or faith communities.

Looking at Robert Raymond's *Systematic Theology*[197] highlights this difficulty. Speaking of the nature of saving faith, Raymond writes:

> According to Scripture, saving faith is comprised of three constituent elements, knowledge (notitia), assent (assensus) and trust (fiducia),
>
> - Knowledge (notitia) is the cognitive foundation or basis of faith.
> - Assent (assensus) refers to the intellectual or perceptive conviction that the knowledge about Christ is factual.
> - Trust (fiducia) is conviction passed on to confidence.[198]
>
> And it is particularly this third element of trust or confidence that is saving faith's most characteristic act, as the sinner cognitively, affectively, and volitionally

---

[197] Robert Raymond, *A New Systematic Theology of the Christian Faith* (Thomas Nelson: Nashville, 1997) 726.

[198] We note here that all three elements of actualising faith in a normative neurotypical manner, as defined here by Raymond, are contained in Romans 10:9–10. There is no issue here with this definition except that it intellectualises faith and has the tendency to make faith the sole providence of the normative neurotypical person. The concern that this book has with this normative, intellectual definition of faith (exclusively) is that it ignores the essential spiritual element of faith, faith as a spirit gift from God (Eph. 2:8) and can exclude disabled people who suffer from intellectual or neurological disorders who have faith in God and desire to express that faith, in their own language, within their church or faith community. Faith is not a normative construct but a deposit of the Spirit of God within the soul/spirit of that person so saved (Eph. 2:8).

transfers all reliance for pardon, righteousness and cleansing away from him-herself—to Christ."

The three italicised words, *cognitively, affectively, and volitionally*, clearly define the neurotypical intellectual approach to faith. The actualisation of faith, flowing on from this definition, is then based on and dependent upon the believer having full intellectual and cognitive capacity of their mental facilities in a reasoning, assential,[199] neurological, and physiological manner.

I do not deny that this and other definitions of saving faith common in our denominations and faith communities are not valid, but that in the above "definition" we see a fundamental dependence on the prerequisites of cognitive function (intellect), sentient awareness (perception), and personal volition (will) in the actualisation of that faith within churches and denominations that may be disadvantaging those who are disabled in one or more of these areas of their "being."

There are, of course, good reasons for having "creedal-like" definitions and expressions of faith in God, and I do not suggest that we abandon them, but in order to actualise within our churches and faith communities the faith of those who live in the Shadow World, we need to realise that their faith, first and foremost, is a spiritual reality (2 Cor. 4:13; Gal. 3:5, 5:5; Eph 1:13;1 Pet. 2:4f) established and sustained by God in the life of a believer.[200]

---

[199] Assential: A created word—noun adjective—from the verb "assent" with the meaning of the act of giving assent to a proposition, concept, or idea in a mental and sentient manner that constitutes and validates that concept of faith within the intellectual and psychological nature of that person. Again, I face the crux of the matter. How can a person disabled in intellectual and sentient abilities know faith and experience faith in God as a daily reality? Do such people have a split spirituality, one side which knows God and one that cannot cognate that faith in a sentient, normative manner? No, they remain—are one—'spirit/soul'—being. It is that interface, the "communico," that struggles to realise and express what is real and salvic in their life through the disabilities presented to that spiritual reality in the form of their psychological, biological and neurological disability.

[200] A separate discussion, but the general theme of scripture is that God is Spirit (John 4:24), and believers communicate with him primarily in a spiritual manner. This does not negate the engagement of the

> In him you also, when you heard the word of truth, the gospel of your salvation, and believed in him, were sealed with the promised Holy Spirit, who is the guarantee of our inheritance until we acquire possession of it, to the praise of his glory. (Eph. 1:13–14)

Returning to Charles Gourgey's paper on "Faith, Despair, and Disability" for a moment, we find a definition of faith, in relation to those who are disabled, that is important in a congregational and faith community context.

> The faith that is given in the biblical message lies on a stronger foundation. It is not based on our beliefs, but on the activity of the divine Spirit.

We need to remind ourselves that our "being," though present in our material anatomical body in this world, is fundamentally a spiritual reality, (i.e., a spirit/soul) a nondimensional identity—reality—and as such the house of God is defined, primarily, as "a spiritual house" (1 Pet. 2:5).

> As you come to him, a living stone rejected by men but in the sight of God chosen and precious, you yourselves like living stones are being built up as a spiritual house, to be a holy priesthood, to offer spiritual sacrifices acceptable to God through Jesus Christ. (1 Pet. 2:4–5)

Also, as mentioned earlier, disability does not mean dis-able, that is, people who live in the Shadow World of disability are able to respond to the Holy Spirit (within their spirit/soul-being), both knowing and receiving salvic faith and life in Jesus Christ from God. Even though we may not be able to quantitatively define that faith within our faith communities from a purely normative neurotypical perspective—or from within a denominational model of actualisation—in recognition of their faith in God, as Raymond

---

mind and intellect of a person in their spiritual relationship with God, but here in our discussion we need to understand that "faith" and "belief" are primarily spiritual realities (Ps. 51:1f, 118:22; 1 Cor. 2:13–14, 9:11, 12:9; Eph. 1:3, 2:20; Col. 1:9; 1 Pet. 2:2–6).

suggests, this does not negate faith's existence and reality within their life.[201]

So, then, the essential question is:

Can the Holy Spirit regenerate the heart of an intellectually and neurologically disabled person, not just remotely from heaven like a robot, but interactively in a manner in which that person can participate in that regeneration[202] having the actuality of salvic faith in God implanted in them by the Holy Spirit within their personal being (soul/spirit) and that this regeneration be known by them in their inner heart and mind (Eph. 1:13–14)?

As I was approaching this point in the book, in the outline, I thought of this moment with some trepidation for as they say, "when all is said and done," the penny has to be paid, so what is my answer to this question?

"Can the Holy Spirit regenerate the "heart" of a neurologically and cognitively disabled person?'

Yes, I believe so.

It is clear to me that the Holy Spirit can regenerate the heart/mind—soul/spirit of a person apart from, even over and beyond, the limitations of their neurological, cognitive, and psychological condition or disability (Titus 3:5).

---

[201] My argument is not against Raymond as such, for the three prerequisites that he writes about are available to people with disabilities and exist within the framework of their "being," including the anatomical and the spiritual, as fundamental properties of their faith, knowledge, assent, and trust being spiritual are fully attainable to them whatever their anatomical or neurological disabilities. Although they might not be "fully" understood cognitively and empirically, they exist as spiritual realities within the soul/spirit of the person (Eph. 1:13–14).

[202] Regeneration requires working with what is there. You cannot regenerate an old pushbike without working with the old frame and wheels. You cannot regenerate a soulless body; it is dead. In order to regenerate the heart and mind of a sinner, the Holy Spirit, sent from God, interacts with the "spirit/soul" of that person in situ, in their heart and mind, in a manner that is both substantive and meaningful to each, God, the person and the Holy Spirit (Ezk. 36:26).

> But when the goodness and loving kindness of God our Savior appeared, he saved us, not because of works done by us in righteousness, but according to his own mercy, by the washing of regeneration and renewal of the Holy Spirit, whom he poured out on us richly through Jesus Christ our Savior." (Titus 3:4)

Where, then, exactly, does this regenerational[203] "faith" reside?

Faith in God, through the Holy Spirit, resides within the spiritual "being" of a person, in their spirit/soul, which is the essence of that person. As we have previously identified, cognisance, knowledge, and self-awareness are functions of the spiritual nature, "heart and mind," of a person and interact with the anatomical and psychological elements of one's being—existence. Faith, then, as a spiritual reality, becomes a component of their "being" resulting in the believer having an interactive experiential salvic relationship with God inwardly, in their spirit/soul, that is expressed externally through word and action, albeit in some cases impaired, but is still substantively evident.

It is a struggle for me to define "faith" and "being" in this context in the nexus between the material and the spiritual. Our study clearly recognises the impairment of spiritual expression through the disabled material body but determines that the spiritual can still experience, and know, all the benefits and attributes of faith in God unfettered by the material, biological, and psychological elements of one's disability (Rom. 8:16, 26).

> The Spirit himself bears witness with our spirit that we are children of God, and if children, then heirs—heirs of God and fellow heirs with Christ, provided we suffer with him in order that we may also be glorified with him. (Rom. 8:16)

---

[203] Regenerational faith: The Holy Spirit regenerates the "dead" spiritual life of the spirit/soul of a person in such a way that they are redeemed, forgiven, and renewed in the image of God such that they now have peace and a "new" eternal-life relationship with God.

It is in this conundrum "of how (do) we know that they know what they know"[204] that challenges us in trying to address the issues of cognisance and recognition associated with actualising faith in God for the disabled within our churches and faith communities. We need to put into place procedures that can quantify, verify, acknowledge, and accept the faith statements of the disabled within the context of their disabilities.

Discussing theoretical knowledge versus evidential knowledge, Kuhn, in "How Do People Know They Know," suggests that environmental situations can affect knowledge and its justification. This "environment" of knowledge for the disabled varies as does their diagnosis, so the knowing varies in accordance with their disability and quantifying such knowledge, then, must take into account these environmental variables. That is, what a person knows is in some sense determined in how their cognitive and sentient process "filters" information and cognates—determines—and forms that information into ideas and concepts.

It is important, then, for us to consider the knowledge environment in which a disabled person receives that gift of salvic faith in, and from, God, and how they conceive and believe in God through that faith. These biological and neurological "environmental" filters—considerations should form the basis of our interaction with them in actualising their faith statement within the framework of our churches and faith communities.

Let me explain.

---

[204] Deanna Kuhn, "How Do People Know?" *Psychological Science* 12, no. 1 (Jan. 2001), 1–8: "There is reason to think, then, that differing conceptions of what it means to know something influence how people know, in both the narrow sense of knowing how one knows something and the broader sense of how knowing processes operate. The broader claim I have made here is that one cannot fully understand the processes of knowing and knowledge acquisition that people engage in without investigating their understanding of their own knowing. Hence, to understand the acquisition of intellectual values and dispositions, and the ways in which they shape performance, it will be necessary to examine them in the social contexts in which they emerge and develop." The bracketed (do) mine.

There are basically three accepted—conventional—"methods" within Christian denominationalism for the actualisation of faith in the life of a person within that church or faith community.

First, the person could be brought into a communicant relationship with that faith community through the sacraments and services of the church. Second, the person could enter into a faith relationship with God within the life of that fellowship through a personal testimony or declaration of faith. Third, or finally, the person is examined by elders, deacons, leaders, etc., and approved to be accepted into the fellowship of that faith community as part of that fellowship's liturgical practices.[205]

In the Shadow World of disability, any one or a combination of these "methods" of actualisation of personal salvic faith may be unattainable, at least from a cognitive or comprehended point of view, as the impairment of the disabled person's body-soul/spirit-mind interrelated continuum[206] may preclude them from,

- physical involvement in a sacrament,
- vocalisation of concepts in a creedal confession,
- cognizance in the assimilation of knowledge consenting of faith,
- volitional capacity in applying received knowledge or,
- actualising in a congruent mind-soul/spirit interface their sentient belief.

Therefore, when we seek to actualise faith in God in the life of those who live in the Shadow World from within the existing structures of our denominations—faith communities—there is a need to consider the expressional capabilities of the disabled person and, in the words of Susannah Mintz, rethink our views of faith in God, and creatively receive that person and their faith into the life and fellowship of our church or faith community.

---

[205] Please note, I am speaking of a faith community's processes and practices in initiating—actualising and establishing membership within that fellowship or faith community, not specifically the examination of or evidence of faith in God in that person. It is assumed in all three options that faith is established as part of the worship and doctrine of that faith community.

[206] See "Glossary" – continuum, page 268

For, as we embrace the disabled within our church, we need to see that faith in a relational model that overcomes the limitations of intellectual and sentient disabilities that many in the Shadow World suffer from and open the door to a refreshed view of what it means to believe, to be a part of the spiritual community of God's kingdom on earth. As Dr. John Swinton writes in his paper "Restoring the Image," speaking of the changes needed in faith communities when dealing with disability:

> A relational understanding of faith and spirituality as outlined here offers the church the freedom to avoid evaluating a person's spiritual life according to intellectual criteria and to begin to find new ways of preaching the Word (of God) to those who have no words.

So, in essence in this book, disability does not mean dis-abled to believe, and we need to recognise this and work toward solutions relevant to that person, their disability, and their faith.

There are several things we need to understand in actualising faith, believing faith in God, in the life of a disabled person within our church or faith communities.

People with disabilities are fully human in the essential anthropological definition of their humanity in their "being"—that is, they have the same "stuff" spiritually inside them as we do but may be living in a biological or cognitively disabled vessel (body). It is our responsibility as leaders within our respective faith communities—churches—to assist them to articulate and actualise their faith in a manner that is both meaningful to them and to the congregation—fellowship—to which they belong. And, in providing the ability for them to actualise their faith, we express our love for them as they witness to the world in their own language, confirming their faith in and the love of God for them.

Reminding ourselves of Raymond's points above,[207] actualising the faith of a disabled person within their faith community is not beyond the realms of possibility; but it does require some new thinking and the willingness to work with different expressions of spirituality for those who live in the Shadow World.

---

[207] See my comments on Raymond's discussion – footnote 198, page 133

What is good news for the disabled in relation to faith and disability is that several of the papers listed in this discussion refer to a growing awareness within our churches and faith communities of this need for inclusion, and if this book adds to that discussion, then this book has served its primary purpose, for a faith community "completes" the body of Christ within its fellowship when it takes steps to actualise the faith responses of the disabled within their community—congregation.[208]

JUST HANDS

Throughout history, there have been three basic images, concepts, of what constitutes or generally defines what it means to be a human being.[209]

To help us visualise and understand the interaction between the body and spirit/soul of a person in order to grasp the reality of faith as a spiritual truth in the life of the disabled person I suggest we look, for a moment, at the human hand.

---

[208] In a recent conversation at church, I was asked how we can allow people with communication disabilities to take part in communion—membership when they cannot speak or clearly articulate their "faith" so that we can confirm its existence in their life. I'm not a quick thinker, but later these thoughts came to me. There are 100 people in a church congregation who believe in God, but 5 are disabled, cognitively and neurologically, and cannot easily articulate that faith to the elders, deacons, leaders, and congregation. It is communion time, a "spiritual" meal—sharing with God (Luke 22:19-20; 1Cor. 10:16-17). God sees 100 believers in the congregation in need of "spiritual food," and we see 95. I don't need to say anything more.

[209] A very complex discussion across philosophical, religious, and psychological disciplines. This discussion is exhaustive, so my approach is to simplify this discussion on what constitutes "being", and the relationships between body and 'soul/spirit,' into three basic groups, materialistic, one hand; dualism-monism, two hands together; and continuum, interlaced but individual hands, which I term integration, my illustrated representation of a Christian model, "and man became a living being" (Gen. 2:7).

In our first view, image, man is seen as just a singular material reality, a compounding of chemicals, water, electrical impulses, and molecules that interact and produce thoughts, ideas, and knowledge (so defined).[210]

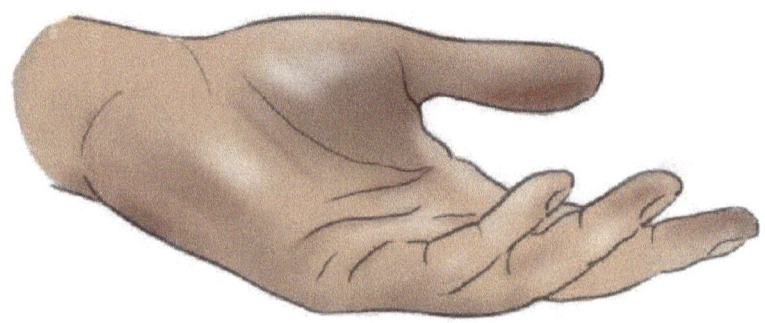

AN OPEN HAND

Our second image has two hands touching each other.

In this model man is seen as a two-part being. That is, man constitutes in a material body in which a spirit resides and gives life, animation, motion, thought, and knowledge to that two-part reality.

---

[210] Basic materialism is a type of Monism (Karl Marx); The three main forms of monism are physicalism, which holds that the mind consists of matter organised in a particular way; idealism, which holds that only thought truly exists and matter is merely an illusion; and neutral monism, which holds that both mind and matter are aspects of a distinct essence that is itself identical to neither of them.

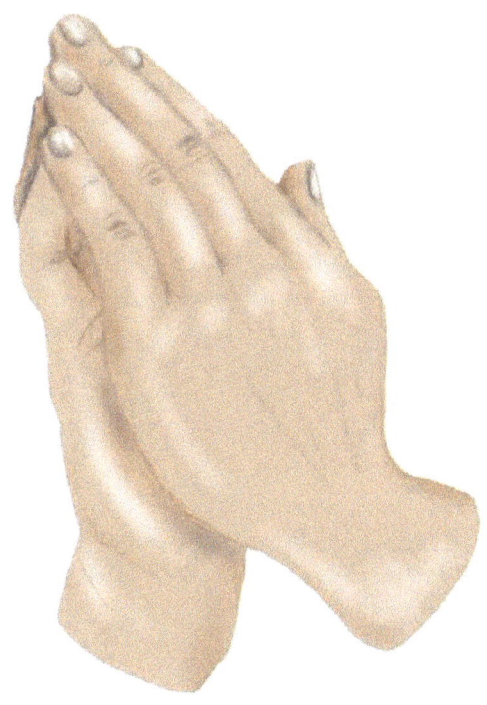

TOUCHING HANDS

However, the two parts remain somewhat separate, as individual entities, yet can connect with one another.[211]

A third view is that a 'human' being is essentially a homogeneous spiritual being where both body and 'spirit' are in a supportive relationship.

That is, it is the spirit/soul of a human that forms the core reality of "man," and that the spirit/soul is interwoven within the material body in such a way that it brings "ontological" life, thought, knowledge and animation to the body in an expression of

---

[211] Cartesian Dualism, with many variants either of substance or property dualism. In philosophy of mind, dualism or duality is the position that mental phenomena are, in some respects, nonphysical, or that the mind and body are not identical.

that inner spiritual "being"; yet, although both are interlaced, the material and spiritual, they have separate defined realities.[212]

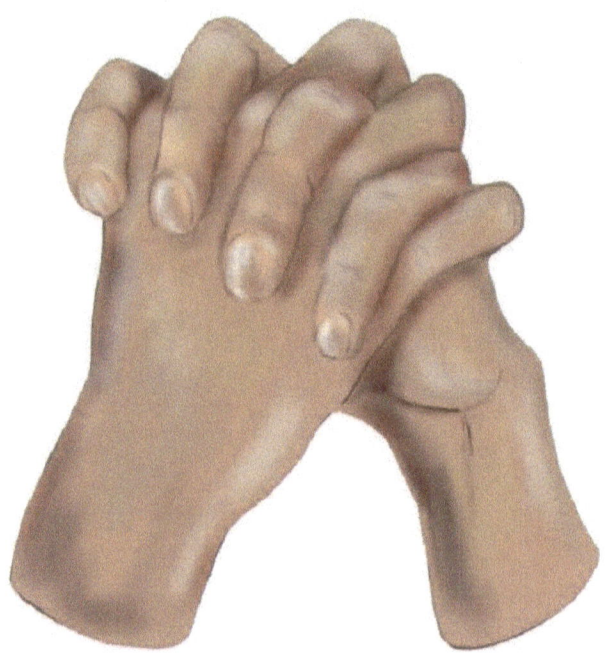

INTERLINKED HANDS

This book follows the third, interlinked hands, model of what it is (means) to be a human being—"to be" (Gen. 2:7). It assumes that the spirituality, the soul/spirit of man, is the essential part of man that defines who and what we really are. This spirit/soul-body union forms the basis of man's essential humanity—reality—"being" in this world.

The Apostle Paul clearly articulates this dependant-independence relationship in Acts 17:28.

---

[212] Realities here means that a human person's 'spiritual' and 'material' elements are interdependent entities in and of themselves. Once given to a person, the 'spiritual', their 'spirit', is eternal. The material body is temporal (mortal), existing only as long as the 'spiritual' remains within that mortal body Job. 34:15, Eccles. 12:7.

> For in him we live and move and have our being. (Acts 17:28a)
>
> - *live*; life, in essence, the spiritual life of man in the soul/spirit,
> - *move*; the material reality of man constituted in the body,
> - *being*; the physical and spiritual continuum which defines the reality of our intra-dependant existence in this world.

The spirit/soul, in this third model, impacts upon the body (material existence), and the body impacts upon the soul/spirit (spiritual existence), yet each have their independence as constituent parts of what it means to be human. The soul/spirit (spirituality of being) can exist without the material body, but the material body cannot exist without the soul/spirit.[213, 214]

This interlaced model, illustrated with our intertwined hands, as used in this book, accepts the reality of the true spirituality of those who live in the Shadow World and opens up a portal for us to enter into their world, a world where their "spiritually," their true inner "being" is the same as ours, and reveals to us the possibility of and ultimately the factuality of "salvic" faith in the Shadow World.

How then do we confirm their faith? We first need to link hands and join them there, in the Shadow World where they live and experience their living faith with them within our churches and faith communities. So, how do we identify "salvic" faith within the Shadow World?

---

[213] In the Genesis account, the body of Adam was created "materially" first (Gen. 2:7), and the "spirit" (soul) was breathed into it by God, bringing that material body to life. This book holds the view that while the 'spirit' animates the material body in a coexistent relationship in mortal life, the spirit of 'man' can exist without the material body, Eccles. 12:7 "and the dust returns to the earth as it was, and the spirit returns to God who gave it." (See also Num. 16:22, 27; Eccles. 3:21, Jer. 38:16).

[214] In this third model, bodily activities are a function—neurologically, of the spirituality of the person, whereas in the second, Greek – Aristotle, model the body may act independently of the spiritual and thus, the spiritual is not necessarily contaminated, made sinful, in the sense of, or as a result of the actions carried out in the body.

CHAPTER 9

LIVING FAITH

FAITH TRANSCENDS DISABILITY

There is a vulnerability in presenting this concept of faith in God, of faith being principally a spiritual reality implanted by God and not contingent upon the normative intellectual neurotypical cognitive sentient awareness model we currently use in our churches and faith communities,[215] that may present us with some difficulties when we attempt to accept, validate, and actualise such faith in the life of those who live in the Shadow World.

It might seem at first that I am creating a disjunction between the interaction of the intellectual and psychological elements of their existence within the soul/spirit—mind—"being" of the disabled person, especially for those who are intellectually and neurologically disabled. It may seem that there is a disconnect between the correspondence (agreement) of their cognitive awareness, particularly when their cognitive capacity may be impaired, and their spirituality such, that there is a disconnect between their awareness of God and the spiritual nature of faith within the disabled person's "being," but that is not the case.

At this point, I am talking about the ability of the disabled person to respond to the gospel within their own personal spirituality (apart from their disability) and for them to know and experience the fullness of saving faith in a manner that is valid to their spirit/soul-being, whatever their disability mix, just as we

---

[215] As I have mentioned earlier, I do not advocate casting out current and well-established models of verification and confirmation of faith in God used within our churches and faith communities. I would never advocate such an unbalanced approach to faith in God. In order to confirm and include the faith statements of disabled people, especially in complex cases of biological, neurological, and psychological disabilities, I am suggesting we investigate new ways to verify and include those who cannot meet the current models used in our faith communities.

would experience "spiritually" within our neurotypical normative—cognisant world.

That is, apart from defining new ways to actualise their faith within their church or faith community, for the disabled person there is a second question of the reality—the veracity—[216]of that faith that that person experiences and comprehends within the limits of their disability in the Shadow World.

When probing into areas not discussed much in Christian theology, it is easy to misquote scripture, to make scripture say what you want it to say, and there is a danger in doing this here now, but I do believe that these words of the Apostle Paul, in Romans 8:26–27, give us a clue in our search for understanding.

> In the same way, the Spirit helps us in our weakness. We do not know what we ought to pray for, but the Spirit himself intercedes for us with groans that words cannot express. And he who searches our hearts knows the mind of the Spirit, because the Spirit intercedes for the saints in accordance with God's will. (Rom. 8:26–27)

The word "Spirit," here in Romans 8:26, refers to the Holy Spirit of God, who is first mentioned in scripture in Genesis 1:2, as God's agent of action bringing order out of chaos (Gen. 1:2), and is revealed in the Bible as the conduit of communication between God and man (Ezek. 36:27, John 14:17, 26). The Spirit knows both the mind of God, and the mind of man (1 Cor. 2:10–12) and interconnects a dialogue—spiritually—between both (Rom. 8:27).

Looking closely then at Romans 8:26,[217] we read that "the Spirit himself intercedes," and in the new "light" of this book, I

---

[216] In addition to the issue of the "truthfulness" or "genuineness" (veracity) of the faith of the disabled person, previously dealt with in chapter 7 "Reality of Faith," there is the issue of the spiritual vividness—the vitality of their faith relationship with God.
See "Reality of Faith," page 91, para 5

[217] Interpretations of this passage rightly identify the assistance that the Holy Spirit gives to the believer in moments of intense prayer where matters are pressing, urgent, or human weaknesses in prayer are the topic of discussion. But this also identifies the Holy Spirit as one who works with and supports the believer's spiritual nature, transcending the anatomical and neurological, where necessary, in

believe, as it is written here by the Apostle Paul, the Holy Spirit is able to do work within the Shadow World of the disabled in a "language" that both pleases God and is effectual, salvic—relevant and edifying in the life of that disabled person (Rom. 8:14–17).

Normatively, we usually interpret the words "our weakness" as a spiritual weakness, a property of our sinful fleshly human nature, a failure to follow God and love Him as we should, and I am in general agreement with this. But, having been there in the Shadow World, I ask, why do we limit this intercessory work of the Holy Spirit to the world of the neurotypical as though only the neurotypical would need or could understand this essential intercessory work of the Holy Spirit?

Biblically, the Holy Spirit communicates God's word, will, and purposes between God and man throughout the Old Testament and on into the New. The major difference between the Old and New Testament activity of the Holy Spirit is that after Pentecost, Acts 1:8ff, the Spirit indwells man in a new, lasting manner, John 14:17f.[218]

Part of the attributes of the Holy Spirit of God is that of knowing the mind of God (1 Cor. 2:11); and He, the Spirit, "searches [the] heart of man" (1 Chron. 28:9) and communicates "spiritually" (Rom. 8:16, 27) to the "spirit of man," including the disabled person, an understanding of their need for the salvation

---

order to do so. My supposition is that the Holy Spirit, who can assist a believer, either enabled or disabled, in prayer, can also assist the disabled person in believing in God.

[218] Got Questions: *https://www.gotquestions.org/what-does-the-Holy-Spirit-do.html* "The Bible clearly shows that the Holy Spirit is active in our world. The book of Acts, which sometimes goes by the longer title of 'The Acts of the Apostles,' could just as accurately be called 'The Acts of the Holy Spirit through the Apostles.' After the apostolic age, there have been some changes—the Spirit does not inspire new scripture, for example, but He continues to do God's work in the world."

See Also: *https://www.gotquestions.org/Spirit-Old-Testament.html* "The Spirit performed much the same function in Old Testament times as He does in this current (New Testament) age. The major difference is the Spirit's permanent indwelling in believers now. Jesus said, regarding this change in the Spirit's ministry." "But you know him, for he lives with you and will be in you" (John 14:17, Olive Tree, Ver. 6.0.17, ESV)." Cited, 08/05/2018.

within the soul/spirit-mind—"being" of their person. Not only this, but the Holy Spirit first regenerates, then enables and deposits faith, faith in God, within the "spirit/soul" (heart and mind) of the redeemed person over and beyond any limitations of intellect, cognisance, and sentience that that person may suffer from (Eph. 1:13–14).

There is no greater barrier-breaking verse in the Bible for the disabled person than Romans 8:27, for in it we see that the Holy Spirit communicates the gospel to the heart of the person (here synonymous with their spirituality), communicating the gospel in a language understandable to that person's persona– (i.e., in congruence with their level of understanding and awareness of the fullness of God's grace and love for them) maintaining within their spirit/soul—"being" that gift of salvic faith within them.[219]

> And he who searches hearts knows what is the mind of the Spirit, because the Spirit intercedes for the saints according to the will of God. (Rom. 8:27)

Not everyone in this world speaks the same "language," but throughout this world, daily, people affirm their faith in God in different national languages, but the same spiritual assent of faith is given to God regardless of the language used.

Why then do we assume that faith in God, as a spiritual reality, is dependent upon that faith being understood—verified through a neurotypical model of cognisant authentication in a common[220] "vocal" language used to express and realise that faith?[221]

Put another way, do I believe that the disabled person, particularly those with neurological, cognitive, and psychological

---

[219] In the case of Mary, whom we will meet later in this chapter, Mary communicates nothing, verbally or normatively, into this world; yet, in her 'own' way, in her 'own' language, she enjoys a rich, vibrant, and blessed relationship with God through the Holy Spirit.
See "Mary," page 183, para 1

[220] "Common" here means an everyday language used by nations, tribes, and countries throughout the world.

[221] Knowledge about God is not faith in God; those who say they know about God do not necessarily have faith (in God) as a result of that knowledge. Faith in God is a spiritual attribute, and 'true' knowledge of God comes through faith alone. Unless the spiritual dimension of faith is present in a person's 'heart/mind'–'spirit/soul,' true salvic faith is not.

disabilities, can, in their spirit/soul—"spiritual self," know, acknowledge, and trust in God in a personal sense like the rest of us do in a normative manner in our neurotypical world?

Yes, I do!

God can speak, through the Holy Spirit, in a language unique and understandable to the disabled person communicating to them spiritually, that is to their spirit/soul-being, the same concepts of faith, grace, and love that we often assume are the prerogative of the normative neurotypical world.

And why should we limit the language of a disabled person to that of the normative neurotypical mind as if this "normative" language is the only language that God understands or uses to speak, person to person, with humans?

What we find is that in the New Testament books of the Gospel of John, and 1 and 2 Corinthians, God pulls us into the Shadow World and speaks to us in a language that both God and the disabled person can understand and express fluently, person to person, to each other (John 4:24).

It is the spiritual language of God.

> God is spirit, and his worshipers must worship (him) in the Spirit and in truth. (John 4:24)

> But the Helper, the Holy Spirit, whom the Father will send in my name, he will teach you all things and bring to your remembrance all that I have said to you. (John 14:26)

> And we impart this in words not taught by human wisdom but taught by the Spirit, interpreting spiritual truths to those who are spiritual. (1 Cor. 2:13)[222]

> Now the Lord is the Spirit, and where the Spirit of the Lord is, there is freedom. And we all, who with unveiled faces contemplate the Lord's glory, are being transformed into his image with ever-increasing glory, which comes from the Lord, who is the Spirit. (2 Cor. 3:17–18)

---

[222] Which, of course, we have already identified a person as being.

So, we can say without reservation, that the Holy Spirit experiences no impairments (barriers) in communicating with the spirit/soul of a person living with disabilities in the Shadow World.

The work of the Holy Spirit here is clearly that of an interpreter who overcomes the difficulties of the "language" barrier/s that might inhibit communication between the disabled person's "being'" (in their soul/spirit-heart and mind) and the reality of God's grace in their life whatever the neurological or ontological [metaphysical] status of that believer may be.

> And you also were included in Christ when you[223] heard[224] the message of truth, the gospel of your salvation. When you believed, you were marked in him with a seal, the promised Holy Spirit, who is a deposit guaranteeing our inheritance until the redemption of those who are God's possession—to the praise of his glory. (Eph. 1:13–14)

Note the Apostle Paul's words "when you heard," "when you believed." What does this say to you?

More importantly what do these words "mean" to the disabled person, particularly one impaired in the normative and neurotypical aspects of their "being"? They should mean the same thing that they do to us neurotypicals.

For example, a neurologically and psychologically disabled person living by faith in the Shadow World hears the same gospel, believes the same gospel, is saved by the same gospel and lives with that same gospel in their life, heart, and mind, are regenerated by the Holy Spirit and sealed in that faith by that same Holy Spirit as you and I. There is no distinction.

> There is one body and one Spirit, just as you were called to one hope when you were called; one Lord, one faith, one

---

[223] The word for 'you' ὑμεῖς, (Eph. 1:13), is normative, indicating the subject "you also" is inclusive—individualistic, indicating that the receipt of faith is synonymous with salvation.

[224] The Greek word ἀκούω used here has a sense of more than the auditory; it contains a sense of comprehension, to understand, perceive, and comprehend.

baptism; one God and Father of all, who is over all and through all and in all. (Eph. 4:4–6)

Thus, it is the Holy Spirit, as the agent of change, who interacts with the soul/spirit-mind of the disabled person and transcends any impairments, whatever they may be, bringing to that person the reality of Christ in a manner that can be both understood by them and acted upon by them, within their being (spirit/soul), whatever their neurological capacity for understanding, comprehension, or volition thought might be (Titus 3:5).

> But when the kindness and love of God our Savior appeared, he saved us, not because of righteous things we had done, but because of his mercy. He saved us through the washing of rebirth and renewal by the Holy Spirit, whom he poured out on us generously through Jesus Christ our Savior, so that, having been justified by his grace, we might become heirs having the hope of eternal life. (Titus 3:5)

W. A. Criswell, in his sermon "Why Preach That the Bible Is True," writes on the regenerative and proactive work of the Holy Spirit in bringing the person to a point of recognition of God, the need for forgiveness, and the proactive impetus of the Spirit to bring that person forward to a point of Faith in God. The phrase, "by the Holy Spirit," identifies the Holy Spirit as the "gift giver" who brings new life and faith to the unregenerate (unbeliever), bringing about that regenerational change within their heart and mind that they believe in faith in Jesus Christ.[225]

---

[225] R. C. Sproul, *The New Genesis; The Mystery of the Holy Spirit* (Tyndale House: Wheaton, 1979), Quoting W. A. Criswell, Why I Preach That the Bible Is Literally True, (Nashville: Broadman, 1969), para 1)
"It is to the Holy Spirit of God that we are debtors for the grace of regeneration and faith. He is the Gift-giver, who, while we were dead yet, made us alive with Christ, to Christ, and in Christ. Because of the Holy Spirit's merciful act of quickening, we sing sola gratia and soli deo gloria—to the glory of God alone." http://www.the-highway.com/genesis_Sproul.html Cited, 06/06/2011.

> Without the presence of the Spirit there is no conviction, no regeneration, no sanctification, no cleansing, no acceptable works... Life (salvic life) is in the quickening Spirit.

Craig L. Bloomberg, in the *Evangelical Dictionary of Biblical Theology*, writes on the Holy Spirit, that it is the work of the Holy Spirit to bring a person to a point of faith in Jesus Christ.

> The Spirit is God's agent for bringing people to himself—only through his (the Spirit's) power can individuals first receive God's Word as divine—and those who are saved (are saved) through the washing and rebirth of the Holy Spirit."

Therefore, it is not only possible but is necessary that the Holy Spirit works within the life-soul/spirit—mind and heart—of a disabled person in ways that are *radically different* to our normative neurotypical concepts of conversion in bringing and actualising that faith from God within the disabled person. But this a-normative[226] (transcendent) activity of the Spirit in the life of the disabled person nonetheless does not devalue the validity or reality of that salvic faith which now exists in the life of that disabled person.

In the Paternoster Press's sister volume on theology, *The Evangelical Dictionary of Theology*, faith is defined as truth received. Therefore, giving just intellectual assent to a set of facts or philosophies is inadequate and represents works more than faith. This "truth received" indicates an outside actor is required—necessary for faith to be actualised in the heart-mind (spirit/soul) of the believer and is independent to them in its origin.

Also, this actualisation of faith, salvic—saving—faith by the Holy Spirit within their being, as we have discussed above, may not occur in a manner that we are perceptive of, but it can and

---

[226] "a-normative"—the prefix 'a' signifies anti—against or beside what is normative. "A-normative" is a word I have had to invent to describe the gracious activity of the Holy Spirit in transcending the three normative requirements of Romans 10:9-10 (knowledge, assent and trust) to overcome cognitive, volitional, and sentient disabilities in order to bring faith and life into the soul/spirit—"being" of that disabled person. (Acts 17:28) See page 133, para 3f

does happen effectively—spiritually—in their life and contains all the blessings, certainty, and permanency that God can give.

Faith is not an invention of man; it is a creation of God.

> Yet to all who received him, to those who believed in his name, he gave the right to become children of God — children born not of natural descent, nor of human decision or a husband's will, but born of God. (John 1:12–13)

It would be helpful for us here to state that actualised faith in a denominational sense is only the signature—an external sign of our declaration of faith and salvation. Salvation is found alone in the redeeming work of Jesus Christ, at Calvary, applied to the spiritual life of the sinner through the work of the Holy Spirit (Acts 4:12, Eph. 1:1–14).

> Salvation is found in no one else, for there is no other name under heaven given to men by which we must be saved. (Acts 4:12)

All those who receive faith, salvic faith in Jesus Christ, believe in and are adopted as children of God. This is a universal principle and not only applies to those who live in a neurotypical normative world, who can actualise that faith in ways that we can identify with, but also to those who live in the Shadow World of disability. Therefore, those whose impairments may preclude them from demonstrating or actualising that faith in a neurotypically comprehended manner are no less saved by their faith, a gift from God (Eph. 2:8).

> For it is by grace you have been saved, through faith—and this not from yourselves, it is the gift of God—not by works, so that no one can boast. For we are God's workmanship, created in Christ Jesus to do good works, which God prepared in advance for us to do. (Eph. 2:8–10)

The words of the Apostle Paul, here in Ephesians, calls us to set aside our normative neurotypical perceptions of life and faith and accept with joy the faith of those who live in the Shadow World. A faith that can be actualised in ways that are meaningful to them, God, and us when we take the time and make the effort to become aware, to look and learn and speak their "language."

But to leave the discussion here just gives us a lot of words to think about.

If we are to engage in this debate in order to seek change in how we look at and interact with the issues of disability and faith, we need a new awareness of and willingness to rethink faith and life for those who live in the Shadow World.

Charles Gourgey, in "Faith, Despair and Disability," says of faith, in the life of the disabled, that the external experience—the intellect is not the only way that faith can be experienced but faith itself in a spiritual experience seen in the life of the "heroes" of Hebrews chapter 11, in the Bible, who went beyond self-knowledge and embraced the spiritual nature of faith.

Charles writes:

> "This is faith, the truly spiritual faith that the Bible comes to teach."[227]

This "awareness" of faith that we are talking about may be articulated in a language different from our normative models of communication and responses to God, but faith's existence and expression within the life of the disabled person are, nevertheless, real, and they are valid because it is the Holy Spirit who generates and sustains that faith in the life of the normatively compromised person.

Faith, then, transcends all disabilities, bringing "life" to the spirit/soul of a person, establishing a personal Spirit to spirit relationship with God. This, of course, challenges our neurotypical understanding of faith, our definition of what faith is, and what faith does in the life of a person.

---

[227] Charles Gourgey, "Faith Despair, and Disability," Journal of Religion in Disability and Rehabilitation 1, no. 3 (Haworth Press, 1994): 51–63.

A THEOLOGY OF FAITH IN THE SHADOW WORLD:

In Hebrews 11:1, we find a definition of faith that we theorise heavily but might need to take literally when we enter the Shadow World.

> Now faith is being <u>sure</u> of what we hope for and certain of what we do not see. (Heb. 11:1)

At this point, most assume that "faith" is something that we possess, acquire, believe, have, or find in some manner helpful as an assurance of a relationship with God through Jesus Christ. There is a sense in which this is true; however, in all the listings of the heroes of faith in Hebrews chapter 11, in our English translations, each person—character listed begins with the word "by." The word "faith" in each of these sentences is a noun and stands alone at the beginning of each sentence, or account of a hero of faith, so why do we translate the Greek word πίστει, "faith," as "by faith," adding the preposition "by"?

The word "faith," πίστει in Greek, here is "absolute" in grammatical terms, and in these verses identifies "faith" as the actor—the progenitor[228] of action in the sentence. We would say in our English language that faith itself is a substantive "active" reality in the spiritual nature of that person and is the origin, and source of the outward display of the reality of the existence of "faith" in the life of that person.

Let me explain:

From a neurotypical [normal neurological] perspective, we view faith in this verse as trust, trusting in God's "sure" promises while looking forward to that which we "do not see," but—yet know to be true, by that very faith which we receive from God.

In the Shadow World of disability, "faith," which may be unseen by us, is nevertheless a confident reality for them, they "being sure of what we (they) hope for" and brings with it to them,

---

[228] Progenitor: Here is the origin of action, what comes before action is possible, like a steam engine at the head of a train. The train goes nowhere without the precursor—the engine at the front that brings motion and function to the train.
https://www.dictionary.com/browse/progenitor Cited, 17/05/2021.

in their inner "being," all the promises of God founded on that same gospel all receive, bringing new "spiritual" life and every possible blessing from God in the certain hope of everlasting life and joy with God in eternity to come (Eph.1:1–3, 13–14).

Although those with cognitive and neurological disabilities may be spiritually impaired in their articulation and expression of faith, they, nonetheless, have (the same) saving faith, and the same spiritual experience of that faith, a faith that is dynamic and real, a faith that is defined in new relational ways that God and they may alone understand.

Their spirit/soul may be constrained—impaired in its expression within the vessel, body, that they currently live in, but it, their spirituality (experience of spiritual realities), is not disabled. Likewise, their "faith" in God may be constrained in a neurological cognitive manner, but it is *never* disabled. As a spiritual reality, it stands apart from their disability and consists intrinsically of the same spiritual salvic value as that of any other normative person.

John Swinton speaks eloquently on this and argues that cognisance is not the only parameter through which faith in God can be experienced:

> Secondly, I would dispute the suggestion that an inability to reason at a complex level is necessarily incompatible with meaningful spiritual experience and the development of authentic faith.

To this, I would add that although most accept that faith may exist in the life of a disabled person living in the Shadow World, it, their faith that is, is not seen as containing that same affective[229] value in the life and experience of that disabled person as it would have in the life of a normative, neurotypical person's faith. Faith, for the disabled, always carries with it some residue of their disability—that is, their faith is usually seen as limited

---

[229] I use the word "affective" as opposed to "effective" in order to stress the point that "faith," as a gift from God, affects the spiritual nature of a person transforming them completely (effectually) from a state of sin to that of being justified. Faith always accomplishes what it intends to do—bringing life and affirmation of salvation from sin to that person.

(i.e., only the mind of a five-year-old) in its content and experience.

We acknowledge that at times we may not be able to see tangible "evidence" (James 2:18–20) of such "authentic" faith within one who is disabled, but that does not deny the reality of that faith or the dynamic of its effective relationship within them through which they experience and believe in God in their everyday life.

> You are saved by the Spirit making you holy and by your faith in the truth. (2 Thess. 2:12) [ERV[230]].

What I argue for here is that in that faith, that gift of salvic living faith[231] from God (Eph. 2:8), there is no intrinsic impediment to its experiential reality in the ontological (soul/spirit) spiritual life of that disabled person living in the Shadow World whatever their biological, neurological, and/or psychological disorders.

Also, what may seem to be a "hidden" reality to us is not hidden to them or God in a spiritual sense so that they, in their heart and mind, can, by the reality of that faith that exists within them, look forward with the same joy and expectancy personally,

---

[230] ERV – Easy Read Version, quoted from OliveTree Bible+, Ver. 7.9.2.0. Cited, 10/05/2018. The Greek here is quite complex. Thus, the variety of translations, but the gist of the sentence—phrase—is that the Holy Spirit is the agent of faith and ensures that faith is effective in its redeeming work in the life of the believer.

[231] I realise that I frequently use the terms "salvic faith" and "believers' faith" interchangeably, which might seem slightly confusing. Why, then, do I use the term "salvic faith?" Many will say that they believe that God exists but do they "believe in God," the operative word being "in," as their affective salvation? In order to establish a distinction between believing that God—or a God—exists and actual belief in God as a personal Savior, I use the term "salvic" faith. Salvic faith is that spiritual deposit of faith, through the Spirit of God, that applies the redemptive work of Jesus Christ on the cross, spiritually, into the spirit/soul-being of a person (Eph. 1:13–14). Nor do I wish to create an issue with "additional" things that "salvic faith" is somehow superior to "faith in God." They are the same term, but the phrase "salvic faith" seeks to emphasise the effective value of that "faith" in the life of the person and, therefore, is universally effective and salvific, whatever the neurological or spiritual condition of that person is.

as all who believe, to that new "enabled" life that awaits them in heaven.

Our normative—neurotypical—problem is that we view people from the outside, "from an external world" perspective. We communicate externally, we evaluate externally, and we assume externally so that our collective, outwardly based assessment of their external appearances and communications can overrule our awareness of an internal reality and the possibility of the fundamental existence and veracity of an enduring faith within, ultimately impeding our full acceptance of their faith in God.

My point here regarding the internal reality of their faith gives new meaning and life to the words of the Apostle Paul in 2 Cor. 5:16–17.

> So from now on we regard no one from a worldly point of view. Though we once regarded Christ in this way, we do so no longer. Therefore, if anyone is in Christ, he is a new creation; the old has gone, the new has come! (2 Cor. 5:16–17)

Therefore faith, actual faith in God, in the Shadow World of disability, is permanent, enduring, and consistent with the biblical criteria for faith just as it is in the world of the normative neurotypical.

> There may be, and likely is, a need for us to continue this dialogue between disability and faith in the Shadow World, but Faith in God, applied to the heart of the disabled believer by the Holy Spirit is consistent with an authentic reality in its grounding in the Gospel of Jesus Christ regardless of the neurological-cognitive-volitional-sentient status of that person.[232]

The Apostle Paul writes:

> As Scripture says, "Anyone who believes in him (Jesus) will never be put to shame." (Rom. 10:11)

John Swinton, in his article "Restoring the Image," in the *Journal of Disability & Religion*, writes about this new

---

[232] My quotable "quote" that sums up our paper to this point.

understanding of faith and disability that challenges us to be involved in evangelism in the Shadow World. He speaks of the basic assumptions of the normative view of faith within our denominations and highlights an area of this discussion on faith and disability that we, in any Christian tradition, need to address.

> For many of us whose roots lie within the Reformed theological tradition, there is often the idea that literacy and verbal assent, to intellectual formulations, are inseparable companions in the quest for authentic faith.[233]

This is a key statement in this book—discussion. In our desire, rightly so, to be sure of the truth of and veracity of faith statements made by a person, and in fulfilling our biblical requirements to test that faith, we may have disengaged ourselves from the reality that faith is first and primarily a spiritual attribute and not an intellectual one.

A side effect of this intellectualisation of faith is that we are inclined to preach to the intellect what is primarily a spiritual message and reality. Of course, no one objects to the fact that we need to address the intellect; in theological colleges we are told to "aim" our sermons toward a twelve-year-old audience which implies by nature that intelligence is an important part of faith. However, faith itself, as we now know, can stand and be independent of intellect.

We have already established in this book that salvic Christian faith in Jesus Christ, exists in the Shadow World of disability, even in the most extreme situations of anatomical, neurological, and cognitive disability, so it behoves us to fulfill the call to the proclamation of the gospel to all, including those who live in the Shadow World, "otherwise, how will they hear unless someone is sent, and how will they believe unless they hear" (Rom. 10:14, paraphrase).

Our argument all along has been that we are not determined or identified as a person solely by our level of intellect but by the presence of that essential spiritual "image" of God given to each

---

[233] John Swinton's words are universal in their application across all denominations of the Christian church worldwide and challenge us to re-address our assessment of faith and disability.

of us at conception that establishes and identifies us as human beings and sets us apart from all creation, both material and animated.

This concept of a relational identity established in God is key to our discussion. It is the one thing that all human beings have in common, whether enabled or disabled, whether believing or not believing in God.

Essentially, we are made for relationships, and the tragedy of broken relationships within marriage, family, nations, or faith is evident in all cultures in this world. We are also created, primarily, for a relationship on the spiritual level of life. An essential part of our humanity is our spirituality, the core of our identity as a person and human being.[234] It is also true that a spiritual relationship with God, by faith in Christ, transcends all brokenness and establishes the basis for a life of faith, whether that faith exists in the heart/mind of a disabled or an enabled person.

As John Swinton writes in "Restoring the Image":

> A relational understanding of faith and spirituality as outlined here offers the church the freedom to avoid evaluating a person's spiritual life according to intellectual criteria and to begin to find new ways of preaching the Word (of God) to those who have no words.

On a personal note, I am convinced of the existence of salvic faith in the life of a young disabled girl called Mary,[235] who has not yet uttered an intelligible word in this world. Along with the Apostle Paul, in Romans 8:38–39, I am convinced, by evidence observed from her "unique language" and behavior that neither her extreme epilepsy nor severe dyspraxia "could separate her from the love of God." Even though her "vessel"—body has

---

[234] See chapter 4: "Defining Being," page 31, para 6. Not that we are a two-part thing, but we consist of a "material body—spirit/soul" union that is necessary for life on this earth, that defines our "being," the material giving the basis—an avenue for the verbal and visual expression of the inner spiritual nature of a person.

[235] Not her real name but a young woman now who I first met in 2004 on a disability services conference for families on a weekend at Noosa. We will meet Mary later in this chapter.
See "Mary," page 180

limitations that place stresses upon her "mind"—her intellect—such that she might not be able to articulate this faith to us in a normative manner, yet this faith which she has is as great a veritable reality to her, personally, within her spirit/soul, as yours and mine is to you and me.

We have to understand that in His spiritual transcendence, God can pervade the Shadows of the world of disability and in love implant salvic faith within the spirit/soul—spirituality of the disabled person even if we cannot recognise or verify that faith by, or through, our normative neurotypical criteria within the traditional rituals or procedures of our churches or faith communities.

Faith in God is primarily an internal, spiritual reality, but we don't usually go around the neighborhood with a signboard saying, "I believe in God in my spirit."[236] Yes, we can talk, share, write, and speak about our faith, but that is not faith itself. Faith is the spiritual gift of life that a person receives from God (Eph. 2:6–8) internalised within their heart and mind (spirit/soul), through the regenerative work of the Holy Spirit, allowing them in their regenerated heart/mind—spirit/soul to relate to and communicate with God on a "spiritual" level not possible for them before—that is, in their unregenerate state (Rom. 8:26, 1 Cor. 2:13).[237]

Ezekiel speaks of this spiritual transformation in chapter 36, verses 22 to 32, and this is verified by Jesus speaking of the work of the Holy Spirit.

> And I will give you a new heart, and a new spirit I will put within you. And I will remove the heart of stone from your flesh and give you a heart of flesh. And I will put my Spirit within you, and cause you to walk in my statutes and be careful to obey my rules. (Ezek. 36:26–27)

---

[236] Yes, there are occasions when we might carry a banner in a parade or wear a T-shirt with a Christian slogan, but in everyday life, we look like every other person in our neighbourhood.

[237] Jesus Christ's answer to the Pharisee (lawyer) appears in the three Gospels—Matthew, Mark, and Luke. A Pharisee lawyer and scribe question Jesus on these occasions, and Jesus draws out of that situation the internal reality of faith in God.

> God is spirit, and those who worship him must worship in spirit and truth. (John 4:24)

Likewise, Eric Johnson, speaking of the reception of faith in the life of a person in his essay, "Rewording the Justification – Sanctification Relation with some Help From Speech Act Theory," writes:

> Through faith, they "receive the word implanted, which is able to save [their] souls" (James 1:21), as its illocutions are internalised and their perlocutionary intent brought into being over time.[238]

The internalising of this faith from God is a prime role—activity of the Holy Spirit, who "writes upon the heart these words of God"[239], and in doing so brings new life and faith, in God, to all who believe, whether anatomically or neurologically they are enabled or disabled in body or mind.

Whatever a person's "condition" or ability—disability we all are, in a sense, disabled, separated from God, and impaired in our relationship with Him by our human sin (Eccles. 7:20, Mark 10:18, Rom. 3:23),[240] and it is this regeneration and internalisation of faith that produces the effect of placing that person in a new relationship, spiritually, with God with the ongoing effect of that faith relationship producing perlocutionary

---

[238] Here, Johnson is not specifically addressing faith and disability per se but the process through which God brings faith into the spirit/soul of a human being. We have already established that there is no difference in the spiritual nature of the enabled and disabled person. Hence, his arguments on the salvic process are valid within the context of our book.

[239] Isaiah 59:21, Ezekiel 36:22, 27; 37:14, all used in a national and persona sense, speak of "within," the depositing of the Spirit of God within the person or upon the nation as an internalising reality.

[240] A biblical truth throughout the Old and New Testaments is that the most significant disability any "man" —person faces is sin, sin that separates them from God. It is an impenetrable barrier to a relationship with God that no human effort can remove or erase. Here the word *perlocutionary* comes into effect when the Holy Spirit speaks to the human soul, removes that barrier—disability—and reunites "man," that person, with God (Eph. 1:13).

trust[241], peace and joy with God, a by-product of the work of the Spirit of God in the life of a person, whether they be enabled or disabled.

That is, it is the same regeneration of the heart, the call toward God and the implantation (through the Holy Spirit) of salvic living faith in God in the spirit/soul of a disabled person that sustains this perlocutionary[242] effect on their life spiritually and is the same as that which exists within the life of the neurotypical person living in the world of the normative.

> All this I have spoken while still with you. But the Advocate, the Holy Spirit, whom the Father will send in my name, will teach you all things and will remind you of everything I have said to you. (John 14:25–26)

Thus, I believe, the discussion presented here declares that in the Shadow World faith, salvic faith is valid, articulate, alive, and well in the spirit/soul of the believing disabled person, whatever effect that disability and impairment might be or have upon their neurological, metaphysical, intellectual, or spiritual nature.

The issue for us is, do we accept this as fact and not marginalise the disabled into some fold of "less than human being" status just because we cannot understand their language, or normatively recognise the validity of their faith in the context of our current practices within our families, churches, or faith communities? What we find from our discussion so far is that faith in God is first and foremost a spiritual reality and is not defined by denominational dogma or doctrine, nor is it confined in its reality or experience by the limitations of disabilities upon the body and mind of a person.

---

[241] Perlocutionary trust: in this context, refers to an ongoing regeneration of the heart/mind of a person in its developing relationship with God, primarily on a spiritual level.

[242] Perlocutionary: definition of or relating to an act (as of persuading, frightening, or annoying) performed by a speaker upon a listener by means of an utterance. Here, the Holy Spirit persuades, encourages, and teaches the redeemed soul all that is in the Word of God and necessary to strengthen their Faith in Jesus Christ (John 14:25) https://www.merriam-webster.com/dictionary/perlocutionary Cited, 06/03/2021.

Faith in God lives in the spirit/soul of a person as a permanent deposit of the Spirit of God (Eph. 1:12–14), and thus salvic faith in God in the Shadow World is permanent, enduring, and consistent with the same biblical criteria we accept in our normative neurotypical world.

THE FEET OF HIM WHO BRINGS "GOOD NEWS"

Simply put, how will the disabled person see and "know" of the love of God unless someone tells them, unless they see His "face" in their own personal language, and recognise the message of God's love for them?

It is obvious in cases of complex neurological and cognitive disabilities that using normative conventions in presenting the gospel within our current church and faith community practices could hinder the disabled from "seeing" God. This book identifies that there is a need for practical and innovative means of "preaching the word" of God within our churches and faith communities so that the disabled may be enabled to see God.[243]

In his letter to the Romans, in chapter 10, the Apostle Paul places a serious challenge before churches and faith communities that is relevant to us here in the context of our discussion on disability and faith.

> (For), "Everyone who calls on the name of the Lord will be saved." How, then, can they call on the one they have not believed in? And how can they believe in the one of whom

---

[243] Brian, Woolnough, and Wonsuk, Ma, "Holistic Mission God's Plan for God's People" (2010). Edinburgh Centenary Series. Book 9. *http://scholar.csl.edu/edinburghcentenary/9* Quoted from page 240. "We need to reflect the mind of Christ as Woolnough and Ma indicate in their paper: 'The Marginalized Jesus'. Jesus had a special concern for the poor and all the marginalised, the weak and the socially ostracised. In sharp contrast to his 'religious' contemporaries, Jesus demonstrated a special interest in those who were disabled, children, the old, the lame and lepers (cf. Lk. 7:32–50; 19:1–10). In Jesus' day, lepers experienced terrible ostracism (Lk. 17:12), living alone in awful poverty, shouting "unclean, unclean" lest anyone accidentally touch them. However, Jesus touched the lepers and miraculously healed them, (Mk.1:41)." *https://scholar.csl.edu/cgi/viewcontent.cgi?article=1008&context=edinburghcentenary*

they have not heard? And how can they hear without someone preaching to them? And how are they to preach unless they are sent?" (Rom. 10:13–14)

Understanding and accepting the reality and viability of saving faith in the life of those who live in the Shadow World is our first step forward, but the challenges of bringing the message of the gospel to the disabled, and how we go about evangelism in the Shadow World, is completely another topic that Romans 10:15 might give us some direction and encouragement.

As it is written, "How beautiful (on the mountains)[244] are the feet of those who bring good news!" (Rom. 10:15)

How will they know if they don't "see His face"? It is quite a mystery how the interchange between the human spirit and divine agent in the presentation of the gospel of Jesus Christ works. Both are necessary, but we are certain that the sovereignty of God, in and through His Holy Spirit, works in that presentation of the gospel of Jesus Christ through the human agent to the spirit of the person receiving the gospel. All disabilities present challenges to us, both for the disabled and those who take care of and love them, in the presentation of the gospel.

For human agents this may seem overwhelming. How can we reach into the world of shadows when we see little or no response? Some might say, "God can do anything." Yes, true, but God desires His people to be involved, as the article "Why did God chose human agency..." below[245] states, and, if we don't go there, as commanded by the Apostle Paul in Romans 10, how will they ever

---

[244] (on the mountains): These words are in the original Hebrew text (מַה־ נָּאו֤וּ עַל־הֶהָרִים֙ רַגְלֵ֣י) that the Apostle Paul quotes from Isaiah 52:7. Mountains are hard to climb; you cannot skate-board over them or climb them from the armchair. It takes effort and sweat to get up a mountain. It will take effort and spiritual sweat to climb over the fence (mountain) of negative perceptions about disability and enter into the shadows where many with a disability live. This does not mean that we should not try, for it is imperative that we do so.

[245] James Rochford, Ed. Evidence Unseen, Objection #3: "Why did God choose to use human agency in delivering His message to others?" https://www.evidenceunseen.com/articles/the-goodness-of-god/what-about-those-who-have-never-heard/objection-3-why-did-god-choose-to-use-human-agency-in-delivering-his-message-to-others/

see His face. The traditional issues of actor and acted upon, the divine and human agent-element are irrelevant if there is no message sent, that is, if no one goes into the World of Shadows and presents the gospel to those who live there.[246]

Regarding church culture and practices, then, we need to learn a new language in proclaiming the gospel, as I mentioned in our previous chapter, "Actualising Faith," above—their "unique language," the language that they speak to us daily through their gestures, words, sounds and attitudes. When we speak to them of the gospel of Jesus Christ and converse with them in their world of disability, this is the language we need to use.

Learning and speaking this new language in our presentation of the gospel in the Shadow World is our responsibility, while we trust that the Holy Spirit "translates" the concepts and overcomes the challenges of bringing faith to them in a unique language that the disabled can both see, understand, and comprehend within their spirit/soul. Sometimes this new language that we need to speak is a silent one; sometimes it is a language conveyed through love and care, sometimes a language where actions often speak louder than words.

It is my purpose that this book encourages us to explore new ways of presenting the gospel that not only appeals to the enabled but the disabled alike. Nancy Eiesland, in *This Disabled God: Towards a Liberatory Theory on Disability*, writes concerning our current approach to the gospel and disability that,

---

[246] This is neither the time nor place for a debate on Arminianism and Calvinism (or any other theological position) on the principles of the gospel that needs to be proclaimed (Rom.10:9) and believed in (Rom. 10:10) for faith to be both authentic and alive. When we enter the Shadow World, both systems struggle with the realities of intellectual and anatomical disabilities, which can impact cognition and sentient awareness in the life of a disabled person. It is here that we enter into a new world. Faith, dimensionally, is, in essence, 'Spirit'—spiritual and nonmaterial; it is not based on knowledge and receives its properties from God himself, who alone can overcome the barriers of disability to bring effective faith and salvation to the heart, mind, and soul of a disabled person. Note: It is the same Gospel preached in this new language and the same Spirit of Christ that brings life; it just happens in a manner congruent with the spiritual nature, neurological abilities, and spatial characteristics of the disabled person.

"transformation must be enacted not only in history, but also in imagination and language."[247]

Eiesland suggests to us, in her book, that God has already experienced a form of disability in the incarnation when the eternal God who is without limits was, and now is, spatially and humanly restrained in essence in the person of Jesus Christ.[248]

The Apostle Paul, in Romans 8:39, indicates to us that the challenges and obstacles presented to us by disabilities and events in life are no barrier to the gospel message, essentially the love of God to us in Christ, and therefore, likewise, should be no object or impediment to us reaching into that world and proclaiming the gospel of Jesus Christ (Rom. 8:38–39).

> For I am sure that neither death nor life, nor angels nor rulers, nor things present nor things to come, nor powers, nor height nor depth, nor anything else in all creation, will be able to separate us from the love of God in Christ Jesus our Lord. (Rom. 8:38)

Therefore, as the love of God is supremely displayed in the gospel of Jesus Christ, then, as the Apostle Paul declares to us in verse 38, "I am sure," proclaims the imperative command which we have in response to this call, in Romans 10:13–15, to be involved in the kingdom work of God in the Shadow World.[249]

Charles Gourgey mentions in his paper "Faith, Despair and Disability" the theme of evangelism in the world of disability, that

---

[247] Nancy Eiesland, The Disabled God: Toward a Liberatory Theology of Disability. (Nashville: Abingdon Press, 1994.)
https://www.biblesociety.org.uk/uploads/content/bible_in_transmission/files/2004_spring/BiT_Spring_2004_Eiesland.pdf

[248] See Ligonier Ministries:
https://www.ligonier.org/learn/devotionals/god-christ

[249] A key point in Nancy Eiesland's article—book—is that the divine Son of God, "the Word" (John 1:1–2), experienced the "limitations" of the human form—as a type of disability—post the incarnation (John 1:14). A note of caution here is that Jesus Christ was-is still the divine Son of God and fully human as the Son of Man. The disability Nancy speaks of is the difference in his incarnated person and spatial freedoms while on earth. There was no "limitation"— disability in him being fully God as Jesus Christ.
Nancy Eiesland, The Disabled God: Toward a Liberatory Theology of Disability (Nashville: Abingdon Press, 1994).

God's kingdom extends (transcends) to all the ends of the earth, encompassing all of mankind whatever "world" they live in.

> [Jesus] went way beyond the given apocalyptic framework in presenting the "kingdom of God" as an expression of the unbreakable connection of God to every individual human life.

To achieve evangelism in the Shadow World of disability and fulfill the Great Commission of Jesus Christ in Matthew 28:18ff[250], we will need at times to express the dynamics of the Christian faith in new ways in our interactions with the disabled, their families, friends, and caregivers, using a new language—speech appropriately aimed at communicating spiritual truths of God, grace, sin, and forgiveness, especially with those who live in the Shadow World.

One example of using sensory ideas to communicate Christian faith and concepts to children and the disabled is a book called *The Wordless Book*, which was invented by Charles Spurgeon[251] in the late nineteenth century. It needs to be noted here that caution in the use of this book in child evangelism, particularly with children and adults that have a diagnosis of "sensory overload" should be considered, as the themes that this book brings out might have an "overload" effect on disabled and very young children.[252]

---

[250] Matthew 28:18: "And Jesus came and said to them, 'All authority in heaven and on earth has been given to me. Go therefore and make disciples of all nations, baptizing them in the name of the Father and of the Son and of the Holy Spirit, teaching them to observe all that I have commanded you. And behold, I am with you always, to the end of the age.'" OliveTree Bible+, Ver 7.7.8; ESV Bible.
"All authority" here means all aspects of this creation, life and reality for each and every human person, whether enabled or disabled as we so define.

[251] Charles Spurgeon, The Wordless Book, edited by Bastian, K., @ Kidology.org:
https://www.kidology.org/zones/zone_post.asp?post_id=120

[252] All evangelism with children, and especially the disabled, must consider the effects of the material used upon the senses and their abilities to understand and cognate that material. The Kennedy Institute at Vanderbilt University is an excellent resource for such materials. Other resources are listed at the end of this book under

THE PARADOX—GOD'S PART AND OUR PART IN EVANGELISM

The mystery, anthropologically and theologically, of the interaction of spiritual and anatomical realities involved in the presentation of the gospel does not exclude us from these words of the Apostle Paul. Human "beings" are created as a whole, not assembled out of parts like a kid's toy at Christmas. Each human being is a creation of one person, as a whole, an individual that embodies the material (external) body as well as the spirit/soul of that person.

Yes, the Holy Spirit works in the heart (spirit/soul) of each person "individual" who receives faith, but we, in fulfilling our responsibility and need to engage the mind of that person with the gospel message through whatever "language" the disabled person hears, understands, and comprehends.

Throughout this book, I have been developing the theme of the spiritual aspect of faith, faith as a spiritual gift from God placed within the spirit/soul of the person by the Holy Spirit. I have also advocated that this faith is real and effective in the life of that disabled person, regardless of their anatomical, intellectual, and/or neurological abilities.

What I have not said is that although all of this is in the work of God the Father, through the Holy Spirit, we, as human beings, have a role to play in the bringing of the gospel message of new life to a person, whether enabled or disabled. The imperatives of the Apostle Paul, here in chapter 10, clearly state this. God does His part, but we have our part to do as well. Yes, salvation is God's work as the prime instigator of salvation, but in Romans 10:14 the Apostle Paul leads us into the discussion of our part and responsibility in evangelism within our churches and faith communities.

> How, then, can they call on the one they have not believed in? And how can they believe in the one of whom they have not heard? And how can they hear without someone preaching to them? (Rom. 10:14)

"Bibliography" and "Resources"
https://vkc.vumc.org/vkc/resources/religionspirituality/

The challenge to us is clear. God expects us to do our part in proclaiming His gospel and Word, words of life in Jesus Christ, just as His prophets of old were called and commissioned to do. The great commission of Christ "to go into all the world" in Mark 16:15 applies to the disabled as well as the enabled, and even more so when we see Jesus Christ's interaction with the disabled in His ministry on earth.[253]

So how can they hear unless we speak? But, you say, some are deaf, others cannot see, and others cannot respond in a "normal" cognitive manner to what we speak—say to them in word or visual presentation. It is obvious, then, that my use here of the words "hear" and "speak" must take on a special meaning.

We need to engage with the disabled in their world. Not standing on our side of the fence and throwing "things" to them over the barrier of disability that impairs their mental and intellectual thought—reasoning—hoping that they can catch something of the gospel on the other side of the fence. We need to learn their personal, individual language, a language given to them by God, and we do this through learning their signs and expressions that give us an insight into them, a window into their spirit/soul, and their unique language through the intermediary[254] work of the Spirit of God.

If we accept the challenge to present the gospel in new and creative ways, ways that are true to the gospel of Christ, ways that are God-honoring and relevant to that person's particular "language" and spiritual needs, we can bring the gospel to life in the heart and mind of the disabled person. Of course, this communication is superintended by the Holy Spirit, who translates, as necessary, the gospel of life and applies that "new

---

[253] We learn from Jesus Christ in the gospels that in his ministry on earth, he never skipped over the disabled but dealt graciously and lovingly with them and their needs. Yes, he could "see" things we might not be able to, engaging with the disabled person regarding them as much in need of forgiveness and salvation as the everyday people he met in his itinerant ministry throughout Palestine.

[254] Sometimes overlooked in the exchange between John the Baptist and Jesus Christ (both in the womb) is the fact that the Holy Spirit enabled an exchange of communication between the two men (disabled of normative—verbal—communications while in the womb) that was understood and acted upon by each man.

life" to the spirit of the disabled person, thereby leading them to believe in Jesus Christ, but the human agency of man is not negated in this divine process.

> And how can they preach unless they are sent? As it is written, "How beautiful (on the mountains) are the feet of those who bring good news." (Rom. 10:15)

Although this section is brief, its import goes way beyond its word length and reaches out into the shadows where words, language, and normative approaches to the gospel may not easily apply. It is a mountain to be climbed but one that must be conquered if our churches and faith communities are to fully love and embrace in the gospel of Jesus Christ those who live with disabilities in the Shadow World.

Therefore, the need for evangelism in the Shadows is imperative. But how?

CHAPTER 10

FAITH IN THE SHADOWS

Keeping in mind that practical evangelism in the Shadow World is to be driven by the diagnosis—situation—that is, the dynamics of the world that that person lives in, one initiative—one method of evangelism—in the Shadow World that can be quite effective, and I suggest way before its time, is the *Wordless Book*.

The *Wordless Book* is a visual concept book originally brought out by Charles Spurgeon (c-1886) which has been adapted and enhanced over the years but retains the basic concept of different colors to represent or indicate certain aspects of the Christian gospel. Its use would be limited to those with some cognition, but as an example of how best to evangelise the very young or disabled, it has few equals.

The *Wordless Book* is a set of full-color pages, edge bound and covered. [255] The colors are, black, red, white, gold, and green. Each full-color page has a Bible verse that goes with it. The "language" and talk—discussion to be used with the book is "keep it simple" so that it does not take a lot of time but still communicates man's lost condition, and our need for faith—salvation in God. It is a visual presentation that represents the key elements of the gospel in an easily understood manner.

This, of course, does not mean that a disabled person who understands and believes, given their particular neurological-cognitive capacity, the concepts that the book teaches about sin,

---

[255] Charles Spurgeon, Public domain:
The Wordless Book is an example of using "visual" sensory ideas to communicate Christian faith and concepts to children and the disabled. This is a particularly good place to start. However, as I mentioned, the *Wordless Book* must be used with caution, for its graphic nature can reverse affect some disabled people. I would add an additional white page at the start and say that in the Garden of Eden, as first created by God, Adam and Eve were good, but Adam sinned in the Garden of Eden, and, as a result, sin entered into the world. Sin is when we do and say things that displease God.

God, and Jesus Christ receives a less—than full faith. We have already established above that their faith in God, as a spiritual reality, is fundamentally as full, complete, and real as is ours, or that of any other normative believing person.[256]

I believe Paul, the Apostle, understood that the challenge—the call for evangelism into all the world[257]—includes the world of disability. As a principal element of grace, grace that is both active—regeneration, and effective—salvic, the gospel embraces and overcomes any disability in the life of all who come to Christ, for all born of Adam are alike disabled, at least spiritually, if not anatomically or neurologically (2 Cor 4:7, 16).

Additionally, over the time of research for this book, I have encountered some examples of evangelism in practical terms that accommodate and work with disability in a manner that might help us understand and meet the challenge of evangelism in the Shadow World of disability.

NORMAN:

Norman is a man Charles Gourgey speaks about in his paper "Faith, Despair, and Disability," and lists "a personal anecdote" on their relationship giving a personal and practical example of evangelism in the Shadow World that might also help families, churches, caregivers, and faith workers.

Charles speaks of a period of weeks in which he, and a nurse at the hospice, "spoke" (communicated) with Norman through music, and not any type of music, but the recognisable classic "masters" of Christian music, Handel, Bach, and others. The

---

[256] As proposed earlier, it is imperative that we engage the cognitive and psychological attributes of the disabled person as much as possible. Although many times this might not be available to them or us, in doing so, we give them the ability to process within themselves whatever information they can in their anatomical and cognitive (personal) self. Yes, she may have the mind of a five-year-old (in our opinion), but that five-year-old mind can (and should) be engaged, for through that mind, whatever its age or state, she can respond to the grace of God in her life and express that faith in our normative world.

[257] The gospel mandate, the great commission, in Matthew is usually taken as going into "all the world" ethnically and nationally, tribe by tribe. Does not "all the world" include disabled people also?

expressed and reciprocated love that existed between them at this time was an important part of the exchange between Norman, George himself, and the attending nurse.

> Norman was dying (from AIDS) in hospital. and by the time I saw him, he was very sick. He could not move from his bed, and he needed an oxygen mask to breathe. He could hardly speak. Yet in spite of all his physical limitations, I could see he had a great capacity for love. He showed me love by letting me know how much the beauty of the music I shared with him meant to him. I was surprised by the peacefulness of his spirit in spite of his physical discomfort and his knowledge of the imminence of his death.
>
> Somehow Norman must have struggled within himself to reach the capacity for this love at a time when most people in his position might feel needy and disinclined to be giving. I do not know the course of his struggle; I saw only the fruits.
>
> But I believe it was his love more than his esoteric practices that saved him and brought him a divine response that enabled him to cope with his fear of death.

If we follow only our denominational dogmatics neurotypically cognised model of determining the fact and veracity of the existence of faith in Norman, then there is little basis for us to assume that Norman, severely disabled as he was by his illness and barely able to speak a few words, could have entered into a real salvic faith—in a spiritual—relationship with God.

However, The Bible challenges us to think differently.[258]

---

[258] One of the things that happened to me as I wrote, and reviewed this book, is that Bible verses have taken on new meaning. Not that I have gained some "higher knowledge" or proclaim another gospel (as Paul mentions in Gal. 1:6), but in reading the Bible, with an understanding that the intrinsic spirituality of the disabled is not incapacitated by their anatomical, neurological, or psychological disabilities, verses in the Bible have come alive as they open doors to my understanding of the workings of the grace and love of God in new and spectacular ways for those who live in the Shadow World.

> If anyone acknowledges that Jesus is the Son of God, God lives in him and he in God. And so we know and rely on the love God has for us. God is love. Whoever lives in love lives in God, and God in him. In this way, love is made complete among us so that we will have confidence on the Day of Judgment, because in this world we are like him. There is no fear in love. But perfect love drives out fear, because fear has to do with punishment. The one who fears is not made perfect in love. (1 John 4:15–18)

Prior to this unusual mode of evangelism, Norman had a dread and great fear of dying. What transformed this attitude, what changed this position of his heart from one of "fear" to "peace"?

It could be argued that Norman's earlier experiments with meditation had some effect on his outlook on life, but this was all before his contact with Charles and the nurse in the hospice, and Norman's explorations into Eastern religions, meditation, and traditions in the past had not transformed his outlook and attitude to life, especially his fear of death and dying as a person.[259]

I would suggest then that faith in and the love of God came to this man, spiritually, through the evangelism of Charles and the nurse; and that the "language" of Christian music used as a medium to communicate that love of God was effective, along with the demonstrated love they both gave, in reaching into the heart of this man through the Holy Spirit bringing to Norman new life in Christ. This mode of evangelism was one that Norman, in his distressed condition, could understand, actualise, and receive as that gift of faith from God.

Charles Gourgey concludes (and I agree with him):

> This must be an example of what Paul meant when he said that nothing "in all creation, will be able to separate us from the love of God in Christ Jesus our Lord." (Rom. 8:39)

Charles indicates that the "spectacular" changes in Norman's outlook on life and death could not have come from any other source than God who had placed in Norman that gift of "faith" and

---

[259] This is a precis of Charles Gourgey's article regarding his time with Norman. See footnote 227, page 155

life. Through His Spirit, God spoke, and speaks, to Norman in a "language" that both God and Norman could understand through his pain and suffering. Charles writes about Norman's continuing struggle with pain and the reality of his impending death.[260]

> The path is not easy, but we do not have to do it all ourselves. "The Spirit helps us in our weakness" (Rom. 8:26). As our struggle opens our hearts, we find room for the working of the divine Spirit.

It is not the outward things of life that determine faith, but the inner heart of man in tune with the God who gave that life, life itself.[261]

SUSAN:

Another example of evangelism in the Shadow World that I present here, as an example of effective disability evangelism, is the case of a young girl (now woman) called Susan. Susan, whose diagnosis of Autism—Asperger's syndrome (high functioning) was only discovered in her very late teens, has some early developmental disorders and lessened motor skills.

For many years Susan attended Sunday school, church, and a variety of Christian activities with her parents. There was no external indication, or moment in time event, which indicated that "faith" in Jesus Christ had come into the life of this young person, just a growing awareness of her developmental differences from those around her. Gifted with art, the young teenager began to draw what she heard in church, Sunday school, and Bible studies.

As time passed, her parents noted that she responded to certain visual stimulations, rather than conversational conventions, especially in her "cartoon-like" drawings. At that time the children's program, the King, Snake, and the Promise (a

---

[260] I have been advised by Charles Gourgey, since the initial writing of this book, that "Norman" passed away peacefully some months after this interview with Charles, in a manner not before able— accessible to Norman without the work of God in his heart.

[261] In his paper, Charles speaks of the "realm of faith", telling us that it is an area of existence in which scientific and philosophical studies still struggle to fully understand the working of the divine God in the human realm, especially where disabilities can be challenging.

CD-based program) was running at her church in the Sunday school.

A bit of a loner, the parents encouraged their young daughter, and she began attending these classes, continuing with her drawings, bringing them home to show her parents. Looking at the drawings and the "stories" they told, it took some time for the parents to realise that the gospel was being presented to their disabled daughter, albeit in a radically different way, by the Holy Spirit.

They began praying, and supporting Susan, even attending some of the classes themselves. At this time, the young girl began also to draw pictures of the "classes" and sermons she heard each Sunday morning at church.

Eventually, as the girl became a young lady, the question of faith, communion, and membership of her church arose. During classes with her pastor, the girl began to present her drawings of the communion classes to her pastor. Although the young lady could speak, words were not easy for her to use, though through her drawings it became clear to all that this young woman was a believer in Jesus Christ.[262]

The time came for that evening service where she was to take her first communion. As the pastor approached the young lady, she presented her sketches and drawings to the elders and congregation as a slide show and answered the questions, as able, asked of her with her drawings.

Definitely not your standard neurotypical communicant service, but it was effective in demonstrating that the Holy Spirit had enlivened her heart and mind to the love of God in Jesus Christ, and of her receiving that gift of faith from God through the Holy Spirit.

Today this young woman, seriously disabled with autism spectrum disorder—high functioning Asperger's syndrome, continues with her church fellowship, growing in grace and the love of God her Savior.

---

[262] These communion classes were spread over eight months, meeting fortnightly, when the normal communion classes at her church took three months meeting fortnightly.

Susan's evangelism was slow and mostly visual in context. The "time" of her conversion—coming to a realised faith—is uncertain, but contextually it happened in a visual world. Words were not that important—or understood cognitively—as Susan has complications in understanding complex concepts and has since been diagnosed with additional "executive dysfunction disorder."[263]

JULIE:

I became aware of another instance of "shadow evangelism" while discussing this book with a friend at church. One of our elders was speaking with a church member, Julie, who is disabled both with IDD[264] and Down's syndrome.

Speaking with "Julie," the elder asked her one day why she sits at the front of the church. Julie answered that she sits there so she can "hear the music." "Why?" asked the elder. "So that I can see the songs," was Julie's reply.[265] The elder then asked, "What song do you like the best?" Julie answered, "Shine, Jesus, Shine."

There is a lot packed into this song, but the key issue is that Julie understood, in her own, personal, way—in her own "spirit"—its message to her. That is the issue of this book. What God communicates to the disabled, whatever their disabilities may be, is both understood, within their heart and spirit/soul, and is beneficial to them in their spiritual "being," and their life in God in this world.[266]

---

[263] Susan: Susan is diagnosed with Executive Dysfunction Disorder (EDD) and, in Vineland II assessment, is categorised as having a cognitive function level of 0.01% of young women her age in Queensland, where she lives.

[264] IDD: Intellectual Development Disorder

[265] Julie is slightly deaf and has poor vision because of her medical condition.

[266] In this world, we often assume that the disabled have problems "enjoying" life and looking at the complications that some have, it seems to us that life is nothing more than a drawn-out pained existence awaiting death. In her spiritual "being", Julie enjoys the fullness of her relationship with God (Eph. 1:3) even though her expression of and experience of that relationship with God anatomically and psychologically in this world might be muted or impaired by her material and cognitive disabilities.

MARY:

My final example is of a young girl, Mary, (now a young adult) who is severely disabled to the point where communication with those who live in our predominantly neurotypical world, on our side of the fence, is limited to groans, hand movements, and body gestures. There are no discernible cognitive or illocutionary[267] vocal responses to words spoken to her or written down for her to read.

My first visit to the family was one of discovery. This young girl, Mary, came up to me and leaning against me began to tap my shoulder and leg to be picked up. This "touch" language developed in the relationship between us, which continues today. Over the period of a few years, I grew to learn Mary's unique "language" and could increasingly determine the moods and phases of her personal expression.[268]

What occurred one afternoon while sharing time and coffee with her stay-at-home dad was quite astounding, and, in a large part led to the writing of the original academic paper, Faith in the Shadows in 2012, upon which this book is based.[269]

While playing with my mobile phone looking for songs on YouTube, some music began to be heard by Mary who was close

---

[267] Illocutionary: Essentially, the ability to convey in a defined and understood manner, vocally, the thoughts and reasonings of one's heart, mind, and emotions. Mary is constricted in all three of these essential elements of illocution.

[268] I am not a psychologist, but if current theories on disabilities placing limitations upon the spirituality and ontology of a person hold valid, then, this young girl's spirituality—her essential being—should have been disabled to the point where expression—communication, and cognisance of her "feelings"—would be impaired. However, as is the case here, and in many other situations that present, caregivers and parents can tell you that their severely disabled child is either happy or sad and can articulate—process—express emotions, albeit in their 'own' distinct language, just like neurotypicals, would indicate to us that their personality, essentially their spiritual soul, is not impaired and in reality can process—demonstrate personal awareness, organise and facilitate perception, reasoning, and judgment within the abilities of their person and being.

[269] I delivered the original paper this book is based on in 2011 at the International Conference on Academy and the Church at St. Lucia University of Queensland in Australia.

See "Introduction," footnote 16, page 4

by. As the songs came and went, we noticed a marked change in Mary's mood and "personality" (persona) and her different responses to music that we would term as Christian traditional "church" music and secular pop culture music.

Not a word was said either way between Mary and those who were listening, but after some time her parents mentioned that whenever they played their classic Christian "church" music in her hearing, their daughter would become calmed and relaxed.

Mary's home also has two other routinely active children who have and use mobile phones, iPods, tablets, watch TV and DVD movies, so a wide range of music—audible sounds—were part of the family's normal lifestyle.

However, as mentioned above, whenever classical Christian music was played, and Mary could hear it, the change in Mary's persona was noticed by her family.

All this, Mary's responses to different types—genres—of music, of course, can be put in the anecdotal basket and dismissed as conjecture; however, a similar case of music and spiritual responses, but in quite different circumstances, presents itself in the Bible and can certainly speak to us in this situation.

> Whenever the spirit from God came upon Saul, David would take his harp and play. Then relief would come to Saul; he would feel better, and the evil spirit would leave him. (1 Sam. 16:23)[270]

Theologically this is a quite different situation to that of our young girl, Mary, but the example of the ability of music to speak to the soul/spirit inner "being" of King Saul is clearly articulated here, and it is in this manner that I apply this verse to our discussion (Prov. 18:15, Matt. 6:22, Luke 8:15, Rom. 10:17).

We are not told of the physical transformations that occurred in King Saul, but it is stated that the music of the shepherd David "calmed his soul." What is noticed with Mary is the external transformation that comes over her when music is played in her

---

[270] Theologically, this is quite a different situation for our young girl. However, the example of the ability of music to speak to the 'soul/spirit' of King Saul is clearly articulated, and it is in this manner that I apply this verse to our discussion.

hearing. When the traditional Christian hymns are played, in vocals or music, her body relaxes, and her eyes express a peace that is not noticeable when she is otherwise active.

> The eye is the lamp of the body. If your eyes are healthy, your whole body will be full of light. But if your eyes are unhealthy, your whole body will be full of darkness. If then the light within you is darkness, how great is that darkness! (Matt. 6:22-23)

Yes, Matthew 6:22 does not indicate that one can look into a person's eye and see their soul or the state of their mind; but their eyes can express emotion, as we all know. One thing that is often overlooked in 1 Samuel 16:23, is that David observed the heightened state of Saul and knew to play the harp that would calm Saul the king. David saw the playing of the harp (music) as a ministry of grace from God that he could perform for King Saul.

It is important in our discussion, then, to take notice of the effect that church-based music has on Mary. With all the disruptive effects of chronic epilepsy, cognitive incapacities and sentient IDD disabilities upon her Mary speaks and expresses herself, primarily, and sometimes only, through her body language—attitude and her eyes.

We all acknowledge that we can "see" the emotions of joy, love, sadness, anger, hate, and even amusement through the eyes and physical body language of a person. Are we then reluctant to accept that we could see "faith," belief in and peace with God, through the eyes and bodily responses of this disabled young girl as divine love and contentment with life?

If we can "see" human inner emotions and attitudes expressed through the body and "eyes" of a person, why not faith? Have we been so conditioned over the past centuries of neurotypical normative forms that faith can only be gauged through vocal, illocutionary, and volitional assent?

For this young teenager (now young woman) who will never achieve vocal illocution or normative assent, can we accept that her eyes and body are her language, her window into this world, and the one through which she expresses her faith in God?

Like Charles Gourgey says earlier with Norman,[271] I am convinced of the existence of and reality of salvic faith in this young girl, not only because I know her well but because I know the God who knows her better.

I admit that the examples of faith in the Shadow World presented here are not tested in rigorous statistical analysis or university sample studies, and it may seem like an easy way out to just put forward these examples of "faith" in such complex situations as proof of concept, or thesis, but there are objective results in each case, hidden in some, but they are there if we are open enough to look.

Whatever our "take" may be on the examples given above, what is more important to our discussion here is that evangelism in the Shadow World is an imperative given to us by Jesus Christ (Matt. 28:18–20), which is affirmed by the Apostle Paul in his challenge in Romans 10:12–15 (see Mark 16:15–16).

> All authority in heaven and on earth has been given to me. Go therefore and make disciples of all nations, baptizing them in the name of the Father and of the Son and of the Holy Spirit, teaching them to observe all that I have commanded you. And behold, I am with you always, to the end of the age. (Matt. 28:17)

This principle of universal application, not only geographical but social, and of the call to evangelism by Jesus Christ is reiterated by the Apostle Paul.

> For there is no difference between Jew and Gentile[272]—the same Lord is Lord of all and richly blesses all who call on him, for, "Everyone who calls on the name of the Lord will be saved. How, then, can they call on the one they have not believed in? And how can they believe in the one of whom they have not heard? And how can they hear

---

[271] See "Norman," page 176, para 6

[272] It might cause me some flak from theologians and exegetes. However, there is no difference between enabled and disabled, communicative and mute, cognitive and impaired (normatively) etc., as far as the Gospel, salvation, faith, and life in Jesus Christ are concerned.

without someone preaching to them? And how can anyone preach unless they are sent? As it is written: "How beautiful are the feet of those who bring good news!" (Rom. 10:12)

These verses are an imperative that will challenge us to rethink faith, and encourage us to present faith in God, in Christ, "in new and radical ways"[273] in the domain of the Shadow World where real people live (Matt. 28:18–19, Mark 16:15) and need to hear the words of grace that the gospel brings to all who believe.

Charles Gourgey writes in his paper "Faith, Despair, and Disability," in summation, "We are in the realm of faith now, and no biological or scientific proof can be given." However, although they may be subjectively presented here for this book, they are nevertheless real examples of faith in God in the lives of those portrayed.

We have also learned that faith, spiritual believing faith in God in Jesus Christ, transcends disability, not only in theory and theology but also in practical terms of the experience and spiritual aspects of that faith within the life of the disabled person.

The words of the Apostle Paul remind us of this:

> Praise be to the God and Father of our Lord Jesus Christ, who has blessed us in the heavenly realms with every (πᾶς) spiritual blessing in Christ. (Eph. 1:3)[274]

Thus, the disabled, who have faith in Christ, have "every spiritual blessing" (all - πᾶς) and thus have the same level of spiritual blessings as the enabled—neurotypical—person has. To say different means that they, the disabled, are somehow evaluated or considered as having a "less than" faith—in their understanding of and relationship with God. They are often appraised, if we assume so from a neurotypical attitude, to be deemed to have a different type of faith or a "disabled faith," which, as a consequence, is seen to be "less than" in its experience

---

[273] Susannah Mintz, *Disability Studies Quarterly* 26, no. 3 (2006), "Ordinary Vessels: Disability Narrative and Representations of Faith," para 30.

[274] Note that the Apostle Paul uses the Greek word πᾶς here in verse 3, which means, generally, 'all things'—*every*.

and reality in their life—or, at worst, may even be ineffectual in their salvation.

That is, if we assume that neurotypical normativity is needed to fully experience and express faith in and sustain a personal interaction with God, then we judge these people in the Shadow World, who have "every spiritual blessing in Christ (Eph. 1:1–2), to be lacking, somewhat, in their relationship with God.

Our affirmative statement on the other hand is that faith in God in Christ for the disabled person is salvic faith, period, or it does not exist at all. Faith, as defined in this book, is held fully, or not at all. You cannot have three-fourths of faith or be three-fourths saved; it is always full faith and fully saved.[275]

We can conclude, then, that there is no such thing as "a disabled faith" and that no disabled believer has the faith of a five-year-old. Faith, in those enabled and disabled alike, is intrinsically whole, complete, and full—both in experience and salvic endeavor.

We define "living faith" in God as both factual and observable in the life and experience of the disabled if we are prepared to look at the effectual outcomes of that faith in the "language" of that disabled person.

Bringing the challenge of faith into the Shadow World, therefore, is a necessary part of the ministry and responsibility that a faith community has to its people, whatever "world" they may live in.

Yes, understanding *Faith in the Shadows* brings challenges. But knowing that faith exists in the Shadows bridges the fence between two worlds and bringing faith into the Shadow World is a gospel imperative.

As the General Council of the Assemblies of God states:

---

[275] I am continually humbled and amazed at this book, even as I review its work years after its initial writing. What has become apparent to me is that, for parents of disabled children, we have intellectualised faith to the point of exclusion where only the intellectually capable can have, know, or understand faith's effect on their life. What this book has done for me, to my mind, is to open up what the Scriptures say about the spirituality and life of a disabled person. Passages that we previously held in the normative realm are now beautiful in the hearts and minds of those who love and care for disabled people.

> People with disabilities are essential to the wholeness of our Faith Communities. They are people created in the image of God possessing dignity, value and purpose.

The examples presented to us above may need further discussion, but that discussion should not dissuade us from entering into the Shadow World of disability to proclaim the gospel of Jesus Christ in a language that those who live there may understand, relying upon the Holy Spirit to enact change within the life of both the one who brings the good news and the one who hears the good news in their own, personal, fundamental language.

The challenge to our churches and faith communities is to cross over that "fence" of disability, no matter how difficult or demanding it might be, to accept "living faith" in the Shadow World that uses a different language. How these challenges are met over the decades ahead will define our obedience to the call of Jesus Christ to take the gospel into all the earth (Matt:28:18—20).

TWO BOTTLES

Imagine a table where there are two bottles. One is clear, and the other is opaque—dark blue. Both contain a liquid. We can see what the liquid looks like in the clear bottle, but we are not so certain what the liquid is like in the opaque (blue) bottle, its contents are a bit mysterious, clouded.

For the purpose of our illustration (discussion), we will accept that the liquid in the two bottles represents a person's spirituality, their spirit/soul—that source of life—the breath of God—that each one receives from God that defines them, and their personal reality.

The "clear" bottle, in our illustration, represents a neurotypical person, and the "opaque blue" bottle represents someone you may know, or one of the disabled people we have been talking about.

In accepting this analogy there are questions we can ask of our two bottles.

- Is there the same amount of "liquid" in each bottle, the clear and opaque bottle?
- Is the 'liquid' of the same "quality" – and properties?

When someone says that a disabled person "has the mind of a five-year-old," does that mean that that person has less of the spiritual stuff inside them than there is in a person who has the mind of a normal (neurotypical) person? That is, does a disabled person (our opaque blue bottle) have less "spiritual" stuff inside them than there is in a normal neurotypical enabled person (our clear bottle)?

Immediately we answer, No!

Then, why do we frequently hold to the view that only an enabled person (our clear neurotypical bottle) can understand faith, can know faith, can express faith and experience faith, and live by faith in Christ, in their life in a fulfilling and meaningful manner, and that the person living in the cloudy, murky "opaque" bottle in the Shadow World cannot!

Clearly, we need to approach "faith" (our topic) in the "blue" opaque bottle with our eyes open to the fact that an equal amount of "spiritual" stuff in the opaque "blue" bottle means an equal amount of faith exists in this opaque, shadowy person's life. Here a reminder of Ephesians 1:3 might help:

> Blessed be the God and Father of our Lord Jesus Christ, who has blessed us in Christ with *every* spiritual blessing in the heavenly places. (Eph. 1:3)[276]

In our churches and faith communities, we have a vast array of bottles, from clear to cloudy,[277] to fully opaque. Some we can open and drink from and taste their faith, through conversation and interaction; others, like the "opaque" bottle are sometimes closed to us; but this does not mean that their faith does not exist,

---

[276] Italics mine.
[277] Cloudy Bottle: We will meet the cloudy bottle in our discussion on accountable faith in chapter 12, "Accountable Faith."
See "Three Different Bottles," page 226

nor does it mean that their faith is shallow—less than, like that of a five-year-old.

What we discover instead is that "faith" in the opaque "blue" bottle is the same, full and complete faith, as it is in the "clear" bottle; it just has a different language and expression than that of the faith we are used to in the clear bottle.

TWO BOTTLES

Faith is experienced fully in both bottles.

It brings knowledge and strength for life, and confidence in the reality of God in their life. This faith, salvic faith, is more than faith in the "things" of life; this faith goes far beyond the material, beyond what we can see and reason. It touches the very core of our being in spirit and soul.

Charles Gourgey writes:

> "But this faith is more than just a "leap"; it is more than just belief. It is based on the assurance that love always responds to genuine love, an assurance we can feel at the very core of our—their "being."

Charles is right; love through faith exists to its fullest extent in both bottles, the clear one as well as the opaque dark one. Faith is alive, well, and living in the Shadow World; however, it needs our encouragement to grow and flourish.

Chapter 11

Encouraging Faith

As we approach the subject of encouraging faith in those who live in the Shadow World, our remarks in chapter 9, "Living Faith,"[278] would suggest that we need to "see" them, and their faith, from a new perspective, to look at them in a new way, with eyes opened to the true beauty of their person, and the reality of their faith in God.

FEARFULLY AND WONDERFULLY MADE

However, decades of images, projected values, concepts, and ideas about what defines beauty have left us blindsided, clouded so to speak, preconditioning us into accepting a superficial "visualised" picture of what beauty really is. In art and film and over the age's past, the external "form" is often the prescriber of what defines "beauty"—our TV ads, commercials, and media presentations often reinforce this external Aphrodite-style image of what constitutes beauty.

What is needed here in this discussion (debate) on faith and disability is not only a new language in communication but a new definition of human beauty. That is, a definition of human beauty that embraces the beauty of their "being" extant—external to their earthly attributes. We require a new definition of what it means to be lovely and lovable in real personal terms whatever anatomical and/or neurological "profile" one presents to us in our visually accentuated world.

Psalm 139 has something to say to us toward discovering and establishing a fresh new definition of beauty, of "being," of our identity as a person. The definition of beauty of "personhood" in this psalm moves us away from the visual, the external (superficial) toward the inward beauty of a person and opens up the discussion on an important outcome of such a definition in life

---

[278] See "Living Faith," page 171, para 3

for the disabled that presents to us their positive value in the community and society in which they, and we, live.

> For you created my inmost being; you knit me together in my mother's womb. I praise you because I am fearfully and wonderfully made; your works are wonderful; I know that full well. (Ps. 139:13–14)

For those who are disabled, their parents, family, and friends, reading this book the quotation from Psalm 139 above can be both comforting yet at the same time challenging, confronting, and even sometimes confusing.

It is challenging in that the questions arise of how or why a good God could allow a person to be born and live their life as a disabled person. It is confronting from the point of view of accepting that one so disabled as Mary (who does not have any normative means of communication and social interaction) could be "fearfully and wonderfully made" by God.

It is also confusing from the standpoint that we usually associate "wonderfully made" with that which is visually and emotionally attractive, stimulating, and enjoyable. Terms that we cannot easily apply to the "images" perceived by the normative world of those who are severely disabled.

My hope in the next few pages is to turn us away from this superficial, external, "visualised" perception of beauty that we have become accustomed to toward a new definition of "beauty in being," not in a sentimental or affrontive manner, but clearly defining what it means to be "wonderfully made," bringing comfort, joy, and assurance to all alike of the beauty of the disabled person and glory to God who made them.

The question then is, "How can a disabled person be 'fearfully and wonderfully' made?"

First, with quiet humility, I would suggest that we look at our disabled child, friend, or family member from the perspective of their spirituality, their inner being (spirit/soul) rather than just looking at them—or evaluating them as a disabled person living in a neurotypical enabled world using our visually driven external sensory perceptions of and ideas about—what constitutes beauty.

This is not a diversion but a reminder to us that they, and we, are primarily "spiritual" beings and even though they—and we—may be somewhere on the spectrum of disability (everyone is in fact), it is their spiritual attributes—that essential, nonorganic, inner spirit/soul that defines them as a "wonderfully made" human being.[279]

If we can do this, we will be moving in the right direction, taking us away from the externals to the reality and beauty of their full being, making our first steps toward being able to see our disabled child, family member, or friend as "fearfully and wonderfully made," accepting them primarily (and essentially) as a person—a fully human "being" who is momentarily (i.e., in this mortal life) living within a disabled vessel—body.

To be alive in this mortal world intrinsically requires a union between body and spirit/soul and this "spiritual" presence within the mortal earthly body, itself of the essence of God who is Spirit, is the defining image of their beauty.

A verse previously quoted from Acts 17:28 states that "in Him (God) we live, move and have our being." Here, in this verse in Acts the Apostle Paul reminds us that it is God who gives life and "being," through the breath of life (Gen. 2:7) "breathed into" the body in which we live. It is God, who creates life (Ps. 139:13–14), who sees the beauty of life in "man," which is in part the beauty of himself, and whatever the condition in terms of disability or ability in the life of a person we all are living, moving human "beings" (Acts 17:28) having and experiencing their "beauty" as a person primarily defined by God.

It may also take the scales off our eyes, allowing us to see the disabled person in the beauty of their true "humanity," including their spirituality, inclusive of and over and above their disability whatever its anatomical and neurological mix.

So, to answer our first question in Psalm 139, is this challenging? Yes, it is! It is a challenge to redefine "beauty" in our

---

[279] Throughout this book, humanity is defined as a spiritual attribute that distinguishes human beings from all other forms of life on this earth and universe (Gen. 1:27, 2:7).

minds and eyes when our current visual "appearance"[280] driven model—social convention seeks only to "value" someone by their externals. To realise that it is God who defines their beauty just as He does for all His children, as David tells us in this psalm, is the challenge and call we all must face to love that which, at first, does not seem visually appealing.

As we consider a new definition of "fearfully and wonderfully made," *love* is the measure of beauty, the compassionate love of God for *all* His children, as an example of true love, challenges us to respond as it is clearly stated in the Bible.

> Beloved, if God so loved us, we also ought to love one another. (1 John 4:11)

God has already demonstrated His side of this love.

> For God so loved the world[281] that he gave his one and only Son, that whoever believes in him shall not perish but have eternal life. (John 3:16)[282]

Here the word "world" (κόσμος - cosmos in Greek) includes the Shadow World in which your—our—loved ones live, and, more importantly, it is in this Shadow World that we have discovered

---

[280] Appearance, not only visual but emotional, as we "see" them in our daily interactions and conversations. Recalling my friend Bill, see footnote 187, page 125. Bill had IDD and ICD disabilities and was very direct in his presentation and communications; there were, at times, little or no perceptive inhibitors between thought and speech in his personal communications. This was, at times, incredibly challenging, confronting even, as Bill would come up to you, invade your personal space, and about six inches (10 cm) from your face ask you a straightforward question. It took me several years of not leaning back to learn to love and appreciate Bill as a friend. Bill did not look after his external appearances very well; it was not a priority in Bill's life, but he had, as a born-again Christian, a devotion to God that would shame many, me included, with his outright approach to faith and God. My point is that Bill, in this life, was someone we might not, at first, on "appearances," give much time or credence to in our circle of friends.

[281] Used here inclusive of all things that exist, materially and spiritually, both in the natural, animal and human worlds. (Gen. 1:1-31, 2:7)

[282] This should be the primary verse for the inclusiveness of the grace of God in the gospel.

(chapter 7) that their faith, spiritually, is a thing of beauty, that their faith is salvic, real, tangible, and life-giving (Rom. 8:38–39).

The second question, which naturally and usually follows, is, "is God responsible for their disability?"

Is God, as the giver of life (Gen. 2:7) and the one who forms—knits them together in the womb,[283] responsible for the disability of that person who is part of your community, family or friend, or work colleague?

My approach here in answering this question of theodicy[284] may, at first, seem a diversion from an up-front answer. The question of whether God is complicit or culpable in allowing a disability to continue to exist in the life—the body—of our loved one is not what we are really asking when we ask the question, "Is God responsible?"

As Charles Gourgey says:

> "What the question (of theodicy) really asks for [is] there the possibility of faith that resists despair."

At first, this seems like an avoidance quote, but whenever we ask a question, we always have a point of view in mind (or at the back of our mind) or have a secondary question awaiting an answer to the first. So, the "Is God responsible" question is not the actual query in itself. The person already believes that God is responsible, and their questions about theodicy presuppose God being responsible, in their viewpoint, and is a lead-up statement for the inevitable follow-up question/statement of, "Yes, He is, so why should I believe in Him?"

Yes, it is God who brings life (actually all life on earth) to "man" as Genesis 2:6–7f confirms, and it is that moment of "nesama" - נְשָׁמָה'[285], the giving of the breath of life to each person

---

[283] Psalm 139:13

[284] Theodicy: Theodicy is an apologetic defence—justification of a deity, especially regarding the presence of evil and suffering in this world, particularly a work of discourse justifying the ways of God. A fuller discussion of theodicy is found here: *https://www.gotquestions.org/theodicy.html*

[285] The Hebrew words for "spirit—breath—life" generally when used to donate spiritual life in man are - ruach - רוּחַ nefesh נֶפֶשׁ, - and this reference to 'breath of life,' neshama - נְשָׁמָה, - in Genesis 2:7 -

individually, that enlivens the material (physical) body of that human being "spiritually" and sustains that material body, while in union[286] with its spirituality, as the direct act of God.

But external factors of life—accidents, health, genetics, and environment—may bring a different outcome in the "mother's womb," or after birth, than that which was expected for that developing life. At times, there may be no apparent "motive" for these variations in neurological and physical—bodily development, in early or later life, which may lead to a disability in a person, and, in some cases, disabilities can be the result of illness or accident that occurs after the conception and birth of that child—person.

Nor is there a causality[287] that overrides God's gift of life. That is, the supreme gift of God is life itself. The gift of life in this world is in and of itself a miracle, but life in this world is flawed and even the "normative," those that are considered neurotypical in body and mind, are touched by life and circumstances often beyond their control. Nor is fatalism or introspection an answer to this vexing question. It is our current "external" superficial concept of "beauty" that gets in the way and clouds the discussion on God's accountability in the creation of life. The beauty of life in the gift of that "spirit" that first establishes, enables, and then sustains life in a disabled person (Gen. 2:1; Job 12:10, 33:4) becomes overshadowed by what we, not God, define as being "beautifully and wonderfully made."

---

which do not contradict each other but present different aspects of the human "soul/spirit" as presented in scripture. However, nesama - נְשָׁמָה here in this initial giving of "life" to Adam represents the primal creative act of God in Genesis in forming "man" as a living being separate from the "animal" kingdom.

[286] The union of body and soul/spirit is a well-held view of life from early ages. Genesis 2:7 clearly states that it is only when the "breath of God" entered into the formed body that that body and spirit union became a living "creature"—that is, a human being (Gen. 2:7, Eccles. 12:7, 1 Cor. 6:17, 1 Thess. 5:23).

[287] Causality: The relationship between the cause of an action and the effect of that action upon an object, person, or event: the principle that everything has a cause.
https://dictionary.cambridge.org/dictionary/english/causality

It is when we define "beauty" from an anatomically "external" neurological viewpoint, as we currently use in today's society, rather than one of spirituality that the true beauty of those who live in the Shadow World fades into the distance. It is when their "spirituality" is no longer the primary definer of the quality of and beauty in their life that we begin to question—to blame God for creating something "fearfully and wonderfully made" that we, in our speculative—visualised and externalised manner, do not recognise or acknowledge as such.[288]

There is no concise answer to this question of accountability, and any attempts to apportion blame, or responsibility[289] on God, the parents, the environment, the accidental, or fate, etc., distracts us from the true beauty of that life itself, a beauty that is

---

[288] Please do not think me flippant or off-handed here, but I have friends who like and dislike certain car manufacturers intensely, namely Ford and Holden (GM). Sometimes it is a lot of fun; sometimes it is serious. I like many cars but prefer Ford, but I drive a Nissan X-Trail. Why? Because it accommodates our aging bodies getting in and out better. Our car manufacturer rivalry is similar to our debate on disability and beauty. Generally, we, and the world, prefer neurotypical people; we like to be around them. They think and act as we do and do not do strange things or respond in a manner that we might find confronting. That is, we prefer to be around Ford people; Holden people we find strange—different—even challenging, but they are still people, just like Ford people.

[289] Our definition of the word "responsible" today has a negative connotation of prosecutorial accountability that drives our world to a confrontational viewpoint such that when something "goes wrong," someone has to be held "accountable." In a world obsessed with perfecting the imperfect, there will always be a clash of ideals of what is perfect and acceptable, resulting in a constant push to achieve a world where nothing is poor, disabled, wrong, or faulty. Thus, the concept that if something goes "wrong", someone has to be held accountable and responsible for that failure often dictates what we consider "good or bad." Disabilities, accidental or at birth, often fall into this categorising, and beauty is redefined as what might—could have been for that person. If instead, we see—redefine "beauty" in a person—as their "spiritual" reality and not in their anatomical a-normative external attributes. If we "see" that every human being has a perfect 'spirit' from a "perfect" God, then the "beauty" of a disabled person is assured within their spirituality. Disability is not an issue in accountability as God has responsibly given them "perfect" beauty in their spirituality, separate from but existent within their anatomical/neurological disabilities in their life and experiences in this normative world.

internal and is independent of the body—vessel within which that fully human "spiritual being" lives and experiences life in this world.

What the question of theodicy, in relation to disability, really asks, as Charles Gourgey discusses in his paper "Faith, Despair and Disability," is "who has the despair," you, me, or the disabled person?

There might not be enough space here to fully answer this question, but *do* we know that the disabled person, in the case of one severely compromised with moto-neuron and cognitive disabilities (Mary, for example), actually suffers despair? Or, in other words, put another way, do we transfer our despair at their "condition" from us to them in assuming that they experience, feel, or know the "same" despair that we feel or experience at their condition?

I realise that this may be seen as an anecdotal testimony, but Mary, in chapter 10, exhibits no visual or expressional signs of distress as such over her life situation[290], and, when you "learn her language," she clearly expresses the emotions of joy, sadness, annoyance, and love in the same manner as the normative child her age would do.

Conversely, it is also well evidenced that where some level of cognition is present in an interactive cortical[291] spiritual exchange,[292] and the disabled person is unable to articulate

---

[290] Mary enjoys life; she does not seem concerned about not going to university, being a space astronaut, a doctor, or a mother. Mary experiences life, joy, and sadness and has very "visible" moods that every child (now a young woman) her age would—could—experience. She does not seem to be distressed over lost opportunities or missed experiences. It seems that her life is more relaxed than mine as I struggle daily with the pressures of life.

[291] Cortical "cortex": In layman's terms, the "general exchange" of information within the human brain where sensory, motor, and perceptional life experiences are received, organised, and language is formed in response. See: *https://www.thoughtco.com/anatomy-of-the-brain-cerebral-cortex-373217* See also: *https://en.wikipedia.org/wiki/Cell_cortex*

[292] "interactive cortical spiritual exchange" A new study area in metaphysics on the interface between the "spiritual" and the physical (material) cortex in the human brain. Lisa Miller, Iris M. Balodis, Clayton H. McClintock, Jiansong Xu, Cheryl M. Lacadie, Rajita

(neurologically) their spiritual experiences and "feelings" as such, then some level of despair may be experienced and exist within the life of the disabled person.

Barbara Barnum writes in her paper "Spirituality in Nursing," speaking of the cycle of disability, loss, and despair, that despair itself, in the life of our disabled person, may have a profound purpose:

> In what way does spirituality contribute in such situations? Are these the exact situations that might turn a person towards the spiritual?

Our propensity to see the negative in disability, as one of the "bad things" (just watch the daily news broadcasts) that happens in life, often clouds the positive that may result from the disability. If we take a more composite view of "happiness," including the internal beauty of a person rather than just the external observable normative (neurotypical) view of happiness, we may see the true hope in disability and not despair.

This does not diminish the sadness we might feel, or distress we experience, at the discovery of a disability in a loved one, but it does give us the opportunity to see the good that may come from the discovery of that disability, a desire to understand what life is, and a new way of defining life that is not based on our normative externalised—visualised models.

It is in this context while acknowledging that despair is often associated with disability and its discovery that we are here, in this question of theodicy, given the opportunity to look again at disability through the eyes of faith and see the attractiveness of their "inner" spiritual being, and that we view them, not overlooking or dismissing the pain and suffering that disability may bring to them or their family, as people "fearfully and wonderfully made," rejoicing in the personal "beauty" of their humanity, in their inner—spirituality "being," a beauty not limited or defined by their disability or our preconceptions of what defines beauty.

Sinha, Marc N. Potenza: Neural Correlates of Personalized Spiritual Experiences; Cerebral Cortex, June 2019;29: 2331–2338 doi: 10.1093/cercor/bhy102

But does this make God responsible for that disability?

As stated earlier, the question of God's accountability asks an underlining query as to why we ask this question. If God is sovereign over the earth and its creatures, which He is, then we could see accountability as a direct respondent, but this does not account for the other attributes of God, namely His grace and love.

Charles Gourgey writes, in his paper "Faith, Despair and Disability," an apologetic note, that we should take notice of here.

> "If God is love, then God can neither will the existence of evil nor wish to inflict pain."[293]

This goes part of the way in answering our question, is God accountable as the source of the disability, and any associated pain and distress in the life of our loved disabled one, or family member, or friend?

Charles continues to write:

> Nevertheless, something in the nature of love itself requires the existence of pain in order to effect its realization.

God is a God of grace and love (1 John 4:16), grace and love that can overcome and transcend whatever disability your child, spouse, friend, or family member may have or endure daily, for God himself identified with human limitations[294], pain, and suffering in His Son, Jesus Christ at Calvary.

---

[293] Charles Gourgey, "Faith, Despair and Disability," Journal of Religion in Disability and Rehabilitation 1, no. 3 (1994): 51–63.
https://www.tandfonline.com/doi/abs/10.1300/J445V01N03_07
http://www.judeochristianity.com/disabled/faith.htm Charles Gourgey's paper, "Faith, Despair and Disability", is a good read on the topic of disability and faith, realigning our assessment of disability and the people who live with disabilities.

[294] Often forgotten in this debate of theodicy are the first fourteen verses of the Gospel of John, where we read—learn that the divine nature of Jesus Christ (the Word) was pre-existent, with GOD, with no material limitations upon his person. In becoming man, in Bethlehem, the Word first experienced the severe limitations of the human body and its need for daily sustenance, sleep, and movement.

Charles writes further:

> There is a deep mystery involved in the question of God and suffering which the usual form of the question of theodicy totally obscures. The New Testament theology of the cross teaches that in some mysterious way, pain and God are connected.

This connection between God and pain is critical if we are to grasp the issues of theodicy and understand better the deep issues of faith and spirituality that exist in the Shadow World of the disabled. In the life of Jesus Christ, God became "personally" acquainted with humanity and suffering, observed disabilities, and experienced how they impacted on His creatures, as He, Christ, walked the streets of Roman Palestine.

As Charles Gourgey writes on the subject of theodicy:

> What the question really asks for is the possibility of a faith that resists despair. It is the need to resist despair, rather than abstract speculation about God, that drives us to ask the question of theodicy. Thus, to address the question properly we need not to advance theories about God, but to look into the possibilities of faith under extreme conditions.

Ultimately, your disabled child, spouse, friend, or loved one is fully human, "fearfully and wonderfully made," in the image of God with all the wonder and beauty that that image entails, including the ability to believe, love, fellowship, and have faith in God.

So, is God responsible for that disability your child, family member, or friend suffers from? The up-front answer then is no, God is not responsible for the disability in your family member, but He is responsible, as the giver of life, for that spiritual gift of life that defines your child, family member, or friend as a person, "fearfully and wonderfully made."

In fact, you could say that the (pre-existent) Word, Himself, became, in a sense, disabled!

See also: Nancy Eiesland, *The Disabled God: Toward a Liberatory Theology of Disability*. Nashville: Abingdon Press, 1994. Cited, 11/07/2018.

This is comforting, in a positive way, and we can go forward in the knowledge that our loved one, friend, or family member is primarily and always will be a beautiful human being, wonderfully made in the image of God. Whatever the disability a person has, the "beauty" of their being is a reality.

It is God, through the Holy Spirit, who brings to the disabled person new life and hope in this world in which they live, and the hope of eternal life that they will, one day, receive a new heavenly body complete without any defect, perfected and eternal, "fearfully and wonderfully made" in every aspect.

> Now we know that if the earthly tent we live in is destroyed, we have a building from God, an eternal house in heaven, not built by human hands. Meanwhile we groan, longing to be clothed with our heavenly dwelling, because when we are clothed, we will not be found naked. For while we are in this tent, we groan and are burdened, because we do not wish to be unclothed but to be clothed with our heavenly dwelling, so that what is mortal may be swallowed up by life. (2 Cor. 5:1–7)

For those who live in the Shadow World, it is ultimately their spirituality that defines their beauty and not the preconceptions that are frequently associated with their disabilities.

The problem is that more by default rather than intent we are prone to transfer the characteristics of the disability of a person, particularly of those with cognitive—sensory—psychological—and illocutionary disabilities, onto their "spirituality," a sort of transference, as it were, whereby we create a corresponding disability in their spirit/soul, spirituality, as a visual (if not mental) manifestation of the nature of their disabilities that we assume affects their very "being," and therefore they who are disabled in body and mind then also become the "disabled in spirit."

This is not the case!

Although the spirituality of a person may be, in a sense, impaired in its expressional cognizance, by the limitations of the biological human temporal (earthly) body in which it (that spirit/soul) currently lives, their intrinsic being, their "personal" spiritual identity, as a human being, remains untouched.

Yes, the spiritual interfaces with the temporal (the material body) and the temporal with the spiritual, but there is a boundary that separates them as individual realities. The temporal (material body) does not become spiritual, and the spiritual does not become temporal, yet in the mystery of life—of "being"—they are intra-dependent upon each other for their "temporal" existence in this world. Nor does this intra-dependence mean homogenisation, for each has its distinct properties in order to fulfill its purpose and function in one's physical existence "being"—self—reality in this world.

The material body exists, the spirit/soul exists, and both, essential for life here, are fearfully and wonderfully made by God in a union that brings to that human being, person, a unique existence—"an awareness of being"—and a sense of oneself who belongs in this world.

As Barbara Barnum writes:

> That is, Spirituality refers to meaning, direction, purpose, and connectedness with the sacred. Spirituality is internal, affective, spontaneous and private.

If we can take—or make—this mental step in our minds and change our viewpoint on the disabled, seeing them anew, apart from their disabilities, which we do not deny are at times grievous, we can grasp that they are in fact "fearfully and wonderfully made" with all the potential to experience God from their side of the fence in ways that are often beyond description and out of this world.

> For you formed my inward parts, you knitted me together in my mother's womb. I praise you, for I am fearfully and wonderfully made. Wonderful are your works, my soul knows it very well. My frame was not hidden from you, when I was being made in secret, intricately woven in the depths of the earth. Your eyes saw my unformed substance; in your book were written, every one of them,

the days that were formed for me, when as yet there was none of them. (Ps. 139:13–16)

In our verse in Psalm 139 above, which started our discussion on disability, God, and theodicy, King David uses very direct language.

Here, in Psalm 139 David is utterly convinced that prior to his birth, even before any ability or disability that he may have had could be identified or experienced, that he was "fearfully and wonderfully" made.

David's sublime rendition of the sovereignty and grace of God in his "forming" allows us to see a connected God, not one who is disinterested or disconnected from our daily life but one who is intricately involved in our lives for our good.

Looking beyond the shadows, then, we can agree that all, disabled and enabled, *are* "fearfully and wonderfully made" by a good and gracious God.

And the Shadow World is a real place where real people live, albeit at times on a different dimension to ours, but fully human nonetheless "fearfully and wonderfully made" with desires, needs, aspirations and hopes, which all born of Adam might feel and express daily.

Ultimately, the reality and existence of faith in the world of disability brings us back to God in faith and causes us to rely upon Him in that place where we often cannot go, into the Shadow World of our loved ones.

GRACE IN THE SHADOW WORLD

As I come toward the conclusion of this paper, I feel rather inadequate, humbled by the knowledge that although I may have been given a neurotypical existence here in this world I, like all born from Adam whatever our ontological or neurodiversity, am also saved by the same grace as are my brothers and sisters living in the Shadow World, and this all to the praise of God's grace and love upon us all.

The concept of grace in the face of disability seems at first to be a contradiction in terms. Surely if grace from God is real, then no one should be born, or become, disabled.

The Apostle Paul has much to say about this question. The apostle himself was once blind, Acts 9:8–9[295], and lived, served, and worshipped God with a disability in his body (2 Corinthians 12:7–9). There is much speculation about what this disability was, but Paul experienced this disability for all of his life (2 Cor. 12:8). However, Paul's disability did not detract from his understanding of God's grace in his life.

> But because of his great love for us, God, who is rich in mercy, made us alive with Christ even when we were dead in transgressions—it is by grace you have been saved. (Eph. 2:4–5)

Faith, as we have established, exists and is real in the spiritual and personal lives of those who live in both worlds, in the Shadow World and the neurotypical world, where faith as a gift from God through grace is experienced and known by all who believe through the love of God who made us.

Our discussion on "theodicy" above has answered many of the vexing questions and challenges of grace and disability; however, we need to add here that God brings life and faith as a gift, into both worlds, theirs, and ours, as there is no earning of "faith," or biological-neurological condition contingent upon its gift.

Faith is a free gift from God!

> For it is by grace you have been saved, through faith—and this not from yourselves, it is the gift of God. (Eph._2:8)

The discussion on this verse in Ephesians usually centers around which noun, grace or faith, the phrase "gift of God" is referring to here. Is it grace or faith? Grammatically, the correct answer is both, which is difficult, I admit, but faith as a gift from God is the individual result of His grace upon that person, as that

---

[295] Acts 9:8–9: "Saul rose from the ground, and although his eyes were opened, he saw nothing. So, they led him by the hand and brought him into Damascus. And for three days, he was without sight, and neither ate nor drank." OliveTree, Ver. 7.7.8., ESV Bible. Used with permission.

act of love through which He brings the gift of faith and salvation into the life and being of all who believe.[296]

Not only are all who are saved by grace fully saved, but they are also included in the family of God, whatever their anatomical or neurological-psychological profile or abilities or disabilities are in this world.

> And you also were included in Christ when you heard the word of truth, the gospel of your salvation. Having believed, you were marked in him with a seal, the promised Holy Spirit, who is a deposit guaranteeing our inheritance until the redemption of those who are God's possession to the praise of his glory. (Eph. 1:13–14)

It is also through this faith, this spiritual gift from God, that we can identify with those who live in the Shadow World, whatever their neurological and/or physical impairments may be, sharing with them that faith which they have in their spirit/soul—"being" within the body of Christ (Eph. 4:5–6) here on earth.

> For we are God's workmanship, created in Christ Jesus to do good works, which God prepared in advance for us to do. (Eph. 2:10)

Faith in the Shadow World is ultimately a product of the grace and love of God.

HOPE IN THE SHADOW WORLD

You may have noticed throughout this book that I have not made much mention of this—the love of God—for those who live in the Shadow World of disability. This has not been a deliberate oversight on my part, but my decision to establish the reality of the spirituality of their being, the fact of the veracity of their faith within that spirituality—in their inner being—within the life of the

---

[296] John Mark Ministries: *http://www.jmm.org.au/articles/3769.htm* Cited, 19/05/2021. Quoting William Barclay: The Apostle Paul wrote: "For it is to grace that you owe your salvation through faith. The whole process comes from nothing we have done or could do; it is God's gift. Any achievement of ours is ruled out to make it impossible for anyone to boast." (Eph. 2:8–9) William Barclay, Daily Bible Study Commentary (Westminster Press: Philadelphia, 2006)

disabled has taken precedence in this work to this point as the foundation of the authenticity of their beauty and life before God.

I believe emphatically that God both loves and cares for those who live in the Shadow World of disability equally as He does for all his children, and I need to state firmly that I also believe God's love for them is great, greater than any disability or impairment that they may have, suffer from, or endure in the Shadow World (Rom. 8:35–39.[297]

Apostle John reminds us of the impactedness of this love of God upon mankind whatever world one of His children lives in at this point in time.

> How great is the love the Father has lavished on us, that we should be called children of God! And that is what we are! (1 John 3:1–2)

Not only that, but the love of God remains within them and unites us to them and them to us in Himself as part of the family of God.

> And so we know and rely on the love God has for us. God is love. Whoever lives in love lives in God, and God in him. (1 John 4:16–17)

As is so often the case, when we encounter someone who lives in the Shadow World, rather than seeking to engage with them, meaningfully, in their language" and dealing with the issues of God, "love" and faith in their context, we often drop a standard Bible verse like "God is love" and bolt for the door. Rather than work through the issues of comprehending and actualising faith in a way that is uplifting and meaningful to them, so that they may experience hope and the love of God in each and every day, we often avoid the words "the love of God" in our conversation with, about, or to them.

Nor am I evading the question of God, love, and disability that frequently arises in discussions on and about disability in our

---

[297] "For I am sure that neither death nor life, nor angels nor rulers, nor things present nor things to come, nor powers, nor height nor depth, nor anything else in all creation, will be able to separate us from the love of God in Christ Jesus our Lord." (Rom. 8:38–39). OliveTree, Ver. 7.7.8, ESV Bible. Used with permission.

world, but rather I want us to consider how we can bring hope and the love of God to those who live in the Shadow World.

I have also, in our text—discussion—here avoided those Bible texts that are so often used as a type of soothing lotion or remedy for the disabled whom we sometimes refer to as those "pour souls" (sic), and in an unintentional manner commiserate with those who care for and love those who live in the Shadow World; verses like Jesus with the children at Judea (Mark 10:13–15, Matt. 19:13), or verses like Matthew 18:14, "that no little one should be lost."

> Then were there brought unto him little children, that he should put his hands on them, and pray: and the disciples rebuked them. But Jesus said, "Suffer the little children, and forbid them not, to come unto me: for of such is the kingdom of heaven." (Matt. 19:13–14)

This is not because I believe that they are irrelevant to our topic, but because I believe that such verses tend to steer us away from the deeper issues of disability, faith, hope, and salvation that confront parents, family, and friends of the disabled who seek a deeper understanding of God's love and grace upon their disabled child or family member and them, themselves, as caregivers.

It is important for us, as families and friends, to understand that their disabled family member, friend, or loved one is not outside the limits of God's grace and love. But here, in order to bring hope to all, I would rather speak of the disabled person's ability to spiritually respond to God's acts of grace and love upon them in a manner that we would recognise and accept in our neurotypical world.

The Apostle Paul, in Romans chapter 8 writes:

> For I am convinced that neither death nor life, neither angels nor demons, neither the present nor the future, nor any powers, neither height nor depth, nor anything else in all creation, will be able to separate us from the love of God that is in Christ Jesus our Lord. (Rom. 8:38–39)

It might seem a little stretched here, but I believe that Paul's words, "nor anything else in all creation," are relevant to our discussion. They help us to see that whatever life presents to us as parents, family, and friends of the disabled that God's love reaches to the ends of the earth, transcending disability invading and pervading the Shadow World bringing light, faith, life, joy and hope in the face of despair and lossness.[298]

Charles Gourgey says:

> Perhaps to Paul's list of "rulers" and "powers" we may also add the most devastating forms of disability.

Disability, which in many cases can be compound, brings with it its own set of issues and limitations upon the human body-soul/spirit-mind continuum, and it is essential that we understand here that these limitations and impairments cannot suppress or limit the love of God for His children whatever their life situation. It is to their families, friends, and caregivers that I say that God is not limited in His scope or ability to reach into the spiritual depths and innermost being of your disabled loved one or family member and bring joy, hope, love, and salvation.

The real issue is not whether this gracious and loving activity of God can or does, in fact, take place within the Shadow World, but rather that a conceptual limitation in our minds, from this side of the "fence," of its happening is more an issue of our neurotypical way of thinking—or mind-set which causes us to question—or doubt—the veracity of "faith" and the love of God for those who live in the Shadow World.

The truth and reality we need to engage with[299] instead is that the love of God can touch the heart-soul continuum, whatever the neurological or metaphysical dimension a person lives in, communicating with that spirit/soul within the disabled person,

---

[298] Lossness: A sense of hopelessness with sorrow for what might have been or was. See "Glossary" – lostness, page 270

[299] I worked through this paragraph with a friend as part of a morning discussion. We determined that while we accept, believe, and outwardly acknowledge that God's love and grace extend into the Shadow World, we don't often engage with disabled people there on a 'spiritual' level. For example, while walking through the plaza near my home, I often encounter disabled people with their caregivers or families going to the shopping centre. As much as I believe, accept, and acknowledge that these are 'spiritual' creatures, fully human, I still, on occasion, take a step back as they approach me. I know the reality of their spirituality, but I don't act like I do.

without any impediment, bringing faith, hope, joy, grace, and spiritual life to them now, and the certain hope of life eternal and the assured expectancy of a radiant new existence in and with God in the life to come (Eph. 1:13–14).

> In him you also, when you heard the word of truth, the gospel of your salvation, and believed in him, were sealed with the promised Holy Spirit, who is the guarantee of our inheritance until we acquire possession of it, to the praise of his glory. (Eph. 1:13)[300]

Also, there is nothing in the life and soul/spirit—"being"—of your disabled child, family member, or loved one that God is not intimately aware of. He is the God of love and grace, and His love and grace extends—reaches into the deepest regions of the life, both bodily and spiritually, of your loved one (Ps. 139:7–8).

In addition to the evidence of God's love and grace upon them, the disabled believer, by faith, brings an element of hope in the face of despair into their faith community. And it is in this hope, an essential element of faith, that they bring, as a spirituality of life, that that community needs and as such they, the disabled, contribute to the spirituality and worship life of that faith community. Without this hope and faith accepted and actualised, from within the Shadow World, made present and evidentiary within that faith community, then that faith community is spiritually the lesser.

George White writes in his paper "People with Disabilities in the Christian Community":

> "(2) each person with disabilities, no matter how severe, contributes (through faith) something essential to and for the body of Christ; (3) people with disabilities become the

---

[300] As mentioned, numerous times before regarding this verse, we need to get over the neurotypical idea that this verse in Ephesians is the prerogative of the volitional, cognitive, sentient neurotypical only; it is as relevant in the Shadow World as anywhere else in this universe of God.

paradigm for what it means to live in the power of God and to manifest the divine glory (p. 89)."[301]

This essential "spiritual" nature of faith is adequately read in Hebrews 11:2, where faith, hope, and conviction are embodied—personified in the worship life of our faith communities as evidence of the love and grace of God upon us all, enabled and disabled alike.

> Now faith is being sure of what we hope for and certain of what we do not see. This is what the ancients were commended for. By faith, we understand that the universe was formed at God's command, so that what is seen was not made out of what was visible. (Heb. 11:1-3)

Our concern in this book is that the current "neurotypical" "intellectualised"—confessional approach to faith takes and understands verse 1 in conjunction with the words following in verse 6, "without faith no man shall see God," from a neurotypical stance, and creates an artificial barrier for the disabled that never existed.

> And without faith it is impossible to please him, for whoever would draw near to God must believe that he exists and that he rewards those who seek him. (Heb. 11:6)

Our viewpoint here, confessionally, needs to change. We need to be able to accept that faith in God is established, primarily, as a spiritual[302] reality in the inner being—spirit/soul of a person, by the Holy Spirit (Eph. 1:13–14), outside any limitations of the body and mind that may exist within that person; and it is through this view of faith as a spiritual reality, in their inner being, that the disabled person actually experiences the reality of the hope, grace, mercy, and the love of God that that faith brings to them. In

---

[301] George White, "People with Disabilities in the Christian Community," *Journal of the Christian Institute on Disability* (*JCID*) 3, no.1, Spring/Summer 2014.

[302] Spiritual, in the sense of the definition of faith in this work, Faith is Spirit, and not just a connotation of new age thinking but a reality that is intrinsically embedded within the spirit/soul of a person and identifies them, uniquely, as a child of God.

encouraging faith in the life of the disabled, we need to remind ourselves of this, that faith, both spiritually and experientially, is a gift from God, a gift of love and grace.

There is no disability that the love of God cannot transcend or overcome.

ALL GOD'S CHILDREN BY FAITH

What is important is not to focus simply on the disability of a person, and how we "cope" with that disability, but to consider as important as anything else in our discussion the real "inner" person, their spiritual nature, which defines their true humanity, their beauty and being, as they live with us in our church fellowship, community, family, and social world.

With a new definition of their true "beauty" in mind, we still might find ourselves lost in a world of questions and concerns over accountability, either ours or God's, and a sense of loss, lost hope that the issues we face as caregivers, parents, and family members of those disabled, who live in the Shadow World, will continue to need to be addressed.

It is with this in mind that I now move on to some final—summary conclusions, but these in and of themselves are not the conclusion to this discussion; the discussion goes on until we are enabled, by grace, to receive these people into our lives, families, churches, and faith communities with all the respect and dignity that their true humanity in God requires.

There is no greater gift than a life of faith in God, in Jesus Christ, actualised and accepted with genuineness within our churches and faith communities, faith that is hope-giving and the basis for a never-ending continuing conversation essential for those who live in the Shadow World.

What we must not forget is that books, papers, and documents come and go, but the people we love who live in the Shadow World remain. What we need to recall from this discussion is that helping them live out their faith in the Shadow World is an important part of the culture and life of our churches and faith communities.

What we are all called to do is revisit our conceptions and a-priories[303] stepping into the Shadow World where faith and spirituality are intertwined in the life of our disabled loved one, family member, or friend.

JUST WINGS

To help us do this, let us consider the song "The Wind Beneath My Wings" [304]written in 1982 by Jeff Silbar and Larry Henley and sung, amongst others, by Bette Midler, which fits with our theme of living faith and hope in God in the Shadow World.

In the song, as Bette Midler sings, we discover that she thanks God for being the wind beneath her wings; that is, the one who lifts her up when she is falling, who picks her up from a low place and takes her to the heights of the sky to reach out and touch God, to experience joy and peace with God.

Who do we thank for the "wind" beneath the wings of our disabled child, brother, sister, relative, or friend, surely it is God? It is thought, as many have said, that Isaiah 40:29–31 is possibly the source of the theme of this song, and I quote it here.

> He gives strength to the weary and increases the power of the weak.[305] Even youths grow tired and weary, and young men stumble and fall; but those who hope in the LORD will renew their strength. They will soar on wings like eagles;

---

[303] Definition: a-priories; ideas—concepts—words we bring to a subject matter or discussion from life experience. See also, *https://www.oxfordify.com/meaning/a_priori* Cited, 25/08 /2021.

[304] © Title: *"The Wind Beneath My Wings,"* written by Jeff Silbar, Larry Henle, Lyrics © BMG Rights Management, Warner Chappell Music, Inc. 1989: [Woollomooloo, N.S.W.]: Warner Bros. Music Australia: Warner/Chappell Music [distributor], 1989.

[305] The Hebrew word יָעֵף ya`ep̱, translated here in the NIV84 version as "weak", gives a wrong impression in today's usage of the word "weak." However, it more means being disadvantaged by external causes, to be or grow weary, be fatigued, be faint, to be wearied; and be fatigued; figuratively, exhausted— faint, weary." *Isaiah 40:29–31*, Strongs Dictionary, e-Sword Ver. 4.5.01; - Cited, 25/01/2011; Bible Quote: OliveTree Bible+ Ver. 6.1.1; NIV – 1984. Cited, 11/01/2019.

they will run and not grow weary, they will walk and not be faint. (Isa. 40:29–31)

In aeronautical terms, to "fly," aircraft wings need "lift" to work properly as our diagram suggests. However, to gain that lift, they need thrust to move them forward through the air generating that lift needed as they pass through the air.

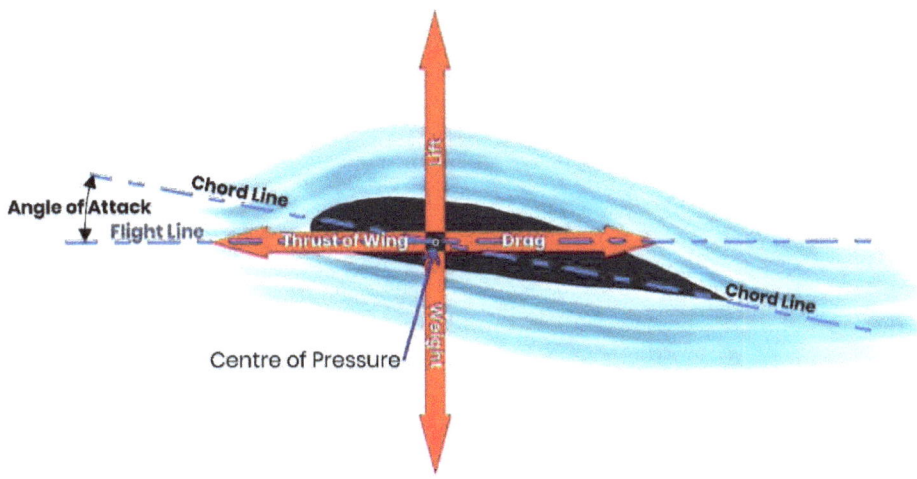

AIRCRAFT WING AERODYNAMICS

However, the weight of the aircraft (through gravity) continually seeks to pull the plane downward; its engines provide the thrust, and power to pass it through the air, and produce the "lift" needed to overcome the barrier of gravity and allow the plane to fly.

Wings are fragile things and have some serious limits. The wrong profile, shape, too great an angle of attack to the wind, and lift is lost, and the wing stalls; the plane stops flying even though

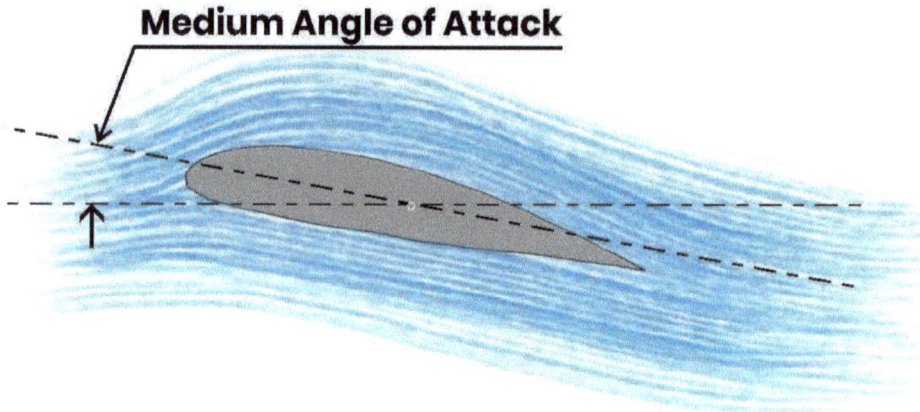

it might be moving forward. Aircraft usually maintain a 'low' angle of attack for safe flight.

For climbing after take-off aircraft can maintain a medium angle of attack to gain altitude and overcome obstacles that may be near the airport from which the aircraft is taking off.

On occasions, due to weather conditions, aircraft systems mall-function, or pilot error, an aircraft might experience an excessive angle of attack.

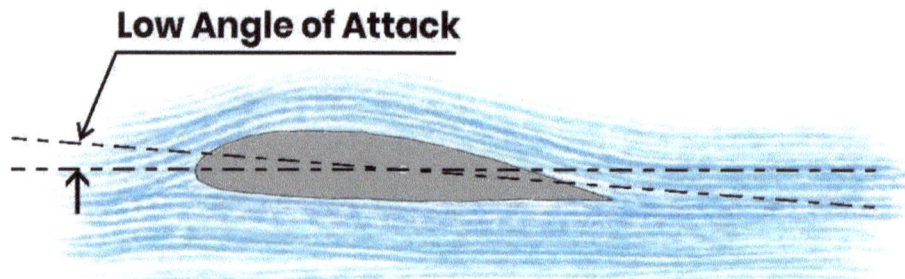

The angle of attack, as well as loss of thrust (forward movement), are the main causes of what is called an aerodynamic "stall." We might think that we are moving forward in our debate on faith and disability, but there is a danger that if we do not break through the barrier, the "fence," of our misconceptions about faith and disability in our faith communities, we might stall.

We might feel or be overwhelmed by the angle of attack of our subject matter and stall, or we might run out of thrust to move forward and deal with the issues of faith in the Shadow World. To both those who live in the Shadow World and those who love and care for them, from the other side of the fence, there is a Bible verse that brings us a ray of hope.

> No, in all these things we are more than conquerors through him who loved us. For I am sure that neither death nor life, nor angels nor rulers, nor things present nor things to come, nor powers, nor height nor depth, nor anything else in all creation, will be able to separate us from the love of God in Christ Jesus our Lord. (Rom. 8:37)

Yes, I am convinced that with God as our "thrust" and the correct angle of attack we can move forward and overcome any tendency to stall in our drive and desire to reach through the barrier of disability into the lives of those who live on the other side of the fence.

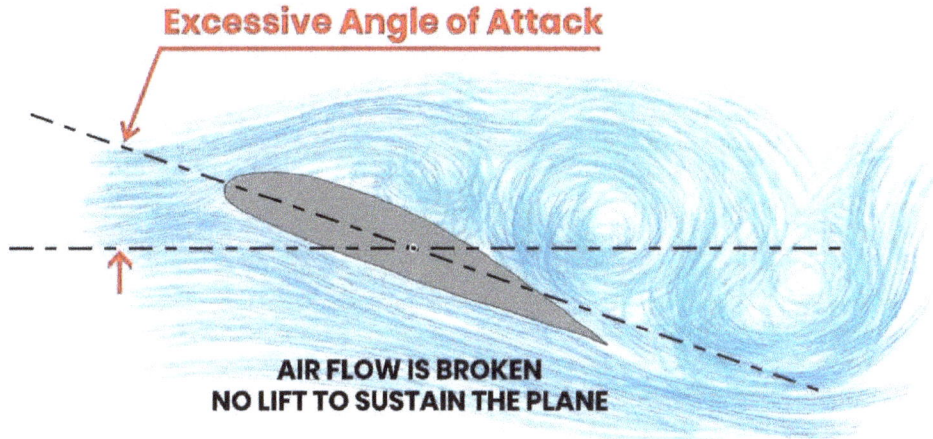

It is God, in whom faith is found, who provides the thrust to carry us forward and provides the "wind beneath their wings"—the *lift* that overcomes the gravity of our subject, on both sides of the fence, and it is His Spirit that gives us the thrust, drive, to go forward and see those who live in the Shadow World "soar to new heights" in their faith and experience of God.

Thus, the church of our Lord Jesus Christ, as the earthly representative of the heavenly reality on earth, should be the leader in providing opportunities for "all" people to connect with the Spirit of God. We may not fully understand how the Spirit connects with a person with mental or cognitive—neurological disabilities, but as the General Council of the Assemblies of God states:

> We must give opportunity for the Spirit of God to speak to such a person at their level of comprehension.[306]

Such opportunity requires us to be inclusive of the disabled and open to new methods of sharing and proclaiming the gospel of Jesus Christ within and without our faith communities. Bringing faith into the Shadows is, therefore, a gospel imperative (Rom. 10:14).

The General Council of the Assemblies of God council states further:

> People with disabilities are essential to the wholeness of the Faith Community. They are people created in the image of God possessing dignity, value and purpose.

It is with these thoughts in mind that we now move forward to our concluding arguments in support of our thesis, that faith in the Shadow World is an authentic reality and life experience for those who live there.

It is God who lifts them up above every disability and gives them wings to fly.

---

[306] © General Assemblies of God, USA: "Ministry to People with Disabilities: A Biblical Perspective," Assembly Paper, August 2000. para, 4. The General Council of the Assemblies of God, used with permission. *https://ag.org/Beliefs/Position-Papers/Ministry-to-People-with-Disabilities* Cited, 28/02/2017.

> He gives strength to the weary and increases the power of the weak. Even youths grow tired and weary, and young men stumble and fall; but those who hope in the LORD will renew their strength. They will soar on wings like eagles; they will run and not grow weary; they will walk and not be faint. (Isa. 40:29–31)

We have, by now, reached the conclusion that "faith" in the Shadows is a true reality and experience for the disabled, even in cases of severe neurological and biological disabilities; but what about the question of accountability, accountability in actualising that faith within their—our faith communities.

Chapter 12

Accountable Faith

In our journey into the Shadow World, one question remains, accountability. How do we establish accountability for a person so disabled that the normative manner of establishing accountability in statements of faith is not available to them in declaring their statement of faith? That is, how do we determine that they know what they know and that they understand this in relation to their statement of faith in God?

Let us review three main points in our book thus far.

Our chapter "Defining Being" clearly identifies the enlivening life-giving "breath of God"—as that fundamental spirituality that we gain from God, the spirit/soul of man, as that essential key element of life that defines us as human beings.

From our chapter "Defining Disability," we learn that disability may impair, or completely disable, communication with the outside world on the other side of the fence, but disability, whatever its composition on either side of the fence, cannot disable the integrity of the spiritual persona—being—of that person (that breath of God which defines human life, Genesis 2:7).

And, in our chapter "Defining Faith," I said:

> With regard to what we term as "salvic faith" in this book, that is, faith in Jesus Christ, there is no distinction or disjunction in its efficacy, character, and nature between that of an enabled person, here taken as the general neurotypical mass of humanity, and the disabled person living in the Shadow World. [307]

When we come to the concept of the "age of accountability," the age of reason—validation, maturity and understanding in

---

[307] See "Defining Faith," page 85, para 1

matters of faith accountability is more a question of experience, language and conversation. With some disabilities affecting "maturity" and intellectual development, we can find ourselves asking the question, can a person so disabled in normative—sentient reasoning (objectively or subjectively reasoned by us) and life "skills" give assent to the concepts and ideology of faith in God that is substantial and evidential?

I have to this point deliberately avoided the topic of the "age of accountability" in our discussion on faith and disability. This is not because of any particular sociological, theological, or doctrinal position I hold regarding the issue of accountability, but because I wished to establish the reality of *Faith in the Shadows* before I engaged with the difficult question of accountability—normativity; that is, do they know what they know, and how do we know that as fact.

Generally, the discussion on the term "age of accountability" in religious avowals is usually taken to be that period of time in one's life—or that age of personal maturity at which point—that person is judged to have sufficient cognitive, reasoning, and volitional skills to be able to make a self-aware substantive declaration of faith within their faith community or denominational fellowship.

In our brief inquiry into faith in the Shadow World of disability we have discovered, in our preceding chapters, that faith is essentially a spiritual "reality"—attribute;[308] that is, it is understood and known in the spiritual realm prior to, and above, its external evidence in the quantifiable world in which we live.[309]

On the other hand, if we say that a "confession of faith" is only comprehended in a neurotypical volitional manner and is "obligatorily" required for membership and inclusion in a faith community, usually at an "age of accountability" (maturity), then we may deny those living in the Shadow World of neurological and

---

[308] See "Defining of Faith," page 88, para 7; and "Actualising Faith," page 160, para 3

[309] The discussion of spiritual maturity is a complex subject. The "spirit" of a person, being a nonmaterial eternal entity, does not grow old, age or "mature" as a human body usually does. However, from a young boy to a man, Jesus "grew"—matured in His understanding and knowledge of God and man (Luke 2:40).

metaphysical disorders the ability to express, verify, and share their faith within their faith community.

This is an interesting point when we are assessing those who are disabled in cognitive reasoning and volitional skills; that is, where we might have concerns over their "age of accountability" in terms of normative maturity or questions that the disabled person may not be able to be assessed in neurotypical terms given the variety of disabilities, both neurological and psychological, that a disabled person may have.

While we seek to deal with the challenge of the age of accountability in our chapter here there is a range of disabilities that we acknowledge might deny those living in the Shadow World full cognitive, volition, and/or sentient ability commensurate within themselves, impairing them, as we may assess or see them, from attaining that "age of accountability" that we assume is essential within our liturgy and dogmatics that would otherwise enable them to express or actualise their faith, albeit in radically different ways[310] to our neurotypical viewpoint, within their, and our, faith communities.

In all who believe, whether they are capable of cognitive, sentient, volitional expression of belief or whether their current body-soul/spirit-mind continuum impairment brings challenges to us, limiting the acceptance of and actualisation of faith to our normative neurotypical protocols, for both them and us, places a further unseen disability upon the disabled person in the expression of their spirituality within their faith community.

We need to remind ourselves here that this perceived impasse of accountability, comprehension, and awareness for the disabled is only viewed from our side of the fence. On God's side of the fence, there is no fence or age of accountability or issues of comprehension and personal awareness of faith in the life, spirit/soul, of that disabled person (Ps. 139, Jer. 1:5).

The crucial issue of faith in the Shadow World, then, is not about their disability, or how its impairment may impact upon

---

[310] A term phrased by Susannah Mintz in "Disability Studies Quarterly 26, no. 3 (2006), "Ordinary Vessels: Disability Narrative and Representations of Faith," para 30 *http://www.dsq-sds.org/article/view/722/899*

their expression of that faith, but that their faith, whatever its composition, is first salvic, spiritual, real, true, personal, and experiential for those who live there.

The ability and willingness of God to overcome—to transcend any impairment—or barrier that may impinge upon the cognitive reality and life experience of a disabled person, in bringing that person to a point of faith and new life, is astounding!

John Swinton, in "Restoring the Image," writes:

> Scripture reveals God as unceasingly accommodating himself to human inadequacies throughout history, and ultimately in the Word becoming flesh, so also he accommodates himself to the communication of love to cognitively disabled people through loving relationships.

The real-life experience of Jesus Christ as a child adds a dimension to our argument for *Faith in the Shadows*.

In John 1:1, we are introduced to the eternal "Word," λόγος - logos, the Son of God, divine, eternal, unlimited, God in essence and reality. In John 1:14, we are introduced to the incarnate Word of God, Jesus Christ, (who became flesh, John 1:14), and we see the infinite becoming finite, the omnipotent becoming constrained, the omnipresent being restricted, the omniscient becoming limited (Luke 1:80; 2:40, 52) in the human sense, and we see Jesus growing in "wisdom and stature" of God, limited in part as it were to the material reality of life in this world, growing in knowledge, experiencing the human limitations of hunger, thirst, weariness, and all the implications of temporal life on this earth.[311]

Who, then, better than God himself in Christ Jesus who understood the limitations that come from human existence in this world whatever that context, to learn of the "human" spiritual

---

[311] Basically, the omnipotent, omniscient, omnipresent God in the incarnation of Jesus Christ became man. The freedoms and power of divine life He once experienced in eternity as the Logos were now bound in human form (John 1:1, 14). Although a fully enabled man, a perfect man, Jesus Christ, as the Son of God, experienced physical and human constraints we cannot imagine. Of course, this is the mystery of the incarnation and is an entirely new—different—discussion, but it must be noted here.

and material constraints whether they be anatomical or neurological, as is often the case, identifying with those living with disabilities in the Shadow World and thus becoming intimately aware of human limitations, both experientially and personally, to care for those who live in the Shadow World?

Therefore, to "concentrate" on the disability of a person alone, and the issues of accountability and cognizance that this may present to churches—faith communities—in accepting and actualising the faith of the disabled, misses an important element of Christ's victory at Calvary, which is to overcome the limitations of mortal human life, including anatomical human disabilities, and restore creation and man to the true image of God, spiritually, bringing salvation to all who will believe in Him whatever their neurological or metaphysical status may be.

Charles Gourgey, in Faith, Despair and Disability, comments on the disparity that often exists between perceptions of faith in the neurotypical world and the perception of faith and its experience for those who live in the Shadow World of disability. He writes:

> Having a disability can lead to the destruction of one's sense of life's meaning not because the disability in any way diminishes the intrinsic value of one's life. People with disabilities are often seen by mainstream [neurotypical] society as "other," in some marginal category, not whole, not fully human.

The Bible, correctly read and understood, presents a different view of disability and faith. In the Bible, the saving work of Jesus Christ is all-encompassing. It does not "work" in one way in the neurotypical normative world and in another way in the Shadow World of disabilities; it is uniquely transparent across all areas of life, for both the enabled and disabled alike.

In the article "Transcendent Love and Shrimp,"[312] the author quotes John Swinton's article, "Restoring the Image: Spirituality, Faith and Cognitive Disability," and makes the point that intellect

---

[312] Author unknown: "Transcendent Love and Shrimp." https://transcendere.wordpress.com/2009/10/11/transcendent-love-and-shrimp/

and cognitive abilities are not the essential elements of faith. Faith, says the author, is defined by God and is active, reactive, and interactive between God and the redeemed soul whatever the "state" or "level" of that soul's cognitive and intellectual abilities.

> Each person's faith journey takes different turns: while some may find fulfillment by intellectual studies of faith, those without that ability are just as valuable in the eyes of God. For the cognitively disabled then, the Holy Spirit is the primary channel of faith, and those like Forrest Gump can still form "authentic loving relationships which are not restrained or determined by the confines of intellect." (Swinton, 25)

Although the "language" of faith may be different in the Shadow World, the salvic effects of Christ's work at Calvary produces the same result in the life of all who receive faith from God, and this faith from God opens up for them and us a portal for acceptance, recognition, and accountability, in a spiritual sense, of faith in the Shadow World of disability that is real, salvic, and experiential.

The Apostle Paul makes an interesting opening comment regarding the nature of the pervasiveness of the love of God for his people in his letter to the Romans.

> No, in all these things we are more than conquerors through him who loved us. (Rom. 8:37)

Many are familiar, of course, with Romans 8:38–39 below; however, verse 37, which introduces Paul's thoughts in this passage, deserves mention as well. The image of "more than" gives us a sense of the completeness of Jesus's victory at Calvary, more explicitly. Not only was death conquered, but as Stephen Homcy, in "To Him Who Overcomes," writes, "we are winning a most glorious victory" over anything that could, or would, separate us from the love of God.

> For I am sure that neither death nor life, nor angels nor rulers, nor things present nor things to come, nor powers, nor height nor depth, nor anything else in all creation, will

be able to separate us from the love of God in Christ Jesus our Lord. (Rom. 8:38–39)

The words of the Apostle Paul, "for I am sure," echo here our statement that faith in the Shadow World is as real and relevant to the disabled person as it is to the normative person living on this side of the fence. The words "not able to separate us" cement the victory of Christ over everything that might impede God's grace overcoming the most complex disability in the life of a person and confirms to us the victory of that faith in Christ, as our thesis has demonstrated, and that although the normative expression of that faith may sometimes be impaired by their disability, of whatever composition it may be, that disability cannot, and will not, separate them from the love of God and His amazing gift of faith to them (Eph. 2:8).

Also, these verses in Romans chapter 8 hold hope for those who live in either world—the world of the neurotypical or the Shadow World of disability—that joy, hope, love, grace, faith, and a life in God overcomes any human condition.

Although a disabled person may have a range of disabilities that affects their experience of life in this world, essentially, at its core their spirituality, their "inner being" (spirit/soul) remains intrinsically whole and can respond to and intelligently (in a language all of its own) communicate, experience, and verify that gift of faith that exists within them in their spiritual interpersonal relationship with God.

Ultimately, then, accountability is first and foremost an issue between the person of faith and God. That is, as it is God who first generates that faith in the heart and mind (deposits that faith within the spirit/soul, Titus 3:4–7) and maintains that faith in the life of the person, in their spirit/soul (Eph. 1:13–14), and that person so saved is first accountable to God. What we call accountability is a human-generated dogma, and as valued as it is in the neurotypical world, does not, and cannot, rule over the acceptance of the faith of the disabled in God's world.

I would hope that we can see those who live in the Shadow World are fully human, fully spiritual *beings* just like us; defined not by their disability but rather their God-given spirituality and are no lesser recipients of God's grace and love than we (neurotypicals) are, and that they, in living the Shadow World, have objective factual salvic faith in Jesus Christ and can experience that faith in all its fullness.

And that everyone, enabled and disabled alike, who believes in Christ Jesus receives from God the same spiritual blessings both subjectively and objectively in the reality of their spirituality and "being."

> Praise be to the God and Father of our Lord Jesus Christ, who has blessed us in the heavenly realms with every spiritual blessing in Christ. (Eph. 1:3)[313]

I hope that we can see accountability in faith in a new light, the light of God's grace and love for those who live in the Shadow World of disability and engage with them on an accountable platform of grace and love learning of their faith and "language" enabling them to become a part of our church and faith community.

THREE BOTTLES

Before we move on to the next chapter in this book, I would like you to think for a moment of three bottles (we have added one from our last illustration).

As you can see, one is clear glass; the other two are made of colored glass. Each bottle contains a liquid that has been poured into them. You can easily see that there is a liquid in the clear bottle and just see something in the cloudy blue bottle, but the opaque blue bottle is a bit of a mystery, if, at all, it contains any liquid.

When we open the bottles and pour out the contents, into three separate clear glasses, we will discover that all three have the same-looking liquid inside them. If we take a step further and taste the liquid from the three bottles, we will find that all three bottles contain water, the same liquid in each. What does all this mean for *Faith in the Shadows*?

---

[313] The "us" in our verse here includes everyone who believes, whether enabled or disabled.

FAITH IN THE SHADOWS

THREE DIFFERENT BOTTLES

It means that if we are willing, prepared to look, to take the time to taste, to "see" into the life of people living in the "cloudy" and "opaque" blue bottles, in the Shadow World of disability, for a moment we will find that the same "spiritual" material (stuff) exists within the life of everyone that God has made, whatever "bottle" they live in (Gen. 2:7).

This same spiritual stuff that gives us our life, our distinctive existence as a human being—that is, the breath of God (Gen. 1:27, 2:7), in our neurotypical world, is the same spiritual stuff that gives life and being to those who live on the other side of the fence, in the Shadow World (of disability) in the cloudy and opaque bottles.

It is here in the Shadow World, in the world of our colored bottles, that these new dimensions of faith exist for the disabled. A new and exciting dimension in which they experience and actualise that same spirituality and experiential faith in their personal relationship with God as do those who live in a neurotypical world—that is, in the clear bottle.

Accountability for them, the disabled then, is the same as it is for us. The life-giving and sustaining work of the Holy Spirit (Eph. 1:13–14) within them bringing faith to them, in their inner being, establishes their accountability before God, an accountability that they display before us in their own unique language. It is our work to learn that language and be prepared to acknowledge their accountability before God in and through that language, whatever it might be, in order to engage with them and hear their conversation within our churches and faith communities.

It will take a lot of effort for us to realign our thinking on faith, disability, spirituality, and accountability, and may require a huge leap of faith for us to overcome the fence we have built around the disabled in our minds, in our dogma, doctrine, and liturgy within our faith communities in order to open the portal of grace and love to their inclusion.

In our conclusion to come, we take the first steps toward how we answer this question in practice, doctrine, dogma, and liturgy within our churches and faith communities.

CHAPTER 13

CONCLUSIONS

In the introduction to this book our opening thesis placed a question before us that we needed to answer.

"Is disability a barrier to faith in God?"[314]

I went on to expand this opening statement and ask the question with the following comment.

"That is, can a seriously compromised (disabled) person have the same joyful and fruitful faith relationship with God as a normal (enabled—neurotypical) person would have and experience?"[315]

In providing an answer to this question, we entered on a journey into the Shadow World of disability and discovered new concepts and ideas on faith that have both challenged and encouraged us to rethink our a-priories on life, disability, faith, God, and grace.

In doing so, we discovered that.

The Shadow World of disability is, at times, a place where customary liturgical and creedal practices used in our faith communities are often inoperative or at worst ineffectual. In the Shadow World, we need to learn a "new language" if we are to understand, recognise, and process the faith responses of those we love and care for. Particularly when their disabilities may prevent them from communicating or expressing their faith in a neurotypical, cognitive, vocal, volitional, sentient manner that we are accustomed to, or accept as a reality, in our world.

Have we then answered our question above?

---

[314] Our initial question in the "Introduction." See page 7, para 3
[315] See "Introduction," page 7, para 4

I would hope so, otherwise we have not progressed forward or learned from the discussion throughout this book that life, on both sides of the fence, is essentially the same, principally in spiritual matters where faith in God is involved.

Let us then, in conclusion, remind ourselves of the topics and arguments put forward to support our thesis that faith in life, essentially a spiritual reality, is identical in its knowledge of God, spiritual experience, and existential reality for those who live in the Shadow World as it is for those who live in the neurotypical world on this side of the fence.

We have looked at essential definitions of life, disability, and faith, redefining them in the light of our "being" as a spiritual person, while hopefully avoiding the cliché responses, either out of unawareness or discomfort, that we often give in association with the circumstances of a disabled person within that person's life, family, social networks, and faith communities.

We have discussed along the way that being disabled does not mean dis-abled in matters of faith, experience, and knowledge of God, that those who live in the Shadow World are real people with true spirituality in need of the same grace and love of God in their life just as you and I are.

We have learned a little about what it is like to live in the Shadow World, the isolation, the loneliness, and fears that can haunt that world and how we can, as a friend, or family member, or church, or faith community, embrace those who live in the Shadow World in our denominational life and fellowship, bringing new meaning to them of what it is to be a spiritual human being in the body of Christ on earth.

We have recognised that saving faith in God is a reality in the Shadow World, just as it is in ours, and that our approach to its veracity and place within our churches and faith communities has been challenged and hopefully changed.

Have we then supported our thesis with sufficient "evidence" that confirms its major proposition; that is, that the essential spirituality of the disabled person is not impaired by their anatomical and neurological-psychological disability/s, acknowledging that although disability can affect cognizance and expression, real salvic faith in God in their world, both objectively and experientially, remains untouched by their disabilities just as it does in ours?[316]

Yes: I believe so, and more than this, we have presented a new dynamic—added a new dimension to life for those who live in the Shadow World, a spiritual dimension that has lain dormant in the history of our churches and faith communities awaiting a fresh look at this topic of faith and spirituality in the Shadow World of disability.

FAITH IS SPIRIT

No longer is faith a synonym for intellect and knowledge; no longer is intellect a prerequisite of faith; no longer does knowledge alone define faith. Although knowledge is part of the faith experience, faith is redefined as primarily a spiritual reality, a gift from God to those who believe (Eph. 2:8–9).

---

[316] It may be surprising to you and me, but everyone is disabled in some sense—or form–no one has the "perfect" body or mind; we all lack some ability to excel above the average to perfection, and it is interesting that we, assuming that our neurotypical status (whatever its capacity) gives us a higher existence than a classified disabled person (a very subjective analysis), we regard ourselves as being nondisabled. Disability is a spectrum with a wide slider. It is only a matter of which end of the scale you are on that we determine whether you are officially classified with a disability. Moreover, note that all on the spectrum are fully human, fully spiritual, and capable of a complete and full 'spiritual' relationship with God.

Simply, in essence, faith is Spirit.[317]

We have discovered that spirituality and faith are inseparably linked in the Shadow World and define, for those who live there, a new dimension of what it means to be a human being on the spectrum of mankind.

Growing in faith then becomes a journey of hope, a journey whose destination is freedom and life in their inner "being," not yet fully attained in this life in the Shadow World of their disability but becomes a journey of promise to all who live in the Shadow World and believe in God.

But have we answered all the questions in Romans 10:9–10?

No. I say no because an important part of the answer to Romans 10:9–10 lies with you and me on this side of the fence. It is a fact that barriers to the acceptance of and belief in the veracity of faith in the life of a disabled person are not constructed by the disabled person but by our a-priories on this side of the fence as to what determines and verifies the existence of faith in the life of a person.[318]

Also, partly because we have not answered every question that arose in this debate to date or learned every language required to understand and verify that faith that exists within the disabled person living in the Shadow World.

Nor have we addressed at length the fob–off phrases like "She only has the mind of a five-year-old" or "only God knows those who have faith" which are often used out of fear of the Shadow World or unawareness of the crucial nature of this topic for those who live in the Shadow World.

Nor do these fob–off lines and phrases touch the reality and pain of those who live in the Shadow World or engage with the

---

[317] As mentioned before in this book, the capital 'S' is deliberate. See footnote 141, page 82

[318] We recall here our previous point that the disabled believer has no barrier to the veracity and reality of their faith which is known to them 'spiritually' through the work of the Holy Spirit. Faith, the deposit of the Holy Spirit, assures them of this, whatever their cognisance and neurological experience of that faith may be.

debate or struggles that they have with the issues associated with this subject but are a lazy man's way of dealing with a complex and emotive subject.

As Jody Plecas wrote to me:

> One aspect of this colourless, darkened, sometimes foggy, mysterious place is also an awesome overpowering fear of the unknown, from both sides of the fence.[319]

The challenge to us then is that this journey into the Shadow World should continue as long as that world exists, and we, on our side of the fence, need to overcome our fears and ignorance or lack of knowledge of what exists there and cross over into their Shadow World.

Yes. Yes, I do believe that this book has taken us part of the way at least, and, like that first journey of Captain Kirk and his Star Ship *Enterprise*,[320] going forward into an unknown universe, there is a lot more we need to do and discover if we are to include those who live in the Shadow World, lovingly, effectively, completely and compassionately within the spiritual and temporal life of our churches and faith communities.

In the interim, we can say that faith is a verifiable reality within the heart and soul of those who live in the Shadow World of disability, that those who believe in God there, in that world, experience true faith, and we, on our side of the fence, need to rediscover the beauty and grace of their life and faith within our families, relationships, and faith communities.

---

[319] Jody Plecas, email, 23/01/2015; in reply to her first reading, Jody commented on the original 2015 paper: "The descriptor Shadow World is magnificent and immediately understandable and is also completely understandable as being a place on the other side of a barrier or fence. One aspect of this colourless, darkened, sometimes foggy, mysterious place is also an awesome overpowering fear of the unknown, from both sides of the fence. Thank heavens there are people, like yourselves, who have created portals between the worlds, to sublimate those fears and offer hope. Thank you so much for sharing this with me."

[320] *Star Trek; The Original Series*, 1969—Gene Roddenberry - Hollywood, California, United States. © 2020 CBS Studios Inc. © 2020 CBS Television Distribution and CBS Interactive Inc. All rights reserved.

Humanity and the question of one's "being" is no longer a matter of externals, or of tangible (evaluated) outcomes and responses that we are familiar with in our neurotypical world, but "being"—that is, to be human, is essentially defined as a spiritual condition and is not dependent upon external forms or expressed realities but the internal spirituality of one's "soul/spirit," which is uniquely particular in each and every human being.

Faith has been redefined and is no longer tied to creedal—catechism or dogmatic knowledge (intellectualism) but is set free from the concepts of man and once again given its rightful identity as Spirit and given its place as the vehicle of God's grace, love, and salvic work for mankind (Ezek. 36:27, 37:14).

FAITH IS A SPIRIT ACT OF GOD

Faith, as a spiritual experience of God's grace and presence in the soul/spirit of man, is no longer tied to the "normative" of cognizance and intellectual knowledge and is equally valid on both sides of the fence, nor is its veracity dependent upon external expression, but faith exists in the internal reality of the presence of God in a person's spiritual life and "being."

Faith communities, whatever their denominational stance, historically have a somewhat checkered past and need to revisit the issues associated with faith and disability and establish programs and means of transcending the "language barriers" that disabilities so often present.

Although the Shadow World of disability is, at times, a place where customary liturgical and creedal practices commonly used in our faith communities are often inoperative or at worst ineffectual, appropriate language can be found if we are prepared to work at the issues of disability from a perspective of acceptance rather than skepticism.

It is in this Shadow World where issues of faith and disability frequently meet that we need to learn a "new language" so that we can understand, recognise, and process the faith responses of those whom we love and care for, particularly when their disabilities may prevent them from communicating or expressing their faith in a neurotypically "normal" intellectual manner that we are accustomed to in our world on this side of the fence.

I believe we have established, learned, and demonstrated, that faith is a matter of spirituality[321] and not established on some denominational-based religious—dogmatism with an intellectual declaration based purely on knowledge. At its core, faith is a spiritual reality, a gift from God that pervades every area of the life of the believer, from thoughts to emotions and knowledge, including one's experience of God, rather than some religious concept or idea tied to a system of established doctrine (Eph. 2:8–10).

We have established that there is no difference, essentiality, in the makeup of faith,[322] its content or effect on the spirit/soul of a person, on either side of the fence. That is, what is experienced and known of God by faith on both sides of the fence is the same.

Therefore, I believe that:

- denying the existence and veracity of faith in Jesus Christ in the spirit-soul-life of those who live in the Shadow World of disability, albeit though often unseen from our neurotypical viewpoint, denies those who live there their true spirituality and ultimately their true humanity.
- denying them the joy of actualising and expressing their faith within the fellowship life and practice of our churches and faith communities rejects the reality and existence of their faith and marginalises them as "lesser—than" human beings within that fellowship and the larger community.
- denying the reality of the existence of their faith can no longer be challenged, but to leave this "faith" unrecognised lessens the spirituality of and the

---

[321] We must carefully distinguish the term "spirituality," as used here in this book, from the new-age holistic-lifestyle approach to spirituality prevalent in this multireligious age. Spirituality, here in this book, is succinctly limited to our discussion on the essence, experience, and expression of one's "being"—the "spirit of life" given by God (Gen. 2:7) to each and every human being.

[322] Faith here is defined as 'salvic' faith in God, in Jesus Christ, as testified to and declared in Romans 10:8–11.

effectiveness of the body of Christ to which they belong.

Our journey into the shadowy world of complex needs disability in the search for faith has taken us to places where we might never think of going, and I hope we have a different aspect—view of faith, its reality, and veracity in the life of those who suffer from complex disabilities.

But more than this, I pray as we return to the other side of the "fence," we will not forget what we have learned on our journey into the Shadow World, where we have discovered that:

Disability is no barrier to faith in God in the Shadow World.

Our conclusion and answer, then, to the question of Faith and Disability in the Shadow World, is a resounding, yes! There, in these shadows, where we may not "see" clearly, their faith in God is real—salvic, experiential, and complete.

We can never compromise this position by appealing to human requirements , dogma, liturgy, and preconceptions about what life is like in the Shadow World.

Our position on this important topic should be to open a dialogue with the disabled, in their own language, if necessary, in order to be accepting and inclusive of their spiritual (faith) needs within our churches and faith communities.

Yes, there will be some difficulties to be overcome, but we approach this through the eyes of faith, faith in God who has placed faith in their heart as a "salvic" act and reality.

> For you are all children of God through faith in Christ Jesus. (NLT: Gal. 2:26)[323]

---

[323] © NLT: Tyndale House Publishers. 2004. Holy Bible: New Living Translation. Wheaton, Ill: Tyndale House Publishers.

Therefore, all who believe in God, on either side of the disability fence, are children of God by Faith.

ALL GOD'S CHILDREN IN FAITH

Where, then, do we go from here?

Chapter 14

Postscript: On Our Side

Just as every journey has a destination, similarly, every journey has a starting point!

My starting point on this journey, which has become this book, was the search for faith in the Shadow World of disability. This journey led me to discover the existence of a "fence," a fence of opinion and dogma that often—may exist between our "traditional" concepts of faith and disability and the spiritual "faith" and life of the disabled.

Others have joined me in this journey into the other side of this fence, into the Shadow World of disabilities, and together, along with you, my readers, we learned new concepts of disability, humanity, faith, and spirituality that we can apply to our understanding of disability, faith, spirituality, and life on the other side of the fence.

It is certain from these investigations, this journey, that never again will we be able to look at faith in the same way. Nor can we go back to the somewhat cryptic neurotypical definitions of faith that are based solely upon liturgical or dogmatic knowledge.

Faith, as defined here in this book, is intrinsically a spiritual identity—attribute. It is no longer a construct of words, dogma, intellectualism, and the ideas of men, but a spiritual gift—a dynamic spiritual reality given by God implanted within the spirit/soul of the believer by the Holy Spirit (Jer. 31:33, 40; Rom. 10:10).

Along the way we have also discussed the invisible nature of this "fence," a fence that often exists in our minds. It is this invisible—yet perceptually visible—fence that presents barriers for us in recognising, accepting, and actualising the faith statements of those who live in the Shadow World of disability.

We ask the questions, "How, did this 'fence' get built?" "Who built it?" And "what did they use to construct it?"

WHO BUILT THE FENCE?

Please do not be offended, or misunderstand what I am about to say, but being on this side of the fence, living in our neurotypical intellectually normative knowledge—driven world, comes with its own "brand" of disability that can go unnoticed (unseen). When we make normative evaluations and assessments concerning the spiritual life and "faith" of the disabled without considering "their language" it maybe we who are disabled, unable to "see" what their true reality is.

When we look over the fence into the Shadow World, and "see" visual and intellectual evidence of disabilities, that those who live there experience daily, we can make uninformed decisions—judgments.[324] Yet, do we pause to consider that our perceptions of what is actual—concrete, objective and real, for them on their side of the fence, is often a form of disability?

These preconceptions we have of what is real and tangible for them may frequently prohibit us from being able to accept the reality of their true "being," of their "perfected" faith (Heb. 10:14), and its resultant, personal (and intimate), relationship that they have with God, a relationship which exists in the life of all who believe in Him.

The Apostle Paul clearly articulates in his letter to the Hebrews.

Now faith is confidence in what we hope for and assurance about what we do not see. This is what the ancients were commended for. By faith, we understand that the universe was formed at God's command so that what is seen was not made out of what was visible (Heb. 11:1).

Do they hope in an assured manner? Yes!

---

[324] Yes, I know, it is another footnote; but do they, people with disabilities, "see" their disability as a disability? It is a valid question that has come to mind in this book's final chapter. Do we assume that they "feel" or "know" they are disabled, or does our definition of neurotypical normativity disable them in our mind? It is quite possible that they do not. My point is that life is normal to them, on their side of the fence, as it always has been. We are the ones who use the term disabled, and, ironically, in our evaluation of them, we too might become disabled.

Do they "see" with assurance what is not visually certain? Yes!

We can then say with certainty, from our study in this book, that faith lives in and is real in the Shadow World and transcends all disability for those impaired in mind and body.

In some ways (please don't misinterpret me here), the disabled, who live in the Shadow World may have greater "insight" and "faith" in God than we, living on the other side of the fence, do. Not in a dumbed-down simpleton style way like the earlier comment we noted (i.e., "she only has the mind of a five-year-old,") but, without the influence of neurotypical and biological senses—input that may lead to sinful actions, concepts, thoughts and ideas[325] in our materialistic and rationalistic world, the disabled living in the Shadow World may see and experience God solely from a spiritual viewpoint, in their inner being, without the impact of worldly external inhibitors on their faith.[326]

How differently I "look" at Hebrews 11:1 above, now that I have journeyed into the Shadow World of disabilities, into the other side of the "fence." Like the Apostle Paul, my preconceptions of religion, doctrine, creeds, liturgies, faith in God, what it means to believe, and what it is to be in a spiritual relationship with God, are rewritten. The old intellectualised cognitive models of "Faith" are rewritten, like Paul discarding his dogma of the synagogue and past ideologies, in the light of the revelation of true faith in God.

But whatever gain I had, I counted as loss for the sake of Christ. Indeed, I count everything as loss because of the surpassing worth of knowing Christ Jesus my Lord. (Phil. 3:7–8)

---

[325] Idea and Thought are words often confused regarding their meanings and connotations. The idea refers to a plan or a process that occurs in our mind about planning an activity, task, or duty. On the other hand, thought is a mental process in our mind about an 'idea' and often goes on unabated. This is the main difference between the two words, idea and thought. *https://www.differencebetween.com/difference-between-idea-and-vs-thought/*

[326] This does not dismiss or disassociate disability and sin, for all sin (Rom. 3:23); however, a blind person cannot be tempted by a sexualised image, or a deaf person by lurid music, etc.

So, what is the "fence" constructed with? Was it time, culture, society, tradition, disability, human pride, church dogma, polity, or "self"?

Its materials are intellectual prowess, dogma and ritual, polity, and practices that we have "invented" in order to rightly guard the door to church life, an essential, critical filtering process—but one that became, over time, a barrier that focused more on externals than internals, a process that satisfies our desire for knowledge rather than spirituality in faith.[327]

The answer to "who built this fence" is shockingly simple, and revealing; it is us, living in our neurotypical world, we built it!

THERE IS NO FENCE TO FAITH

Faith in God is a personal spiritual "Spirit to spirit" relational issue, a relationship that exists between a person's "spirit/soul," and God, who is Spirit. God, then, in giving us the gift of salvic faith, which we receive when we believe, gives us that deposit of the Holy Spirit that resides within our "spirit/soul—being" (Gen. 2:7, Ezek. 36:26, Rom. 8:16, Eph. 1:13–14, 2:6–8).

Being and faith are then both spiritual realities, and as God is Spirit, He defines both one's "being and faith" spiritually. As God transcends both worlds, the enabled and the disabled, what defines faith and being on our side of the fence has to be the same as that on the other side in the Shadow World—that is, "faith and being" are defined by God as spiritual realities in both worlds.

The verse below from the Gospel of John is the clearest on this issue.

> God is spirit, and those who worship him must worship in spirit and truth. (John 4:24)[328]

---

[327] "rightly guard": Sometimes bad things start out as good ideas. While I support 'guarding the door' to the church and communion, our process and propensity for the intellectual has placed the disabled at a disadvantage in actualising and participating in their faith community in a fully spiritual manner.,

[328] This does not negate the expression of worship in a neurotypical, biological, and neurological sense, but that faith is a "spirit" reality at its core. However, people disabled in biological and neurological function can still express the reality of that faith spiritually in whatever neurological and biological capacity they have.

Throughout our discussion, in hopping over the "fence', and back, have we have discovered, "faith" is transcendent of both worlds—the World of Shadows and the neurotypical world. Faith from God, as a spiritual reality, brings new dimensions to us of what it means "to be," to be "real," to be "human" in both worlds. Under this definition of faith, then, there is no fence between the disabled, you and I, and God.

WHERE FAITH IN GOD IS CONCERNED, THERE IS NO "FENCE."

Traveling back to our thirteen-year-old girl Mary[329] (now a young woman) who has never spoken an intelligible—audible word in her life, I am profoundly moved as I am certain[330] that this young girl, now a woman, knows and experiences God, by faith, in her spirit/soul—"being" in a profound spiritual manner that tells us all of the love of God for her.

With "Mary" there are no inhibitors in her life that "separate" her from God, from faith and the experience of that faith and her life in Him in a real and tangible manner.

There are no external influences of life, of human knowledge and experiences from the neurotypical side of life, that could cloud the issues of faith in the Shadow World.

Here, on this earth, Mary experiences "true" faith and joy in God every day of her life as we "see" in her diagram opposite.

This is a great challenge for us neurotypicals; and I feel lost for words to describe what I discovered on this journey. A young girl—woman totally compromised in normative communications has a resilient—vibrant life with God by Faith.

---

[329] See "Mary," page 180

[330] This objective reality came through learning her unique "language" and engaging with her and her parents in talking about faith, disability, grace, and God.

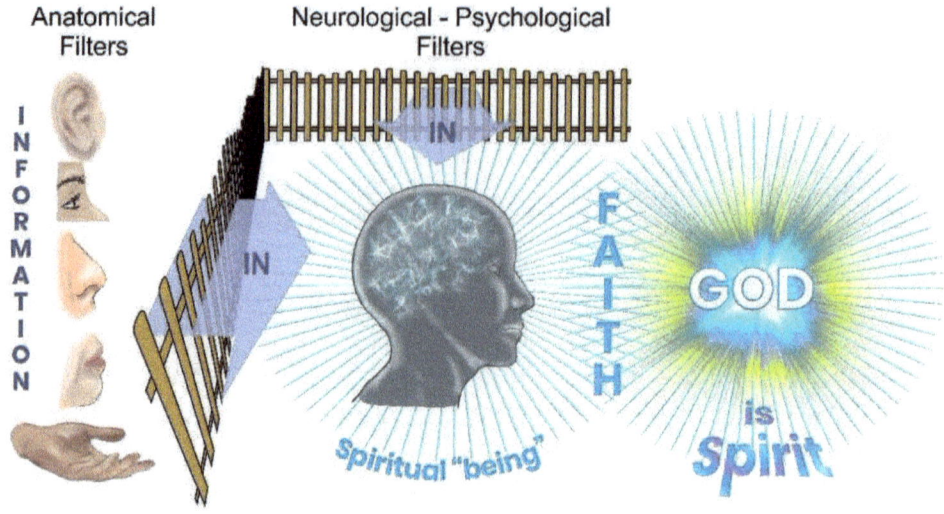

GOD, MARY, AND FAITH[331]

Faith has never been an issue of what we think or know about God; it has always been what God knows of us. With all our neurotypical cerebral powers in place—more or less—it is humbling to know, in a sense of mindfulness, that faith is essentially a spiritual issue between us and God.

A concluding statement pulls our discussion together and places a challenge before us, whichever side of the fence we live on

> Faith in God has, is, and always will be a matter of "spirit"—spirituality. Any other definition of faith is flawed, on both sides of the fence, for it dismisses God who is Spirit as the prime cause and facilitator of faith in those who believe, whatever "world" they live in, and marginalises the disabled whom we may perceive to be incapable of facilitating that faith.[332]

---

[331] Mary: Although we cannot communicate (normatively) with Mary in an everyday conversational sense, and she cannot communicate verbally (normatively) with us, we can get inside the fence and "communicate" with her "spiritually," using her language, just as God can and *does*!

[332] See "The Fence," page 18, para 2

REMOVING THE FENCE

It is essential then that we remove this fence, both the fence of our preconceived ideas about faith, disability, and religious dogma that inhibits inclusion[333] and embrace in the Spirit all who believe in God by faith, whatever their abilities or disabilities are in this present world. For, the enabled and disabled alike have the same universal source of spiritual life and faith from God that unites us all, over and beyond the fences that we may seem to construct in our fellowship and faith communities.

A "new language" of faith is required of us, in order for us to overcome our preconceptions and reliance upon the "seen," when we now know that faith is spiritual, "unseen" by the neurotypical "eye" (Heb. 11:1–2) and dwells within the hearts, minds, and spirit/soul of all who believe in Jesus Christ, on both sides of the perceived fence of disability.

A final concept diagram, adapted from Ms. Jody Plecas's comments, brings us to the conclusion that there is no fence, the fence to faith and inclusion exists only in the minds and attitudes of those who perceive that it exists.

Many good organisations and faith communities are working toward this goal, but it is in our everyday meetings, on the street, in our churches, in faith communities, on social occasions, and at family gatherings that we need to put into practice the things we have learned on our journey into and out of the Shadow World.[334]

This is the challenge presented to us here in this book, a challenge for us to go into all the world, the world of disability and "differentness" and bring the gospel of Jesus, the gospel of life, hope, and faith to all who live in the Shadow World (Matt. 28:16–28).

> Then the eleven disciples went to Galilee, to the mountain where Jesus had told them to go. When they saw him, they worshiped him; but some doubted. Then Jesus came to them and said, "All authority in heaven and on earth has been given to me.

---

[333] Here, I include the actualisation of faith statements and inclusion in the sacraments of our faith communities.

[334] Please see the Appendix for additional material and resources.

Therefore, go and make disciples of all nations, baptizing them in the name of the Father and of the Son and of the Holy Spirit, and teaching them to obey everything I have commanded you. And surely, I am with you always, to the very end of the age. (Matt. 28:16–20)

THERE IS NO FENCE

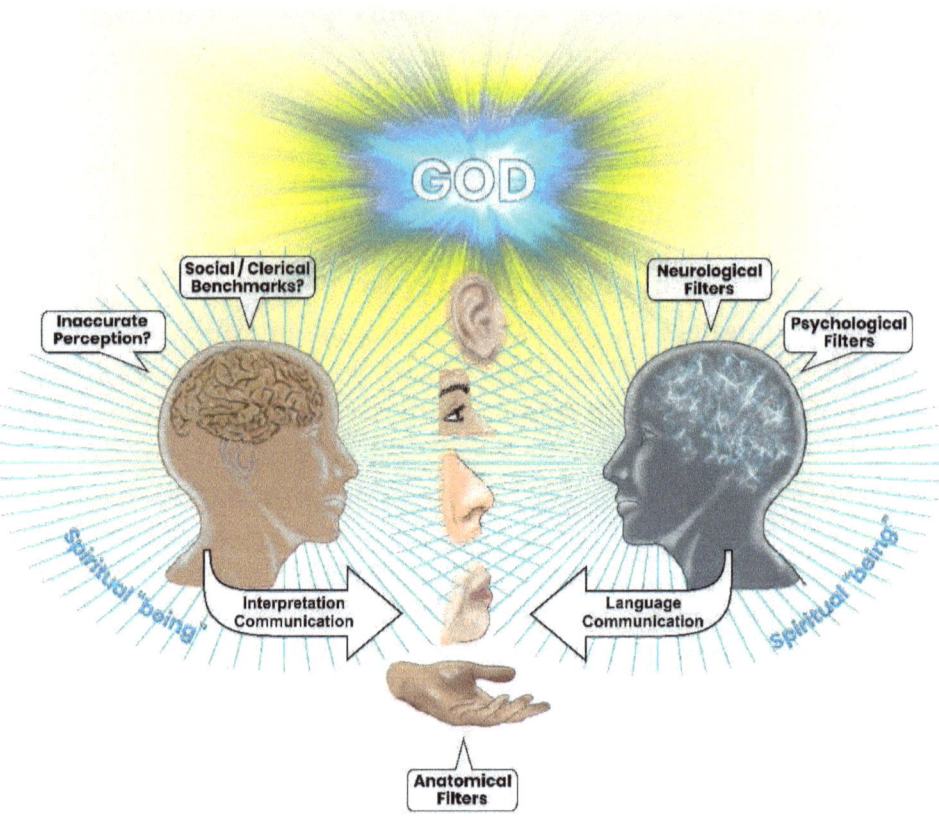

To this end, I dedicate this book.

God be praised.

KEITH HARRIS

BIBLIOGRAPHY

This bibliography does not follow the usual standard alphabetical listing format. It lists resources in the sequence in which they occur in the chapter in the book, and in the order in which they first occur within that chapter. My purpose in this format of bibliography is to provide a resource tool for those who wish to study and investigate faith and disability by theme in each chapter of the book.

Definitions and links to Internet sites follow after the bibliography and are listed in the sequential order in which they occur in this book.

INTRODUCTION

THE SHADOW WORLD

Rifkin, J. *The Emphatic Civilization: The Race to Global Consciousness in a World in Crisis*, (Polity Press: Cambridge, 2010)

Gaventa, W., Coulter D., Ed. *Spirituality and Intellectual Disability* (Routledge: New York, 2011) p 102 [Quoting Diane Burgent, *Come Let Us Go up to the Mountain of the Lord Isa. 2:3,* In Edward Foley, Ed., *Developmental Disabilities and Sacramental Access: New Paradigms for Sacramental Encounters* (Liturgical Press: Collegeville, 1994)

THE FENCE
No references cited.

A BRIEF HISTORY

Munyi, Wa. C. *Past and Present Perceptions Towards Disability: A Historical Perspective*, Disability Studies Quarterly, Vol 32, No 2 (2012) Munyi

Barnes, C. *Disabled People in Britain and Discrimination: A case for anti-discrimination legislation*, (C. Hurst: London, 1991), p13. Cited, 28/02/2017.

Thomas, D. *The Experience of Handicap* (Methuen: London, 1982)

Hanks, J, and Hanks, L. (1980) *"The Physically Handicapped in Certain Non-Occidental Societies"* in Phillips, W. and Rosenberg, J. ed., *Social Scientists and the Physically Handicapped*, (Arno Press: London, 1980)

Schipper, J. *Disability in the Hebrew Bible*, Society of Biblical Literature, *https://www.sbl-site.org/assets/pdfs/TBv2i8_SchipperDisability.pdf* :para 2.

Stiker, Henri-Jaques. *A History of Disability* (University of Michigan Press: Michigan, 2007) p-xi, 36, 69, 76, 180. Cited, 17/02/2017.

Gosbell, L. *The Poor, the Crippled and the Blind and the Lame: Physical and Sensory Disability in the Gospels of the New Testament*. (PhD Thesis Essay) Macquarie University, Department of Ancient History

Metzger, I. *Disability in the High Middle Ages* (Routledge: Abingdon, 2006) example, p50, 54

Miles, M. *Martin Luther and Childhood Disability in the 16th Century; Journal of Religion, Disability and Health*, Vol 5, 2001-Issue 4, p5–36.

Clapton, J., Fitzgerald, J. (1997) *New Renaissance magazine: The History of Disability: A History of 'Otherness'*. Vol 7, No 1. http://www.ru.org/artother.html

Clapton, J. (1996) *Disability, Inclusion and the Christian Church,* Paper Presented at Disability, Religion and Health Conference, Brisbane, October 18–20, 1996, Ibid, Conclusion, para 3.

White, G. *People with Disabilities in Christian Community; Journal of the Christian Institute on Disability* (JCID) Vol.3, No.1, Spring/Summer 2014, p14. Cited, 21/02/2017.

Clapton, J., Fitzgerald, J. *"The History of Disability: A History of Otherness,"* New Renaissance Magazine, Vol. 7 (1997): n.p. [Cited, 14 March 2014]. Online: *http://www.ru.org/human-rights/the-history-of-disability-a-history-of-otherness.html*

Plecas, J. *Review comments Email -* 09/03/2018 (attached see Appendix I), used with permission.

DEFINING BEING

Author Unknown; Philosophy of Spirituality: Article; About the Philosophy of Spirituality, *http://www.philosophy-of-spirituality.org/about-philosophy-of-spirituality.htm?i=1* Cited, 22/12/2106.

Hoekema, A. *Created in God's Image* (Eerdmans: Grand Rapids, 1986) p203ff

OliveTree Bible, Ver.6.0.21, NIV, Zondervan Grand Rapids, 1984

DEFINING DISABILITY

WHO, Disabilities; *https://www.who.int/topics/disabilities/en/*

Gourgey, C. *Faith, Despair and Disability*; Journal of Religion in Disability and Rehabilitation, Vol. 1, no. 3, (Haworth Press, 1994): 51–63,

Gabelein, F. E., Ed. *Expositors' Biblical Commentary*, OliveTree, Ver. 5.4.1, Mark 7:31–37,

World Health Organization, Geneva, *"Towards a Common Language for Functioning, Disability and Health ICF,"* https://www.who.int/classifications/icf/icfbeginnersguide.pdf

Schipper, J. *Disability in the Hebrew Bible*, Society of Biblical Literature, https://www.sbl-site.org/assets/pdfs/TBv2i8_SchipperDisability.pdf

Haenn, J. *Succeeding Together: People with Disabilities in the Workplace*, California State University, Northridge http://www.csun.edu/~sp20558/dis/physical.html

Gibson, B. California State University; *Fact Sheet on the EEOC's Final Regulations Implementing the ADAAA, Technical Letter, HR/EEO, 2011-05, Attachment A* http://www.calstate.edu/HRAdm/pdf2011/TL-EEO2011-05.pdf

Clifton, S. ABC: *Religion & Ethics; Disability and the Dark Side of the Positivity Myth*, http://www.abc.net.au/religion/articles/2014/09/18/4090190.htm

Achieve Australia; *What is Sensory Impairment?* http://achieveaustralia.org.au/people-we-support/what-is-sensory-impairment/

Ochsenbein, M. *Sensory Processing Disorder: It's Not ... Something You Outgrow*: Article listed at Star Institute, Centennial, Colorado. https://www.spdstar.org/node/1134

House With No Steps: *Sensory Disability*, http://www.hwns.com.au/Resource-centre/Types-of-disabilities/Sensory-disability

Doman R., Jr. *Neurodevelopmental Perspectives on Autism and Asperger's Syndrome*: Printed in the Autism Health and Wellness Magazine Volume 1 Issue 3—Autumn 2009. http://nacd.org/journal/0909_autism_spectrum.php

Mintz, S. *Ordinary Vessels; Disability Narrative and Representations of Faith*, Disability Studies Quarterly, Vol26, No 3 (2006)

Disability Services Australia, SENSORY PROBLEMS AND AUTISM *Sensory Integration Dysfunction*: http://www.whynotcare.org.au/wp-content/uploads/2013/08/Fact-sheet-sensory-disability.pdf

Miller, J. *Comorbid-sensory-integration-dysfunction*, Used with permission, Courtesy of the STAR Institute, https://www.spdstar.org/ Quoted from a paper presented at ABILITIESme Symposium & Conference, Abu Dhabi, Feb. 26th, 2015, Quoted in Synapse Fact Sheet, http://www.autism-help.org/comorbid-sensory-integration-dysfunction.htm

Thomas, C. *Cognitive Defects and Spiritual Development: The relationships between Cognitive Defects and Spiritual Development'* (Liberty University: Lynchburg, VA, 2008)

Ontario Brain Injury Association. "What is Acquired Brain Injury." Retrieved 5 March 2011. http://obia.ca/?option=com_content&view=category&layout=blog&id=31&Itemid=41

Rubinsztein, D. C. (October 2006). "The roles of intracellular protein-degradation pathways in neurodegeneration." Nature. 443 (7113): 780–6. Bibcode:2006Natur. 443..780R. doi:10.1038/nature05291. PMID 17051204 https://ui.adsabs.harvard.edu/abs/2006Natur.443.780R

Harris, J., Greenspan, S. "Definition *and Nature of Intellectual Disability*," Springer International Publishing Switzerland 2016 11; N.N. Singh (ed.), Handbook of Evidence-Based Practices in Intellectual and Developmental Disabilities, Evidence-Based Practices in Behavioral Health, DOI 10.1007/978-3-319-26583-4_2,

Monash University; *'Working with People with Intellectual Disability in Health Care'*, Centre for Developmental Disability Health Victoria; CDDH Fact Sheet
http://www.cddh.monash.org/assets/documents/working-with-people-with-intellectual-disabilities-in-health-care.pdf

Turner, S., Hatton, C., Shah, R., Stansfield, J., Rahim, N. Article {JAR:JAR192, *"Religious Expression amongst Adults with Intellectual Disabilities,* Journal of Applied Research in Intellectual Disabilities, V17:3, Blackwell Science Ltd, Issn: 1468-3148,
http://dx.doi.org/10.1111/j.1468-3148.2004.00192.x :p 161.

Plecas, J. Review comments Email - 09/03/2018 (attached see Appendix Part II), used with permission.

American Psychiatric Association: *Diagnostic and Statistical Manual of Mental Disorders, Fifth Edition.* Arlington, VA, American Psychiatric Association, 2013.

Trivedi, J. K. *Cognitive deficits in psychiatric disorders: Current status.* Indian Journal of Psychiatry 2006; 48(1): 10-20.doi:10.4103/0019-5545.31613.
http://www.ncbi.nlm.nih.gov/pmc/articles/PMC2913637/

Millan, M. J. *Cognitive dysfunction in psychiatric disorders: characteristics, causes and quest for improved therapy,* Nature Reviews, Volume 11, Feb 2012,
http://www.nature.com/nrd/journal/v11/n2/full/nrd3628.html

Hill, S. K., Bishop, J. R., Palumbo, D. & Sweeney, J. A. *Effect of second-generation antipsychotics on cognition: current issues and future challenges.* Expert Rev. Neurother, 10, 43–57 (2010).
http://www.ncbi.nlm.nih.gov/pubmed/20021320

Millan, M. J. *Multi-target strategies for the improved treatment of depressive states: conceptual foundations and neuronal substrates, drug discovery and therapeutic application.* Pharmacol. Ther.110 135–370 (2006)
http://www.ncbi.nlm.nih.gov/pubmed/16522330

Grohol, J. M. *The Differences Between Bipolar Disorder, Schizophrenia and Multiple Personality Disorder.*
http://psychcentral.com/lib/the-differences-between-bipolar-disorder-schizophrenia-and-multiple-personality-disorder/000633_p1

Cornah, D., Ed. *The Impact of Spirituality on Mental Health*; Quoting, from; Spirituality and Mental Health Care: Rediscovering a Forgotten Dimension; Swinton, J., Kingsley, J., 2001. ISBN 1-85302-804-5.
https://www.mentalhealth.org.uk/publications/impact-spirituality-mental-health

de Menezes, A., Jr., Moreira-Almeida, A. *Differential diagnosis between spiritual experiences and mental disorders of religious content,* Research Center in Spirituality and Health (NUPES) at Federal University of Juiz de Fora (UFJF), Brazil.

Hoeksema, T. *Protecting Religious Freedom: The Caregiver's Responsibility*; (Calvin College; Grand Rapids, 1994).
https://aaiddreligion.files.wordpress.com/2018/01/protecting-religious-freedom_0.pdf

Rizzolo, M. Council for Quality of Lile, article; *Personal Outcome Measures,* (PDF) https://www.c-q-l.org/wp-content/uploads/2020/03/2017-CQL-POM-Manual-Adults.pdf

Gourgey, C. *Faith, Despair, and Disability,* Journal of Religion in Disability and Rehabilitation Vol. 1, no. 3 (1994) http://www.judeochristianity.com/disabled/faith.htm

de Menezes, A. Jr., Moreira-Almeida, A. *Differential diagnosis between spiritual experiences and mental disorders of religious content,"* Research Center in Spirituality and Health (NUPES) at Federal University of Juiz de Fora (UFJF), Brazil.

Underwood, L. *A working Model of Health: Spirituality and Religiousness as Resources: Applications to Persons with disabilities*; Journal of Religion, Disability & Health, Vol. 3(3) 1999 E, 1999 by The Haworth Press, Inc.

Coulter, D. *Spirituality and Intellectual Disability: Recognition of Spirituality in Health Care: Personal and Universal Implications* (Routledge: New York, 2001)

J. Bishop. *Faith*, The Stanford Encyclopedia of Philosophy (Winter 2016 Edition), Edward N. Zalta (ed.), https://plato.stanford.edu/archives/win2016/entries/faith/

The American Heritage® *Dictionary of the English Language, Fourth Edition* copyright ©2000 by Houghton Mifflin Company. Updated in 2009. Published by Houghton Mifflin Company. All rights reserved. B. B. Collins English Dictionary—Complete and Unabridged © HarperCollins Publishers 1991, 1994, 1998, 2000, 2003

J. Crisp, C. Taylor (Ed.), *Potter & Perry's Fundamentals of Nursing*, (Elsevier: Chatswood, 2009)

Bishop, J. *Faith*, The Stanford Encyclopedia of Philosophy (Winter 2016 Edition), Edward N. Zalta (ed.), https://plato.stanford.edu/entries/faith/

Whitney, W. *The Roots, Verb-forms and Primary Derivatives of the Sanskrit Language (Breitkopf and Hartel: London, 1885)* p 111
http://www.wilbourhall.org/pdfs/rootsverbformspr00whitrich.pdf

Author Unknown, Centre for Systems Philosophy, *Philosophy of Spirituality*: © Centre for Systems Philosophy; http://www.philosophy-of-spirituality.org/about-philosophy-of-spirituality.htm?i=1

DEFINING FAITH

Bishop, J. *Believing by Faith: An Essay in the Epistemology and Ethics of Religious Belief,* Oxford: Clarendon Press, https://plato.stanford.edu/entries/faith/

DeRose, S.L. Bishop, J. *Believing by Faith: An Essay in the Epistemology of Religious Belief.* J Value Inquiry 44, 103–106 (2010). https://doi.org/10.1007/s10790-009-9186-4

Brown-Driver-Briggs *Hebrew and English Lexicon*, Unabridged, Electronic Database, Copyright © 2002, 2003, 2006 by Biblesoft, Inc.

J. I. Packer, "*Faith.*" Elwell W., ed., Evangelical Dictionary of Theology (Paternoster Press: Grand Rapids, 1995)

Helm, P, *John Calvin, the sensus divinitatis, and the noetic effects of sin,* International Journal for Philosophy of Religion, 43: 87–107, 1998

Elwell W., ed. Evangelical Dictionary of Biblical Theology: *Faith and Spirituality* (Paternoster Press: Grand Rapids, 1996)

Butterfield, G. *Doctrine of Faith and Prayer* (WestBow Press: Bloomington, 2012)

Smith, G. B., *The Christ of Faith and the Jesus of History*; Source: The American Journal of Theology, Vol. 18, No. 4 (Oct. 1914), pp. 521-445, Cited, 30/11/2014. *http://www.jstor.org/stable/pdfplus/3154962.pdf?acceptTC=true&jpdConfirm=true*

Fowler, J. *The Regeneration of Man; Christ In You Ministries, Regeneration is the restorational re-lifing of man spiritually with the life of God.* ©1998 by James A. Fowler. All rights reserved. *http://www.christinyou.net/pages/regoman.html*

Samuel, V. *God, Humanity and Disability, Transformation,* Vol 15, No. 4, 1998, pp15–17, JSTOR *http://www.jstor.org/stable/43053893*

Hull, J. *A Spirituality of Disability, The Christian Heritage as both Problem and Potential*; Studies in Christian Ethics, vol.16 no.2, 2003, pp. 21–35 *http://www.johnmhull.biz/A%20Spirituality%20of%20Disability1.htm*

Cagnoni, P. C. *Personhood, human brokenness and the therapeutic calling of the Eastern Orthodox Church: A Pastoral Approach to Mental Health issues and Disability*, Melbourne College of Divinity, Master's Thesis, August 2008

Ray, J. *Practical Theology: In Search of a Disabled God*, (Lulu Publishing, 2011)

Hutchinson, M. *Unity and Diversity in Spiritual Care,* *http://members.tripod.com/~Marg_Hutchison/nurse1.html*

Crisp, J., Taylor C. (Ed.) *Potter & Perry's Fundamentals of Nursing*, (Elsevier: Chatswood, 2009), p480. Quoting P.G. Reed, Spirituality and wellbeing in terminally ill hospitalised adults (Res Nurse Health: 10:335, 1987)

REALITY OF FAITH

Diamond, N. *'The Monkees, I'm a believer'*, Lyrics; © Colgrems Records. *http://en.wikipedia.org/wiki/I%27m_a_Believer*

Schuelka M. (2013) A faith in humanness: disability, religion and development, *Disability & Society* 28 no. 4, 500–513, DOI: 10.1080/09687599.2012.717880, Cited, 22/11/2014. *http://dx.doi.org/10.1080/09687599.2012.717880*

Coombs, M. *Spirituality and Mental Health Care*, Oxford Diocesan Health and Social Care Group, *http://www.oxford.anglican.org/wp-content/uploads/2013/01/Spirituality-and-Social-Care.pdf*

Allen, R. *Faith and Disability: Comfort, Confusion or Conflict?* University of Leeds, School of Sociology and Social Policy; Dissertation Sept 2010 *http://disability-studies.leeds.ac.uk/files/library/allen-RAllen-Dissertation-FINAL.pdf*

Clines, J. A. *The Image of God in Man;* Tyndale Old Testament Lecture (1967), Tyndale Bulletin (1968), 53–103 *https://legacy.tyndalehouse.com/tynbul/Library/TynBull_1968_19_03_Clines_ImageOfGodInMan.pdf*

Liddell, H. G., Scott, R., Ed., *A Greek-English Lexicon; Revised and augmented throughout by Sir Henry Stuart Jones, with the assistance of Roderick McKenzie.* (Oxford. Clarendon Press. 1940) *http://www.perseus.tufts.edu/hopper/text?doc=Perseus:text:1999.04.0057:entry=ei)mi/1*

Gibson, M. D., ed. *Horae Semiticae X;* (Cambridge: Cambridge University, 1913)

Robinson, H. *Dualism*, The Stanford Encyclopedia of Philosophy (Fall 2017 Edition), Edward N. Zalta (ed.), *https://plato.stanford.edu/archives/fall2017/entries/dualism*

Schuelka M. J. (2013) A faith in humanness: disability, religion and development, *Disability & Society* 28, no. 4, 500–513, DOI: 10.1080/09687599.2012.717880.

Hester, R. *Historical Research: Theory and Methods* (ED Tech Press: Waltham, 2018)

Schipper, J. *How Does 2 Samuel Encounter Disability?*, SCM Press Blog, (2018) *https://scmpress.wordpress.com/2018/08/14/how-does-2-samuel-encounter-disability/*

Swinton, J. *Restoring the Image; Spirituality, Faith, Cognitive Disability*, Journal of Religion and Health, Vol. 36, No 1, Spring 1997; *https://www.abdn.ac.uk/sdhp/documents/restoringtheimage.pdf*

Birchenall P., Quoted in; Parrish, A. *Mental Handicap* (London: Macmillan, 1987)

Willows, D., Swinton, J., Ed. *Spiritual Dimensions of Pastoral Care: Practical Theology in a Multidisciplinary Context*, (Jessica Kingsley Publishers: London, 2000)

Erickson, M. J. *Christian Theology*, Vol. 2. (Baker: Grand Rapids, 1984)

Nimmo, A. Centre for Thomistic Studies, Souls and Spirits, Human Soul:
http://www.cts.org.au/2000/soulsandspirits.htm
http://www.talentshare.org/~mm9n/articles/man2/4.htm

Diagnostic and Statistical Manual of Mental disorders; DSM_V,
 (2014) Copyright © American Psychiatric Association, All
 rights reserved
 https://doi.org/10.1176/appi.books.9780890425596

Kane, L. *Including Adults with Disabilities Manual*; Vanderbilt
 Kennedy Center, 2011
 *http://vkc.mc.vanderbilt.edu/assets/files/resources/disabiliti
 esrelmanual.pdf*

Kabue, S. *Disability, Society and Theology: Voices from Africa* (Zapf
 Chancery Publishers: Limuru, 2011)

ACTUALISING FAITH

Butterfield, G. *Doctrine of Faith and Prayer* (WestBow Press:
 Bloomington, 2012).

Gourgey, C. *Faith, Despair and Disability*, Journal of Religion in
 Disability and Rehabilitation, 1, no. 3(1994): 51–63.
 http://www.judeochristianity.com/disabled/faith.htm

Mintz, S. Disability Studies Quarterly, Vol 26, No 3 (2006*), Ordinary
 Vessels: Disability Narrative and Representations of Faith.*
 http://www.dsq-sds.org/article/view/722/899

Elwell, W. ed. *Evangelical Dictionary of Theology* (Paternoster Press:
 Grand Rapids, 1995)

Reynolds, P. *A Whole New Life: An Illness and a Healing* (Scribner:
 New York, 2000)

Cooper, J., "The Current Body-Soul Debate," SBJT 13.2 (2009): 32–
 50.
 *http://equip.sbts.edu/wp-content/uploads/2015/10/SBJT-
 V13-N.2_Cooper.pdf*

Ryken l., Wilhoit J., Longerman T., eds. *Dictionary of Biblical Imagery* (IVP: Leicester, 1996)

Stack Exchange: *Christianity*, Article on *Faith*; *http://christianity.stackexchange.com/questions/31589/what-is-the-background-of-the-words-notitia-fiducia-and-assensus-and-how*

Raymond R. *A New Systematic Theology of the Christian Faith* (Thomas Nelson: Nashville, 1997)

Kuhn, D. *How Do People Know?*, Psychological Science, Vol. 12, No. 1 (Jan. 2001)

Swinton J. *Restoring the Image: Spirituality, Faith and Cognitive Disability*; Journal of Religion and Health, Vol. 36, No. 1, Spring 1997

Kane, L., ed. *Including Adults with Disabilities Manual*; Vanderbilt Kennedy Center, 2011 *https://vkc.mc.vanderbilt.edu/assets/files/resources/disabilitiesrelmanual.pdf*

Hutchinson, M. *Unity and Diversity in Spiritual Care*, *http://members.tripod.com/~Marg_Hutchison/nurse1.html*

LIVING FAITH

Stack Exchange: English Language and Usage; *"Cognisant over Aware,"* Article; *http://english.stackexchange.com/questions/70783/is-it-ever-more-appropriate-to-use-cognizant-over-aware/70790*

Got Questions: *Holy Spirit,* Article; *https://www.gotquestions.org/what-does-the-Holy-Spirit-do.html*

Got Questions: *The Spirit in the Old Testament*, Article;
https://www.gotquestions.org/Spirit-Old-Testament.html

Sproul, R. C. *The New Genesis; The Mystery of the Holy Spirit* (Tyndale House: Wheaton, 1979), Quoting W. A. Criswell, *Why I Preach That the Bible Is Literally True*, (Nashville: Broadman, 1969)
http://www.the-highway.com/genesis_Sproul.html

Criswell, W. A.: "*Why I preach that the Bible is Literally True*"; Sermon Oct 4th, 1980,
https://wacriswell.com/sermons/1980/why-i-preach-the-bible-is-literally-true/

Elwell, W., ed, *Evangelical Dictionary of Biblical Theology* (Paternoster Press: Grand Rapids, 1996), Craig L. Bloomberg, *Holy Spirit*, page 344.

Elwell, W., ed. *Evangelical Dictionary of Theology*, (Baker Books: Grand Rapids, 1995)

Courtney, W. "*Luther, the Catechisms, and Intellectual Disability,*" Intersections: Vol. 2018: No. 47, Article 10.

Wertz, S. R. *Dyspraxia - Movement Difficulties in Children with Autism Spectrum Disorders*; Growing Minds, Autism Programs.
https://www.autism-programs.com/articles-on-autism/dyspraxia-movement-difficulties-in-children.htm

Johnson, E. *Rewording the Justification/Sanctification Relation with Some Help from Speech Act Therapy*; JETS Journal, 54.4, (December 2011) 767—p 55
http://www.etsjets.org/files/JETS-PDFs/54/54-4/JETS_54-4_767-785_Johnson.pdf

Woolnough B., and Wonsuk Ma, ed. International Conference on Evangelism, Edinburgh, *Holistic Mission: God's Plan for God's People,* REGNUM EDINBURGH 2010 SERIES, 1910,

Edinburgh.
https://scholar.csl.edu/cgi/viewcontent.cgi?article=1008&context=edinburghcentenary

Author unknown; Evidence Unseen; OBJECTION #3: *"Why did God choose to use human agency in delivering his message to others?"*
http://www.evidenceunseen.com/articles/the-goodness-of-god/what-about-those-who-have-never-heard/objection-3-why-did-god-choose-to-use-human-agency-in-delivering-his-message-to-others/

Eiesland, N. L. *The disabled God: Toward a Liberatory Theology of Disability*. Nashville: Abingdon Press, 1994.
https://www.biblesociety.org.uk/uploads/content/bible_in_transmission/files/2004_spring/BiT_Spring_2004_Eiesland.pdf

EVANGELISM IN THE SHADOWS

Surgeon, C. *The Wordless Book*, edited by Bastian, K., @ Kidology.org
https://www.kidology.org/zones/zone_post.asp?post_id=120
http://en.wikipedia.org/wiki/Wordless_Book

Author Unknown; *Transcendent Love and ... Shrimp*,
https://transcendere.wordpress.com/2009/10/11/transcendent-love-and-shrimp/

Brown, T. E., ed. Understood Team, *The Difference Between ADHD and Executive Functioning Issues,* Fact Sheet.
https://www.understood.org/en/learning-attention-issues/child-learning-disabilities/executive-functioning-issues/difference-between-executive-functioning-issues-and-adhd
https://www.understood.org/en/learning-attention-issues/child-learning-disabilities/executive-functioning-issues/understanding-executive-functioning-issues

Rachid, G. S. *The Association between Types of Music Enjoyed and the Cognitive, Behavioural, and Personality Factors of Those Who Listen*: Psychomusicology, 19(2). 32–56 ©2007 Psychomusicology.

Travers, P. L. (Pamela Lyndon), 1899–1996. (19721962). *Mary Poppins*. (Scholastic Book Services: New York, 1972)

General Assemblies of God, USA: *Ministry to People with Disabilities: A Biblical Perspective*, Springfield, Montana, Assembly Paper, August 2000. © The General Council of the Assemblies of God, Used with Permission.
https://ag.org/Beliefs/Position-Papers/Ministry-to-People-with-Disabilities

ENCOURAGING FAITH

Lisa Miller, Iris M. Balodis, Clayton H. McClintock, Jiansong Xu, Cheryl M. Lacadie, Rajita Sinha, Marc N. Potenza: *Neural Correlates of Personalized Spiritual Experiences*; Cerebral Cortex, June 2019;29: 2331–2338 doi: 10.1093/cercor/bhy102 *https://news.yale.edu/2018/05/29/where-brain-processes-spiritual-experiences*

Barnum, B. *Spirituality in Nursing: The Challenges of Complexity*, Third Edition (Springer Publishing: New York, 2011)

Mintz, S. Disability Studies Quarterly, Vol26, No 3 (2006), *Ordinary Vessels: Disability Narrative and Representations of Faith*, para 5, *http://www.dsq-sds.org/article/view/722/899*

Boon, J. *The Mystical Science of the Soul: Medieval Cognition in Bernardino de Laredo*, (University of Toronto Press: Buffalo, 2012)

Thermos, V. *Towards a Theological understanding of Psychopathology and Therapy, International Journal of Orthodox Theology*, 2:3 (2011): urn: nbn:de:0276-2011-3064, http://orthodox-theology.com/media/PDF/IJOT3-2011/Thermos-Therapy.pdf

White, G. 'People with Disabilities in the Christian Community', Journal of the Christian Institute on Disability (JCID) Vol.3, No.1, Spring/Summer 2014.

Elder, R., Evans, K., Nizette, D. *Psychiatric and Mental Health*, (MOSBY: Marrickville, 2007)

© Got Questions: Accountability, *Where Do I Find the Age of Accountability in the Bible?* https://www.gotquestions.org/age-of-accountability.html

ACCOUNTABLE FAITH

Reinke, T. "*Disability and the Sovereign Goodness of God* (Desiring God Publishing: Minneapolis, 2012), p4.

Kierman, B. 'The Mentally Handicapped Child', ISBN-13: 9784447353196, http://twittertravels.com/serious-parents-of-severely-mentally.pdf

Smedes, L. "Can God Reach the Mentally Disabled?" http://www.christianitytoday.com/ct/2001/march5/31.94.html

Kayne, L., *Including Adults with Disabilities Manual;* Vanderbilt Kennedy Center, 2011 http://kc.vanderbilt.edu/kennedy_files/IncludingAdultswithDisabilitiesinRelEdMANUAL.pdf

World Council of Churches. *A Church of All and for All*, 02 September 2003, para 6, 22, 24 http://www.oikoumene.org/en/resources/documents/commissions/faith-and-order/ix-other-study-processes/a-church-of-all-and-for-all-an-interim-statement

Whitworth University. *Diversity and Intercultural Relations, A Theological Foundation*; University Council Committee Report, November 2014. para 7 https://www.whitworth.edu/cms/media/whitworth/documents/administration/diversity-equity--inclusion/institutional-diversity-committee-report-2014.pdf

Homcy, S. L. *"To Him Who Overcomes."* JETS 38/2 (June 1995) 193–201 O. Bauernfeind, Theological Dictionary of the New Testament, Vol 9 (Eerdmans: Grand Rapids, 1964) 4:945

Garland, D. E., ed. *The Expositors Bible Commentary*; Longman III, T., *Romans—Galatians*, (Zondervan: Grand Rapids, 2011)

Heschel, A. (Rabbi) *The Older Person and the Family Perspective of Tradition*, In: Aging with a Future. US Govt. Print Office, Washington, 1961, Series No. 1. Quoted in Baylor University, *Reaching Out to the Spiritual Nature of Persons with Dementia.*

CONCLUSIONS

Star Trek; The Original Series, 1969 - Gene Roddenberry - Hollywood, California, United States. © 2020 CBS Studios Inc. © 2020 CBS Television Distribution and CBS Interactive Inc. All Rights Reserved.

POSTSCRIPT

Fatehi, M. *The Spirit's Relation to the Risen Lord in Paul: An Examination of Its Christological Implications* (Coronet Books: Tubingen, 2000)

© IMBD, Quotes; *Mary Poppins*, Quotes from Script for Mary Poppins http://www.imdb.com/title/tt0058331/quotes Cited, 06/02/2015.

Author Unknown; *Transcendent Love and ... Shrimp*, *https://transcendere.wordpress.com/2009/10/11/transcendent-love-and-shrimp/*

GLOSSARY

This glossary lists definitions of terms in this book that I use in a limited and specific way in my writing, or which may be unfamiliar to you. These definitions are all written so that a reader can easily understand the specific context in which I have used these words and phrases. Feel free to refer to this glossary as you need to during our shared journey to the 'Other Side of the Fence.'

actualising: To make real in an inner and outward sense the faith of the disabled person. Not only that we know but that they know we accept and know.

accredited: A business accounting term that means given to, placed into his/her account and is not something that the person previously had or earned in their own right.

adaptive behavior: That process, or conceptual processes, whereby a person receives information and facilitates a response.

agrarian: Relating to the cultivation of land or a society based on farming as its main source of social and financial existence.

alleviate: The act or process of alleviating or relieving suffering, pain or in this case a disability.

anormal: Responses or reactions to normative situations that solicit a response from a person that is considered not normal given the overall circumstances.

a-normative: 'a' - prefix used as an affix – donating being the opposite of something – standing aside from something – a-normative, beside or not the normal generally accepted – see 'normative' below.

a-priori: Relating to or denoting reasoning or knowledge which proceeds from theoretical deduction rather than from observation or experience, a-priors are assumptions about human nature based on pre-conceived ideas.[335]

---

[335] See also, https://www.oxfordify.com/meaning/a_priori

assent: The act of giving acknowledgment to a verbal or visual proposition, concept or idea in a mental and sentient manner that constitutes and validates that concept of faith within the intellectual and psychological nature of that person.

avowal: A statement that declares your faith in something that you support or believe in.

being: Here in the sense of defining the existence of a person in body and spirit/soul of a human being giving them motor and intellectual skills and existence.

causality: The relationship between two events, exploring the degree to which one may have caused the other.

caveat: A statement that limits a more general statement or holds one position as true to avoid misinterpretations.

coalesce: To unite 'two things' into one unified body. Faith becoming part of the constitution of the whole inaugurating a new reality, in the being of a person, whether enabled or disabled.

cognisant: To be conscious of or to know a fact within your cognition.

cognition: Cognition is the process in which people use their brains to perceive and experience the world around them.

cognitive deficit: An impairment in neurological functions that can have a negative impact on one's cognition.

comorbidity: The presence of two or more diseases (disabilities) in a person that compounds the diagnosis and interacts in affecting cognitive and bodily function.

comprehend: One step further than just knowledge to the point of realising and acting upon that knowledge. To understand the meaning and nature of something in the mind.

conditio humana: The general condition of being human as separate from animal and plant life. Life, experience, thought, emotions, and morality are some identifiers of conditio humana.

conditio conscius: The ability to independently generate thought from sensory or intellectual information and rationalise a response.

congruence: A coming together of the anatomical, sensory, and mental neurological functions of a child or person that work in harmony and facilitate responses in an ordered and reasoned manner with understanding and comprehension of that answer—and the outcome so derived.

consciousness: Used here not in the sense of being conscious but able of conscious thought.
continuum: Used to describe the inter-relationships of the elements of our being, spirit/soul-body, at the point of union, interface, while each element retaining their intra-dependence in this world, the body mortal while the spirit/soul remains an "immortal" entity in itself.
commensurate: A thing, idea or concept that corresponds in size or proportion with another. In our case, the combined abilities of a disabled person, within themselves, to express their persona.
cortical: 'Cortex'; Relating to the human cortex, the brain tissue, where cognition, neurological and sensory perception takes place. In layman terms, the organic brain tissue where the general exchange of sensory, motor, and perceptional experiences of life are received, organised, and language is formed. The biological, bodily location where humans think and act.
criterion: A standard or set of standards that are used to make a judgment or assessment for admittance to or passing a test—in common term—a yardstick.
developmental disability: A disability where life skills and adaptive behavior presents as underdeveloped to the norm due to biological or neurological disabilities that result in loss of intellectual, communicative and or motor skills.
disability: Any biological, neurological or health condition that restrains full interaction and expression in a person within their community and society.
dogma: A set of principles established by a society or a religious group and held as important to their function and identity.
doxastic: Principals of thought and reasoning related to belief or logical thought concerning a person's belief systems. Faith, as a practical commitment beyond the normal evidence to one's belief that God exists.
doxastic venture: As the word venture suggests, faith that goes beyond rational thought. An active commitment to the truth of faith proposals.
dualism: A "person" is a composite being, the spirit/soul and the material body held in a union that is created by God. The 'spirit' of a person in this world requires the material body, and the

material body requires the spirit of life (Gen. 2:7) to give movement, expression and being to that person.

edify: To encourage an individual to live with or deal with life situations. Especially to encourage intellectual, moral, or spiritual improvement. To improve especially in a moral and religious knowledge

existential: Of, relating to, or dealing with existence based on experience; empirical. What we know about life from personal experiences and events

faith: Confident belief in the truth and value of an idea, a person or religion. In the Christian sense Faith is Spirit, a deposit of God's Spirit as a gift to the believer.

galette: A French flat cake. In our context here a term for a flat muted response, impassiveness, in our case with some disabilities a lack of expressed emotion or realisation of—or to surroundings.

homeostasis: The propensity of molecular systems to maintain a state of order and resist change. A state of balance to survive.

human life: Life defined in terms not associated with the animal world but distinct spiritual life originating from the Breath of God, everlasting life that separates mankind from the animal kingdom.

illocutionary: The notion of a locutionary act, which describes the linguistic function of an utterance, a vocal response to internal and external stimulation. The ability to convey vocally, in a defined and understood manner, the thoughts and reasonings of one's heart, mind, and emotions. Mary is constricted in the essential elements of illocution.

incarnation: In Christianity, the doctrine that the Son of God was conceived in the womb of the virgin Mary, by the Spirit of God, and that Jesus is both true God and true man. See Colossians 2:8–9

intellectual disability: Generalised loss of normal neurodevelopmental processes, either through biological or accidental causes that impair mental function and expression.

interface: My usage of the word interface is about communication between two separate entities, God, and man.

intra-dependence: 'Intra' means to transact within boundaries, between two things, and although we have boundaries between the spiritual and bodily self, we are not two a 'two parts' person (i.e., interstate highways).

liturgical: Relating to words used as a set convention in music, song, and ceremonies (rituals) within a religious framework, especially with denominational Christianity.

lossness: A sense of hopelessness with sorrow for what might have been or was.

mental disorder: Disorder or mental patterns that affect the way a person behaves, feels, thinks, or responds to external vocal and natural stimulations or situations that cause significant distress or anormal reactions to otherwise normative situations.

meta: The meaning of "meta" varies with use but is generally a term used as a self-reflection upon the following word. Meta-data means data about data. A metajoke is a joke about jokes.

metaphysics: A branch of philosophy that examines the fundamental nature of reality, experience, and reactions in order to set normative guidelines which are used to then assess normative human behavior.

meta-theory: The investigation of theory, usually from within that theory—-field of study itself. The concept of self-examination in order to improve knowledge and awareness of the subject matter.

meta-value: The investigation of the theory of value. What makes something valuable to us or in a material sense how much is it— or thing worth.

mind-body problem: My approach is to simplify this discussion of what constitutes 'being' and the relationships between body and soul/spirit, into three basic groups, Materialistic, one hand, Dualism-Monism two hands together and Continuum, interlaced but individual hands, which I term integration, my aspect of a Christian model, "and man becomes a living being."

neurodegeneration: A loss of neurological function, due to cerebral cortex and or neuron decay, that affects one's thinking. It has many variations but mainly is a slow loss of mental powers that a person used to have in a normative sense.

neurodiversity: To acknowledge the many different ways in which human brains, and therefore consciousness, can develop over one's lifetime.

neurotypical: This is a word created by the autistic community to mean those who experience the world in a 'normal' or 'typical' way.

normative: Used to refer to the generally accepted practices of faith communities in acknowledging and accepting faith statements of their members, statements which are accepted as verifying the internal, heart and mind, commitment that a person is making before the congregation or faith community fellowship. Normative also means the creedal and liturgical practices of a faith community that are accepted as indicative of their belief systems and dogma which identify that communities spiritual and practical structures.

ontology: The study of the nature of being, establishing evidence of one's existence and relationships within reality. The study of who I am and why I am, thus defining ontological life.

organic life: An organism that can adapt to its environment, metabolise energy, respond to stimuli and reproduce. More specific definitions of this are highly controversial.

perception: One's ability in the organisation, identification, and interpretation of sensory information in order to represent and understand the presented information or environment.

perichoresis: (perichoretic) A Greek term or word that refers to the eternal triune God and the interrelationship that exists perpetually between the Father, Son, and Holy Spirit. (περιχώρησις—peri: rotation—around; choresis: progression - going)

perlocutionary act: The act of speaking that is designed to or causes or has an altering—response or challenging effect upon the hearer.

persona: The external—visual—aspect of someone's character that is presented to or perceived by others. How one presents to the world.

perspicuity: The meaning here being the transparency of the gospel and scripture. Disability is no barrier to the spiritual reality of Faith, God, or the Gospel; they can all operate with clarity within the Shadow World.

progenitor: Here the origin of action, what comes before action—movement is possible. Like a steam engine at the head of a train.

The train goes nowhere without the precursor—the engine at the front that brings motion and function to the train.

quintessence: The essential makeup of a thing, idea, concept, or viewpoint. Its basic foundational reality.

relational: How two or more things are connected to or relate to one another in a close relationship. In Christian theology, God is seen as a triune—relational person who interacts with His creation and creatures—especially man. God is active and involved in relationship with others (man).

religious texts: Texts that are related to a religious belief. For example, the Bible and the Quran are significant texts of the Christian and Muslim religions, respectively.

salvic: Salvic 'faith' is that spiritual deposit of the Spirit of God, that applies the redemptive work of Jesus Christ on the Cross, spiritually, into the spirit/soul-being of a person. Believing comes from—and is empowered by the deposit of 'salvic faith' by the Holy Spirit.

sapience: While most animals are sentient, humans are different in that they are also sapient, a word that is more closely tied to reasoning than experiencing.

sentience: Sentience is that spontaneous capacity to feel, perceive, or experience subjectively from surrounding stimuli and process such to generate original thought. When God creates a new life, that life is created as a sentient being.

spiritual disability: A created term to define, if possible, the affect that the biological disabilities of a person may have upon their spiritual nature in that that spiritual nature is impaired in its expression through their biological agencies; yet the spirit nature within that person remains fully enabled.

spirituality: God-given spiritual life, not the alternative meaning that is usually applied to the term 'spirituality' in today's multi-faceted well-being industry or 'mind-body-spirit' holistic view of life, a view which gives the portent of reality but has no foundation on which to build a system of life and faith, where everything is fluid and 'self' is defined in whatever gist has the moment in the froth and bubble of our new-age ultra-post-modern society.

statuted: Established as a statute, a nonremovable objective reality in the life of a believer.

substantive: Having a firm basis and so important, meaningful, or considerable. Having a separate and independent existence that has both an experiential, definable, and existential reality.

systematic: Ordered as opposed to a random, approach to thought, theology, and life that in an ordered, progressive, sequential process seeks to define a topic of life experience in an arranged manner.

theodicy: Theodicy is a defence - justification of a deity, or the attributes of a deity, especially in regard to the existence of evil and suffering in the world; a work or discourse justifying the ways of God.

value theory: Value theory involves various approaches that examine how, why, and to what degree humans value things and whether the object or subject of valuing is a person, idea, object, or anything else. Within philosophy, it is also known as ethics or axiology. (Wikipedia)

veracity: To adhere to the truth. The disabled person has no barrier to the veracity and reality of their faith, that is known to them spiritually as the work of the Holy Spirit and that deposit of the Holy Spirit assures them, whatever their cognizance and neurological experience of the faith may be.

veritable: Something, either an idea, or belief, or concept, or reality that can be verified as true or existent.

volition: Volition or will is the cognitive process by which an individual decides on and commits to a particular course of action.

Internet Links

Wikipedia: Religion
> *https://en.wikipedia.org/wiki/Spiritual_but_not_religious;* Cited, 13/02/2017.
> *http://en.wikipedia.org/wiki/Hinduism,* Cited, 29/04/2011.
> *http://en.wikipedia.org/wiki/Islam,* Cited, 29/04/2011.
> *http://en.wikipedia.org/wiki/Taoism,* Cited, 29/04/2011.
> *http://en.wikipedia.org/wiki/Budhism,* Cited, 29/04/2011.
> *https://plato.stanford.edu/entries/dualism*, Cited, 3/01/2016.
> *https://en.wikipedia.org/wiki/Religious_text* Cited, 07/01/2014.
> *https://en.wikipedia.org/wiki/Mind%E2%80%93body_problem* Cited, 24/01/2017.

Australian ABC:
> *http://www.abc.net.au/religion/articles/2014/09/18/4090190.htm;* Cited, 26/12/2016.

World Health Organization:
> *https://www.who.int/publications/m/item/icf-beginner-s-guide-towards-a-common-language-for-functioning-disability-and-health*Cited, 01/07/2011.

Wikipedia: Mental Disorders
> *https://en.wikipedia.org/wiki/List_of_mental_disorders#cite_ref-1*

Sydney University: Centre for Disability Studies,
> *http://www.cdds.med.usyd.edu.au/news-a-information-66/faqs/48-what-is-developmental-disability*

Got Questions:
> *https://www.gotquestions.org/unclean-spirits.html,*

Cited, 16/04/2018.
https://www.gotquestions.org/psychological-demon.html,
Cited, 16/04/2018.

National Centre for Biotechnical information:
https://www.ncbi.nlm.nih.gov/pmc/articles/PMC3705683/
Cited, 16/04/2018.

Mental Health UK:
Vanderbilt university; Kennedy Centre:
https://www.mentalhealth.org.uk/sites/default/files/impact-spirituality.pdf Cited, 16/04/2018.
http://vkc.mc.vanderbilt.edu/assets/files/resources/denominations.pdf Cited, 07/01/2014.

AAIDD; Religion and Spirituality
http://www.aaiddreligion.org/ Spirituality and Developmental Disorders, Cited, 07/01/2014.
https://aaiddreligion.org/2013/08/05/aaidd-religion-and-spirituality-division-spirituality-and-congregational-participation-action-plan-feedback/
Cited, 07/01/2014.
https://aaiddreligion.files.wordpress.com/2019/12/dimensions-of-faith-2009.pdf Cited 14/04/2023.

Princeton University:
https://www.princeton.edu/~achaney/tmve/wiki100k/docs/Jewish_principles_of_faith.html Cited, 30/11/2014.

Merriam—Webster Dictionary
http://www.merriam-webster.com/dictionary/edify
Cited, 14/02/2015.

Stack Exchange: Christianity, Article on Faith; Cited, 27/01/2017.
http://christianity.stackexchange.com/questions/31589/what-is-the-background-of-the-words-notitia-fiducia-and-assensus-and-how

Stack Exchange: English Language and Usage; "Cognisant over Aware,"
http://english.stackexchange.com/questions/70783/is-it-ever-more-appropriate-to-use-cognizant-over-aware/70790
Cited, 27/01/2017.

Got Questions: What Does the Holy Spirit Do? Cited, 08/05/2018.
https://www.gotquestions.org/what-does-the-Holy-Spirit-do.html

Got Questions: The Holy Spirit in the Old Testament; Cited, 08/05/2018.
https://www.gotquestions.org/Spirit-Old-Testament.html

Got Questions: What was the role of the Holy Spirit in the Old Testament?
https://www.gotquestions.org/Spirit-Old-Testament.html
Cited, 08/05/2018.

Wikipedia Article; *Wind Beneath My Wings;*
http://en.wikipedia.org/wiki/Wind_Beneath_My_Wings
Cited, 25/01/2015.

Wikipedia Article; Spiritual but not Religious;
https://en.wikipedia.org/wiki/Spiritual_but_not_religious
Cited, 13/02/2017.

Software Resources

e-Sword, Copyright © 2020 — Rick Meyers, Ver. 9.9.0, International Standard Bible Encyclopaedia; *http://e-sword.net*; Used by permission. All rights reserved worldwide.

e-Sword, Copyright © 2020 — Rick Meyers. Version 10.3.0; NIV Family Bundle: NIV, NIV84, TNIV, and NIrV for e-Sword PC; © scripture quotations taken from The Holy Bible, New International Version® NIV® Copyright © 1973 1978 1984 2011 by Biblica, Inc. TM Used by permission. All rights reserved worldwide.

OliveTree, Bible+, Ver. 6.0.23.910; © ESV Version, Copyright ©1998-2022 Olive Tree Bible Software.

OliveTree Bible+, Ver 7.7.8; © ESV, Copyright ©1998-2022 Olive Tree Bible Software.

OliveTree Bible+, Ver 7.7.8; NASB, Copyright ©1998-2022 Olive Tree Bible Software.

OliveTree Bible+, Ver 7.7.8; NLT, New Living Translation, Copyright ©1998-2022 Olive Tree Bible Software.

OliveTree Bible+, Ver 7.7.8; New English Bible, Copyright ©1998-2022 Olive Tree Bible Software.

OliveTree Bible+, Ver 7.7.8; Jerusalem Bible, Copyright ©1998-2022 Olive Tree Bible Software.

OliveTree Bible+, Ver 7.7.8; NASB, Revised English Bible, Copyright ©1998-2022 Olive Tree Bible Software.

OliveTree, Ver 6.1.1: © Crossway Classic Commentary; Acts of the Apostles, Copyright ©1998-2022 Olive Tree Bible Software.

Olivetree Bible+, Ver. 7.7.8; Strong's Numbers, Copyright ©1998-2022 Olive Tree Bible Software.

OliveTree Bible+, Ver 7.7.8; Gaebelein F., Ed., Expositor's Commentary, 12Vol, Zondervan, 2009, Copyright ©1998-2022 Olive Tree Bible Software.

APPENDIX I

DISABILITY, RELIGION, AND SPIRITUALITY RESOURCES:

VANDERBILT: KENNEDY CENTER.

Possibly, the best source currently on the internet for educational, spiritual, and care material for those caring for, working with, and helping people who have disabilities within a church—faith community. A stable internet site with immense potential to help organizations develop programs for their disabled people. Too many links to individually list here.

Link: *https://vkc.vumc.org/vkc/*

The Vanderbilt link below leads to resource material for church communities.

Link: *https://vkc.vumc.org/vkc/resources/religionspirituality/*

LEXINGTON THEOLOGICAL SEMINARY

The majority of the links below are based on resources at Lexington Theological Seminary. I have also added resources that I have found in my research for writing this book. Internet links have been checked that they were working at the time of publication.

Link: *https://www.lextheo.edu/wp-content/uploads/2009/01/lts-fe_4_disabilityandspiritualityresourcesforemaillinks.doc*

WEB SITES

AAIDD: American Association of Intellectual and Developmental Disabilities

The following WEB-sites are listed under the AAIDD website with additional resources I have found useful in writing this book.

Link: *http://www.aaiddreligion.org/resources*

> Resources put out by the Religion & Spirituality Division of the AAIDD including Cooperative Resource Exhibit, *Journal of Religion, Disability, and Health*, On the Road to Congregational Inclusion, publications by members and links to other resources.

http://www.nod.org/index.cfm?fuseaction=Page.viewPage&pageId=1563

> This links to the National Organization on Disability's program for disability and religion. Resources include the Religion and Disability Program e-newsletter, accessible congregation programs, various print publications, conferences, interfaith directory of religious leaders with disabilities, seminary project, tools and resources used by congregations who care for and prepare projects for the disabled.

http://www.larcheusa.org/

> L'Arche Communities, founded by Jean Vanier in France in 1964, brings together people, some with developmental disabilities and some without, who choose to share their lives by living together in faith-based communities. The mission of L'Arche is to create homes where faithful relationships based on forgiveness and celebration are nurtured, to reveal the unique value and vocation of each person, and to change society by choosing to live relationships in the community as a sign of hope and love.

http://www.abdn.ac.uk/cshad/

> The Centre for Spirituality, Health and Disability at the University of Aberdeen has a dual focus on the relationship between spirituality, health, and healing and the significance of the spiritual dimension for contemporary health care practices, and the theology of disability. The centre aims to enable academics, researchers, practitioners, and educators to work together to develop innovative and creative research projects and teaching initiatives.

http://www.faithability.org/

> This website links to various resources on disability and religion.

http://www.religionanddisability.org/

> The Center for Religion and Disability Inc. is a 501(c) (3) educational organisation. Their primary focus areas include education and research about graduate theological education, people with disabilities, and the total learning environment, building community supports, strategic planning, and consultation. The Center for Religion and Disability Inc. provides innovative education, consultation, and research about people with disabilities and their families.

http://www.nafim.org/quarterly.php?section=publication&cat=quarterly

> This website allows users to order monthly articles on disability and spirituality for only $1 each.

http://www.loc.gov/nls/reference/circulars/bibles.html

> This site gives links for finding Bibles and other sacred texts in special media including Braille, audio, and large print.

http://thechp.syr.edu/spirituality.html

This links to a resource packet on disability, spirituality, and healing. Documents include *Changing Attitudes, Creating Awareness, Victim Theology*, syllabus used for a seminary course, handouts for courses, retreats, and lectures, and *Disability Awareness: An Empowering Ministry*.

http://www.ncpd.org/

The National Catholic Partnership On Disability is the disability voice of the US Catholic Bishops. NCPD was established in 1982 to further implementation of the 1978 Pastoral Statement of US Catholic Bishops on People with Disabilities, which calls for full inclusion of all persons with disabilities in the church and within society and is a vision they are still urgently working to achieve. The website includes a newsletter, various information resources, and presents Catholic perspectives on disability issues.

http://www.blhs.org/resources/ncrc.asp

Part of Bethesda Lutheran Homes & Services, NCRC provides resources to families of children with disabilities, pastors, volunteers, and other professionals in the field of developmental disabilities throughout the world. NCRC holds workshops, responds to telephone inquiries, and offers a wide variety of other programs and services.

http://www.ou.org/ncsy/njcd/default.htm

This is the website for the National Jewish Council for the Disabled, an orthodox organisation that maintains a national resource center, a national center for inclusion, and "mainstreamed" and self-contained social and recreational activities.

http://www.joniandfriends.org/

This organization's mission is to accelerate Christian ministry in the disability community. Its website includes information about the organization and its programs, a geographical directory of churches and organizations with disability ministries, plus a very nicely organized collection of disability links.

http://www.liftdisabilitynetwork.org/

Lift Disability network includes a family network, learning network, and ministry network for the families and providers of individuals with disabilities. Its efforts are combined with the Christian Council on Persons with Disabilities, and they are associated with over two hundred organizations across the country.

http://members.aol.com/jesna/spedcon.htm

This website, for the Consortium of Special Educators in Central Agencies for Jewish Education, offers some resources for Jewish special education. As expressed in its name, the consortium was developed to strengthen special education through central agencies for Jewish education, and to provide a context in which communities' special educators can build a professional network.

http://www.cjsn.org/Home.asp

The Council for Jews with special needs is a nonprofit human resources agency, composed of concerned individuals working together to ensure that all Jews have the opportunity to fully participate in the richness of Jewish religious, cultural, and social life. The website includes information about the organisation and its services. There are also related articles and links.

ARTICLES

Boswell, B. B., Knight, S., Hamer, M., & McChesney, J. (2001). "Disability and spirituality: a reciprocal relationship with implications for the rehabilitation process." *Journal of Rehabilitation* 67, no. 4:20–25. October 2001.
Link: *https://www.researchgate.net/publication/290289079*

Byrd, E. K., Byrd, P. D. "A listing of biblical references to healing that may be useful as bibliotherapy to the empowerment of rehabilitation clients. *Journal of Rehabilitation*, Washington, DC. Vol. 59, no. 3 (Jul 1, 1993).
Link:

https://search.proquest.com/openview/083966abfb999d63378f96fa648f6f5c/1?pq-origsite=gscholar&cbl=1819158

Byzek, J. "Freaking the Bible. *Mouth Magazine* 13, no. 5: 17–20 (2003).
Link: *http://www.mouthmag.com/issues/75/75_pp3.html*

Byzek, J., "Jesus and the paralytic, the blind and the lame: A Sermon." *The Ragged Edge Online*, Nov/Dec 2000.

Link:

http://www.raggededgemagazine.com/1100/1100cft1.htm

Description: This article urges Christians to help stop the oppression people with disabilities often face. The author gives some examples of inappropriate ways Christians respond to Jesus's healings in the Bible (e.g., people with disability are there solely to show Jesus's glory etc.,) and contrasts Christian indifference with interpretations of Jesus's healings from a more disability-friendly stance.

Chambers, S., "The man upstairs." *Mouth Magazine* 13, no. 5, 22–23. (2003).
Link: *http://www.mouthmag.com/issues/75/75_pp3.html*

Coddington, J. H. "Child of the king." *Mouth Magazine* 13, no. 5, 20–21. (2003).
Link: *http://www.mouthmag.com/issues/75/75_pp3.html*

Cooper-Dowda, R. "Please don't cure me, I'm already healed." *Mouth Magazine* 13, no. 5, 26–28.
Link: *http://www.mouthmag.com/issues/75/75_pp3.html*

Ellor, J. "Reaching Out to the Spiritual Nature of Persons with Dementia," Ed., *Journal of Religion, Spirituality and Aging*, a *Routledge Journal* annual meeting of NCOA/ASA Washington, DC. 03/27/08.
Link:

> *https://www.baylor.edu/content/services/document.php/60623.pdf*

> **Description**: James approaches the subject of dementia and Alzheimer's and their related diseases from the perspective of what the person feels and knows about God. James investigates the spiritual side of knowing God in these conditions and what the person can recall and asks the question does a loss of mental functions disable the human soul. James looks at practical means of helping dementia and Alzheimer's people share in worship. Trigger prompts are suggested as a way that can help the disabled person worship God in a meaningful way. As James says, "Part of being a spiritual person is to be in a spiritual context," and it is this spiritual context that James suggests is the door to their faith and life in God. A highly recommended read.

Gaventa, W. "A place for all of me and all of us: Rekindling the spirit in services and supports." *Mental Retardation* 43, 48–54 (2005).
Link: *https://meridian.allenpress.com/idd/article-abstract/43/1/48/7973/*

Gaventa, W., "End of life, religion, disability, and health: Where all the paths converge." *Journal of Religion, Disability & Health* 9, no. 2 (2005).
   Link: *http://aaidd.allenpress.com/pdfserv/10.1352%2F0047-6765(2005)43%3C48:APFAOM%3E2.0.CO%3B2*

Gourgey, C., "Faith, Despair and Disability," *Journal of Religion in Disability and Rehabilitation* 1, no. 3 (1994): 51–63.
   Link: *http://www.judeochristianity.com/disabled/faith.htm*

   Description: Charles's paper takes us into the world of Alzheimer's and Dementia, asking the question does faith still exist when memory and mental functions can no longer recall the past. In a pastoral and gentle manner, Charles reminds us that mental and physical illness cannot assuage spiritual realities that exist within the spirit/soul of a person nor diminish that person's spiritual experience of God. Opening up new avenues of thought, Charles challenges us to reassess what we believe about and accept as faith in the life and worship experience of the disabled. A highly recommended read.

Gray, M. "A spiritual key for autism." *Faith at Home.* (2002).
   Link:
   http://www.faith-at-home.com/articles/autistic_mg.html

   Description: This article is written by Melissa, a mother of a child with autism, about her child's spiritual needs.

Hersh, E. and Hughes, R., The role of suffering and disability: Evidence from scripture. *Journal of Religion, Disability & Health* 9, no. 3: 85–92 (2006).
   Link: *https://doi.org/10.1300/J095v09n03_06*

   Description: This article focuses on finding models in Old and New Testament scriptures for those who have disabilities and are experiencing suffering. Habakkuk, David, the

Apostle Paul, and Jesus are presented as models whose faith perspective carried them through suffering. Possibilities for application in today's world are presented, with one of the authors presenting his personal story. Individuals, as well as those who work in a pastoral setting with people with disabilities, may find this document to be a resource of hope.

Leidy, P. "If I were God." *Mouth Magazine* 13, no. 5, 24–25 (2003).
   Link: *http://www.mouthmag.com/issues/75/75_pp3.html*

Melchionna, E. M. *Redefining disability through Eucharist: That all must receive*. Yale Divinity School; Yale Institute of Sacred Music (2004).
   Link:
   http://www.samford.edu/lillyhumanrights/papers/Melchionna_Redefining.pdf

Minton, C. and Dodder, R. "Participation in religious services for people with developmental disabilities." *Journal of the American Association on Mental Retardation* 41, no. 6: 430–39 (1993).
   Link: *https://pubmed.ncbi.nlm.nih.gov/14588059/*

Nabi, G. "How to lead a special education ministry." Lifeway.com.
   Link:
   http://www.lifeway.com/lwc/article_main_page/0%2C1703%2CA%25253D161421%252526M%25253D201144%2C00.html

National Council of Churches USA. NCC disability committee leads worship at Chicago seminary. Retrieved January 8, 2008, from: (2007).
   Link: *http://www.wfn.org/2007/09/msg00236.html*

National Organization on Disability (NOD) "That all may worship: An interfaith welcome to people with disabilities."

Link: *http://www.nod.org/index.cfm?fuseaction=Feature.showFeature&FeatureID=99*

Rose, A. "Who causes the blind to see: Disability and quality of religious life." *Disability and Society* 12, no. 3: 395–406 (1997).
Link: https://www.tandfonline.com/doi/abs/10.1080/09687599727245

Swinton, J., (2004). "Restoring the image: Spirituality, faith, and cognitive disability." *Journal of Religion and Health* 36, no. 1: 21–28.
Link: *https://www.jstor.org/stable/27511088?seq=1*

Description: There is a great deal of theological confusion within the church as to the level of participation people with profound cognitive disabilities should be allowed within the orders of the church. For some, sacramental participation without intellectual comprehension is dishonoring to God, while for others, lack of cognitive ability precludes any kind of meaningful spiritual life. This paper sets out some of the various positions and argues that faith and spirituality are not intellectual concepts but relational realities. It is only in and through our relationships that any of us can learn anything about the divine. A relational understanding of faith and spirituality as outlined here offers the church the freedom to avoid evaluating a person's spiritual life according to intellectual criteria and to begin to find new ways of preaching the Word to those who have no words.

Vanover, E. N., "Ads for God." *Mouth Magazine* 13, no. 5, 12–13 (2003).
Link: *http://www.mouthmag.com/issues/75/75_pp3.html*

Weinberg, N. and Serbian, C. "The Bible and disability." *Rehabilitation Counseling Bulletin* 23, no. 4: 273–81 (1980).
Link: *https://eric.ed.gov/?id=EJ229691*

Wolfe, K. "The Bible and disabilities: from "healing" to "burning bush." *The Disability Rag* 9 (1993).

BOOKS

Bishop, M. E. (1995). *Religion and disability: Essays in scripture, theology, and ethics.* Lanham, MD: Sheed & Ward.
    Link: http://www.amazon.com/Religion-Disability-Essays-Scripture-Theology/dp/1556127138/ref=sr_1_1/002-9019454-0531235?ie=UTF8&s=books&qid=1194839837&sr=8-1

Breeding, M.; Hood, D. K., and Whitworth, J. *Let all the children come to me: A practical guide for including children with disabilities in your church ministries.* Cook Communications Ministries.
    Link: http://www.amazon.com/Let-All-Children-Come-Disabilities/dp/0781444047/ref=pd_sim_b_img_3
    Description: This book blends theory and research with practical ideas and strategies for teaching children with special needs and places it in a spiritual and Christ-centered context. Teachers and pastors will find inspiration and information, reminding them that God calls us to include all children, no matter the challenge. Additionally, the book includes wonderfully practical elements with many ideas that can be easily integrated into any classroom.

Carter, Erik. (2007). *Including people with disabilities in faith communities: A guide for service providers, families, and congregations.* Baltimore, MD: Paul H. Brookes.
    Link: http://www.amazon.com/Including-People-Disabilities-Faith-Communities/dp/1557667438/ref=pd_bbs_1?ie=UTF8&s=books&qid=1201101214&sr=8-1

    Description: This is a practical guide on how to include people with disabilities in religious communities. It addresses how faith communities, service providers, and families can work together to support the full participation of individuals with disabilities in the faith community of their choice.

Gaventa, W. and Coulter, D. L. (2001). *Spirituality and intellectual disability: International perspectives on the effect of culture and religion on healing body, mind, and soul.* New York: Haworth Pastoral Press.

Gaventa, W. C. and Abrams, J. Z. (2007). *Jewish perspectives on theology and the human experience of disability.* New York: Haworth Press.

Govig, S. D. (1989). *Strong at the broken places: persons with disabilities and the church.* Westminster John Knox.
Link: *http://www.amazon.com/Strong-Broken-Places-Persons-Disabilities/dp/0804211531/ref=sr_1_3/002-9019454-0531235?ie=UTF8&s=books&qid=1194840130&sr=8-3*

Description: When linked to biblical teachings, understanding disability offers congregations and society the pathway to hope and change. Stewart Govig, himself disabled, provides a practical resource that enables congregational communities to achieve a balance of realism and hope in responding to the needs of all of its members. He examines the attitudinal barriers thrust upon persons with disabilities and investigates the biblical resources for overcoming these barriers. He advocates an understanding of the Christian community that removes social stigma for the disabled.

Medina, K. (2006). *Finding God in Autism: A 40-day devotional for parents of autistic children.* (Tate Publishing: Mustang OK, 2006).

Link: *http://www.amazon.com/Finding-God-Autism-Devotional-Autistic/dp/1598865633/ref=pd_sim_b_img_15*

Description: This devotional book provides scripture readings to restore hope, strengthen faith, and show you that God has a plan for your child's life. Scriptures are listed that direct you to the promise that God is listening to your every prayer, that He is watching over your children and the prayers, works and efforts being done on behalf of them.

Molsberry, R. F. (2004). *Blindsided by grace: Entering the world of disability.* Minneapolis, MN: Augsburg Fortress Publishers.

Link: *http://www.amazon.com/Blindsided-Grace-Entering-World-Disability/dp/0806645725/ref=sr_1_7/002-9019454-0531235?ie=UTF8&s=books&qid=1194840130&sr=8-7*

Description: An active pastor, husband, father, and triathlete, Bob Molsberry was nearly killed in 1997 in a hit-and-run accident on a rural highway. After an extended period of recovery and rehabilitation, he is a paraplegic, Bob has remained active in family, ministry, and athletics. This book reflects on his experience of disability not as a medical condition—disabled person in search of a cure, nor as a tragedy to be pitied, but as a cross-cultural adventure similar to learning to live in a foreign country. Molsberry also offers a biblical and theological reflection that presents Bible's perspectives on disability—that it is a matter of heroic suffering or miraculous cure, and often interpreted as a consequence of sin.

Newman, B. J. (2006). *Autism and your church.* Grand Rapids, MI: Faith Alive Christian Resource & Friendship Ministries.

Link: *http://www.amazon.com/Autism-Your-Church-Barbara-Newman/dp/1592552730/ref=cm_lmf_img_4_rdssss 0*

Pierson, J.; Tucker-Jones, L.; and Verbal, P. (2003). *Special needs, special ministry*. Loveland, CO: Group Publishing.
Link: *https://www.amazon.com/Special-Needs-Ministry-Group-Publishing/dp/0764425471/ref=cm_lmf_tit_3_rdssss0*
Description: This book is a practical, real-world guide to help you learn from the successes and failures of churches with special-needs programs; with helps to launch or further develop a special-needs ministry while gaining insight from experts in the field.

Rapada, A. (2007). *The special needs ministry handbook: A church's guide to including children with disabilities and their families*. Booksurge Publishing.
Link:
https://www.amazon.com/gp/product/1419665472/ref=pd_cp_b_1_img?pf_rd_p=317711001&pf_rd_s=center-41&pf_rd_t=201&pf_rd_i=1557667438&pf_rd_m=ATVPDKIKX0DER&pf_rd_r=1DSH5P617BB79CX4GAAX
Description: This book is a resource for churches to learn how to start a special needs ministry, use inclusion models, involve volunteers, and church leaders, choose and adapt a curriculum for students with special needs, involve students with special needs in the learning process, create a successful experience for students with special needs, meet the challenge of behavior in students with special needs, and stay connected with the special needs family. It includes thirty-plus weeks of conceptual lessons for students with special needs and supplies organizational forms for your special needs' ministry.

Smith, C. R. (2004). *The physician examines the bible*. Whitefish, MT: Kessinger Publishing.

Link: *http://www.amazon.com/Physician-Examines-Bible-Raimer-Smith/dp/1417949252/ref=sr_1_29/002-9019454-0531235?ie=UTF8&s=books&qid=1194839391&sr=8-29*

Description: The physician examines the Bible as to etiology, diagnosis, and prognosis. Medical subjects in the Old and New Testaments and Apocrypha are presented and compared with present-day practices. Dr. C. Raimer Smith, now a physician in general practice, was for several years a specialist in pathology and clinical laboratory science.

Steere, C. (2005). *Too wise to be mistaken, too good to be unkind: Christian parents contend with autism*. Grace & Truth Books.
Link: *http://www.amazon.com/Too-Wise-Mistaken-Good-Unkind/dp/1930133030/ref=pd_sim_b_img_3*

Stillman, W. (2006). *Autism and the God connection*. Naperville, IL: Sourcebooks.
Link: *http://www.amazon.com/Autism-God-Connection-William-Stillman/dp/1402206496/ref=pd_sim_b_img_2*

Description: This book invokes a cosmic cornucopia of ghosts, spirits, angels, miracles, and past lives to make the case that "the seemingly sudden and mysterious surge of children identified with autism ... is our Creator's purposeful plan to refocus us on the importance of reverence for all of humanity." Tales of telepathy, direct communication with animals, spirit interaction, mind reading, and previous lives abound. This barrage of hokum distracts from the touching stories of connecting with autistic people, and though he writes gently, Stillman, who has Asperger's syndrome, mixes unsettling and unbelievable stories with summaries of scientific research and clinical studies.

Swinton, J. (2005). *Critical reflections of Stanley Hauerwas' theology of disability: disabling society, enabling theology.* Birminghamton, NY: Haworth Press.
Link: *http://www.amazon.com/Critical-Reflections-Hauerwas-Theology-Disability/dp/0789027216/ref=sr_1_22/002-9019454-0531235?ie=UTF8&s=books&qid=1194840512&sr=8-22*

Description: Swinton outlines some central aspects of Hauerwas's theology and ethics that relate to the papers in this volume. He clarifies the type of disability that Hauerwas addresses in these papers and draws out the social and political dimensions of Hauerwas's critique.

Tada, J. E. (1993). *All God's children: Ministry with disabled persons.* (Zondervan: Grand Rapids, 1993).
Link: *http://www.amazon.com/Gods-Children-Joni-Eareckson-Tada/dp/0310593816/ref=cm_lmf_img_5_rdssss0*

Description: This is a handbook for pastors, elders, ministry leaders, and laypeople who want to minister to people with disabilities. This edition is extensively revised, especially the chapters on hearing-impaired persons and on getting a disability ministry started. The resource lists have been expanded and brought up to date.

Webb-Mitchell, B. (1997). *Dancing with disabilities: Opening the church to all God's children.* Cleveland, OH: United Church Publishing.
Link:

http://www.amazon.com/gp/product/0829811524/ref=pd_cp_b_2_img?pf_rd_p=317711001&pf_rd_s=center-41&pf_rd_t=201&pf_rd_i=1557667438&pf_rd_m=ATVPDKIKX0DER&pf_rd_r=1DSH5P617BB79CX4GAAX

Yong, A. (2007). *Theology and down syndrome: reimagining disability in late modernity.* Waco, TX: Baylor University Press.
   Link: *http://www.amazon.com/Theology-Down-Syndrome-Reimagining-Disability/dp/1602580065/ref=sr_1_16/002-9019454-0531235?ie=UTF8&s=books&qid=1194839117&sr=8-16*

   Description: This book provides a comprehensive analysis of the philosophical issues surrounding Down syndrome. It also draws on an account of the Holy Spirit, to help us better appreciate how focusing on disability makes us rethink fundamental theological categories—a careful and systematic theological analysis. Multimedia.

Trachtman, I. (producer/director). (2007). *Praying with Lior* [Motion picture]. United States: Ruby Pictures.
   Link: *http://www.prayingwithlior.com/*

   Description: Praying with Lior introduces Lior Liebling, also called "the little rebbe." Lior has Down syndrome and has spent his entire life praying with utter abandon. Is he a "spiritual genius" as many around him say? Or simply the vessel that contains everyone's unfulfilled wishes and expectations? While everyone agrees Lior is closer to God, he is also a best friend, an inspiration, and a challenge, depending on which family member is speaking. As Lior approaches bar mitzvah, the Jewish coming-of-age ceremony, different characters provide a window into a life spent "praying with Lior."

Wisconsin Council on Developmental Disabilities, *Believing, Belonging, Becoming* [motion picture], 2002.

   Link: *http://www.faithability.org/resource/believing-belonging-becoming-building-welcoming-faith*

   Description: This eleven-minute video highlights the stories of four people who have been meaningfully included in the life of their faith communities. See how faith communities have formed worship support circles, fostered one-to-one relationships, and committed resources to promote inclusion. The video includes a brief discussion guide. This is a great resource to use with adult education classes or to share with various committees looking for ways to promote more welcoming faith communities.

Appendix II

EMAIL: JODY PLECAS

Comments on draft paper: Faith in the Shadows; The Other side of the Fence, by Jody Plecas: 09/03/2018, used with permission.

Your approach in this paper attempts to fend off the many areas of bias that colour the readers interpretation of faith in the life of the disabled. It utilizes many theories, quotes and definitions proposed by many people as fundamentals in the first 100 or so pages.

Being a practical, however non-religious person not wedded to any particular dogma, this was heavy reading for me. I found it confusing to wade through the ornate language, observations and determinations of so many people and sources without the validation of empirical evidence. I did find my way through the mist a bit better towards the end.

In one respect this is understandable as I believe I am not the target audience. Would it be fair to say that you are holding your hand out to a secular audience who may already have a black and white mindset in regard to their faith and the disabled,

Having said that I also have the feeling that you were also making room for a larger audience? If so, does this call for a second document that is more reader friendly?

Your paper has a gentle glow of positivity and I hope you will take my views (as an outsider) as affirmative to your aim, perhaps not unlike a disabled person attempting to both learn and communicate from a different plane.

As a non-secular reader I feel that your audience(s) may be better persuaded by uncomplicating the argument in a revised paper where tantalizing questions with reader friendly explanations. will draw the reader forward. Perhaps something in the nature of the following questions:

QUESTIONS:

- What does the bible say? From past to present how do Christians treat the disabled?
- What Biblical words—principals define our thinking and ultimately our actions?
- Does cognitive disability preclude the notion that a fully cognitive "spirit or soul" is merely trapped inside an impaired vessel?
- How does 'good' or 'evil' or 'sin' fit into the context of the disabled person?

These words contain primary judgmental concepts overlaid on a shadowy realm and that hold the attention of us all. Good or evil jump to the fore and become relevant as we consider that although we are all God's children not all his children are good children.

- So, can evil be intrinsic or is it merely a lack of faith?

If a certain percentage of the population may be deemed evil, then it would seem logical that a few of our mentally disabled may actually be spiritually disabled to the point of evil. Are the disabled or the enabled different in God's eyes?

- Are disabled undervalued in Christian communities and if so, why?

The understanding and communication issue (both sides of the fence), consider whether this unrecognised faith in the disabled is actually a type of abuse.

- How can we solve inequity in inclusion from both viewpoints?

For me the strongest elements of persuasion will be those anecdotes from your own life. Tell us more of what you have witnessed. This is proof that you know what you are talking about! You've lived it. Anecdotes from those you have met and know greatly supports and reinforces your conclusions.

Appendix III:

Additional Books Accessed & Read

Ayrault Evelyn W., Beyond a Physical disability; the Person Within (Continuum International Publishing: New York, 2001)

Barnes, C., 'Disabled People in Britain and Discrimination: A case for anti-discrimination legislation', (C. Hurst: London, 1991)

Beates, Michael S., Disability & The Gospel (Crossway: Wheaton, 2012)

Berkhof L., Systematic Theology (Banner of Truth: Grand Rapids, 1949)

Boon J., the Mystical Science of the Soul: Medieval Cognition in Bernardino de Laredo, (University of Toronto Press: Buffalo, 2012)

Bradshaw J., Home Coming; Reclaiming and Healing Your Inner child (Bantam Books: New York, 1992)

Butterfield G., Doctrine of Faith and Prayer (WestBow Press: Bloomington, 2012).

Carter Erik W., Including People with Disabilities in Faith Communities (Paul H. Brookes Publishing: London, 2007)

Coren S., Ward L. M., Sensations and Perceptions (Harcourt Brace: Indiana, 1989)

Coulter D., Spirituality and Intellectual Disability: Recognition of Spirituality in Health Care: Personal and Universal Implications (Routledge: New York, 2001)

Crisp J., Taylor C., eds., Fundamentals of Nursing: Potter & Perry (Elsevier Australia: Chatswood, 2005)

Elder R., Evans K., Nizette D., Psychiatric and Mental Health: Nursing (Elsevier Australia: Chatswood, 2005)

Elwell W., ed., Evangelical Dictionary of Theology (Paternoster Press: Grand Rapids, 1995)

Elwell W., Ed., Evangelical Dictionary of Theology, (Baker Books: Grand Rapids, 1996)

Elwell W., Evangelical Dictionary of Theology, (Baker Books: Grand Rapids, 1995)

Ferguson S., Wright D., New Dictionary of Theology, (IVP: Leicester: 1988)

Free Presbyterian Church of Scotland, Westminster Confession of Faith (Eccles Press: Inverness, 1976)

Grandin T., Duffy K., eds., Developing Talents: Careers for Individuals with Asperger Syndrome and High Functioning Autism (APC Publishing: Shawnee Mission, 2004)

Hoekema A., Created in God's Image (Eerdmans: Grand Rapids, 1988)

Isanon Abe, Spirituality and the Autism Spectrum (Jessica Kingsley Publishers: London, 2001)

Lowther R., Spirit and Gospel (Paternoster: Milton Keynes, 2017)

Merrill F., White w., Nelson's Expository dictionary of the Old Testament, (Thomas Nelson: Nashville, 1980)

Monteith Graham W., Disability Faith and Acceptance (St. Andrews Press: Edinburgh, 1987)

NIV Classic Reference Bible, (Zondervan: Grand Rapids, 1988)

Phillips, W. and Rosenberg, J. ed., Social Scientists and the Physically Handicapped, (Arno Press: London, 1980)

Raymond R., A New Systematic Theology of the Christian Faith (Thomas Nelson: Nashville, 1997)

Reynolds P., A Whole New Life: An Illness and a Healing (Scribner: New York, 2000)

Rifkin J., The Emphatic Civilization: The Race to Global Consciousness in a World in (Crisis Polity Press: Cambridge, 2010)

Robinson John E., Look Me in the Eye (Transworld Publishers: North Sydney, 2007)

Ryken L., Wilhoit J., Longman T., Eds, Dictionary of Biblical Imagery (IVP: Leicester, 1998)

Sproul R. C., The New Genesis; The Mystery of the Holy Spirit (Tyndale House: Wheaton, 1979)

Stiker Henri-Jaques, A History of Disability (University of Michigan Press: Michigan, 2007)

Thomas D., The Experience of Handicap (Methuen: London, 1982)

Welsh, Edward T., Blame it on the Brain, (P&R Publishing: Phillipsburg, 1998)

Endorsement:

JASON FORBES, JERICHO ROAD:

As I said, I'm very excited about the book. To reiterate what I said in conversation, I believe what you are presenting is a spectrum rather than a dichotomy. What I mean by that is, all relationships, whether they involve a person with a disability or not, are based on learning the person's language. In a sense, I know that I'm loved and accepted when people know my language.

To clarify, I am not necessarily referring to my speech impairment. I am referring to when it is known what I'm going to say, why I'm going to say it, and how can the other person engage with my language. When severe disability is involved, the difference in language is significant and it can be difficult to communicate across that difference.

From what I've seen of your book thus far, this will help readers identify those differences in communication and ways to overcome those differences which would allow relationships to develop where all involved can be loved and served in Christ.

I'm very excited for the book and pray for a smooth publishing process.

Rev. Jason Forbes:
Disability Advocate, Presbyterian Social Services (AU)
http://www.jerichoroad.org.au

www.ingramcontent.com/pod-product-compliance
Lightning Source LLC
Chambersburg PA
CBHW061131010526
44107CB00068B/2905